Diplomacy

Also by G. R. Berridge

* A DICTIONARY OF DIPLOMACY (*with Alan James*)

* DIPLOMACY AT THE UN (*co-editor with A. Jennings*)

* DIPLOMATIC THEORY FROM MACHIAVELLI TO KISSINGER
  (*with Maurice Keens-Soper and T. G. Otte*)

* ECONOMIC POWER IN ANGLO-SOUTH AFRICAN DIPLOMACY: Simonstown,
  Sharpeville and After

  INTERNATIONAL POLITICS: States, Power and Conflict since 1945
  (*third edition*)

* AN INTRODUCTION TO INTERNATIONAL RELATIONS (*with D. Heater*)

  THE POLITICS OF THE SOUTH AFRICA RUN: European Shipping and Pretoria

* RETURN TO THE UN: UN Diplomacy in Regional Conflicts

* SOUTH AFRICA, THE COLONIAL POWERS AND 'AFRICAN DEFENCE':
  The Rise and Fall of the White Entente, 1948–60

* TALKING TO THE ENEMY: How States without 'Diplomatic Relations'
  Communicate

* *from the same publishers*

Diplomacy
Theory and Practice

Second Edition

G. R. Berridge
Emeritus Professor of International Politics,
University of Leicester

First published by Prentice-Hall 1995

Second edition published by
PALGRAVE 2002
Houndmills, Basingstoke, Hampshire RG21 6XS and
175 Fifth Avenue, New York, N.Y. 10010
Companies and representatives throughout the world

PALGRAVE is the new global academic imprint of
St. Martin's Press LLC Scholarly and Reference Division and
Palgrave Publishers Ltd (formerly Macmillan Press Ltd).

ISBN 0–333–96928–6 hardback
ISBN 0–333–96929–4 paperback

This book is printed on paper suitable for recycling and
made from fully managed and sustained forest sources.

A catalogue record for this book is available
from the British Library.

Library of Congress Cataloging-in-Publication Data

Berridge, Geoff.
    Diplomacy: theory and practice / G.R. Berridge.—2nd ed.
        p. cm.
    Includes bibliographical references (p.) and index.
    ISBN 0–333–96928–6—ISBN 0–333–96929–4 (pbk.)
        1. Diplomacy. I. Title.

JZ1405 .B475 2002
327.2—dc21   2001052346

10   9   8   7   6   5   4   3   2   1
11   10   09   08   07   06   05   04   03   02

Printed and bound in Great Britain by
Antony Rowe Ltd, Chippenham, Wiltshire

For Simon Kear

Contents

Preface to the First Edition

This book on diplomacy is based on the course that I have taught on the MA in Diplomatic Studies at Leicester University over the last four years. The chapter on mediation has appeared previously in *Talking to the Enemy* (Macmillan: London, 1994), and I am grateful to Macmillan for permission to reprint it here. I am also grateful to those of my colleagues at Leicester and elsewhere who have stimulated me with their ideas (most recently at the LSE and Bristol), and I am particularly grateful to David H. Dunn, Alan James, Helen Leigh-Phippard, Jan Melissen, and John Young for taking the trouble to comment on all or part of this manuscript. I am, as always, grateful, too, to Clare Grist of Harvester for her guidance on editorial matters.

G. R. B., Leicester, October 1994

Preface to the Second [printed] Edition

Those familiar with the First Edition of this book will soon spot that it has been radically overhauled and, I hope, much improved. In addition to revising the whole text, I have made some major structural changes. To begin with, I have changed the order of the main Parts for reasons explained in the Introduction to Part I. I have also added three completely new chapters: Chapter 1 on 'The Ministry of Foreign Affairs', Chapter 6 on 'Telecommunications', and Chapter 8 on 'Bilateral Diplomacy: Unconventional' (though the last is a revised version of a chapter earlier published in my *Talking to the Enemy*). In order to make space for this new work, I have compressed the original two chapters on bilateral diplomacy (law and practice) into one, and sacrificed the long appendix in the First Edition that provided the complete text of the Vienna Convention on Diplomatic Relations, 1961. This did not seem a big sacrifice because this document is now readily available on the world wide web and an indexed version is contained in *A Dictionary of Diplomacy* (Palgrave, 2001), which I published with Alan James. Nevertheless, despite these space savings, the extra chapters, together with the need to fill gaps in the existing ones, have produced a substantially longer book. As a result, I am grateful for the indulgence on this score, as on others, of Alison Howson of Palgrave.

It remains for me to record my gratitude to all of those who have offered suggestions for improvements to the parts of this textbook in which they have special competence. Among these I must note especially Stefano Baldi, David H. Dunn, Brian Hocking, Donna Lee, and Kishan Rana. Any remaining errors of fact or weaknesses of judgement remain, of course, mine. I am also extremely grateful to Simon Kear for bringing out a revised version of the First Edition (without the structural changes or new chapters) as an ebook under the imprint of Allandale Online Publishing in 1999/2001. We were ahead of the market, unfortunately, but at least this kept the book alive – and my interest in it. Finally, I wish to express my thanks once more to my copy-editor, the indispensable Anne Rafique.

G. R. Berridge, Leicester, May 2001

Online Updating

For each chapter in the book there is a corresponding page on my web site. These pages contain further reflections and details of recent developments on the subject in question. The web site also contains resources for students of diplomacy, such as the full catalogue of the Archive of Diplomatic Lists at the University of Leicester and reviews of recent books. It also has suggestions for dissertation topics. Please visit www.grberridge.co.uk

List of Abbreviations

ANC	African National Congress
ASEAN	Association of South-East Asian Nations
CHOGM	Commonwealth Heads of Government Meeting
CNN	Cable News Network
EC	European Community
EU	European Union
FCO	Foreign and Commonwealth Office
FMLN	*Frente Farabundo Martí para la Liberación Nacional* [coalition of armed insurgent groups in El Salvador]
GATT	General Agreement on Tariffs and Trade
IAEA	International Atomic Energy Agency
IGO	intergovernmental organization
ILC	International Law Commission
IMF	International Monetary Fund
MFA	Ministry of Foreign Affairs
MIRV	multiple independently targetable re-entry vehicle
NGO	non-governmental organization
OAS	Organization of American States
OAU	Organization of African Unity
OECD	Organization of Economic Cooperation and Development
P5	Permanent 5 [on the UN Security Council]
PLO	Palestine Liberation Organization
PRO	Public Record Office, London
SAARC	South Asian Association for Regional Cooperation
SALT I	Strategic Arms Limitations Talks [first negotiations, 1969–72]
SWAPO	South-West African People's Organization
UNITA	National Union for the Total Independence of Angola
VCDR	Vienna Convention on Diplomatic Relations, 1961
WTO	World Trade Organization

Introduction

Diplomacy is an essentially political activity and, well resourced and skilful, a major ingredient of power. Its chief purpose is to enable states to secure the objectives of their foreign policies without resort to force, propaganda, or law. It follows that diplomacy consists of communication between officials designed to promote foreign policy either by formal agreement or tacit adjustment. Though it also includes such discrete activities as gathering information, clarifying intentions, and engendering goodwill, it is thus not surprising that, until the label 'diplomacy' was affixed to all of these activities by Edmund Burke in 1796, it was known most commonly as 'negotiation' – by Cardinal Richelieu as *négociation continuelle*.[1] Diplomacy is not merely what professional diplomatic agents do. It is carried out by other officials and by private persons under the direction of officials. As we shall see in Part II, it is also carried out through many different channels besides the traditional resident mission. Together with the balance of power, which it both reinforces and reflects, diplomacy is the most important institution of our society of states.

Diplomacy in its modern form has its immediate origins in the Italian peninsula in the late fifteenth century AD. Nevertheless, its remote origins are to be found in the relations between the 'great kings' of the Near East in the second or possibly even in the late fourth millennium BC (Liverani, Introduction; Cohen and Westbrook). Its main features in these centuries were the dependence of communications on messengers and merchant caravans, diplomatic immunity on ordinary codes of hospitality, and treaty observance on terror of the gods in whose presence they were confirmed. However, though apparently adequate to the times, diplomacy during these centuries remained rudimentary. In the main this would seem to be because it was not called on

1

very often and because communications were slow, laborious, unpredictable, and insecure.

In the Greek city state system of the fourth and fifth centuries BC, however, conditions both demanded and favoured a more sophisticated diplomacy. Diplomatic immunity, even of the herald in war, became a more entrenched norm, and resident missions began to emerge, though employing a local citizen. Such a person was known as a *proxenos* (Adcock and Mosley, p. 160). In medieval Europe, the development of diplomacy was led first by Byzantium (the eastern Roman Empire) and then especially by Venice, which set new standards of honesty and technical proficiency (Bozeman, pp. 457–77). However, diplomacy remained chiefly in the hands of special envoys, limited by time and task.

It was in the Italian city states system in the late fifteenth century, when conditions were especially favourable to the further development of diplomacy, that the recognizably modern system first made its appearance. The hyper-insecurity of these rich but poorly defended states that was induced by the repeated invasions of the peninsula by the great powers from the north after 1494, made perpetual diplomacy with less fanfare essential. No barriers were presented to diplomacy by language or religion. And though communications still depended on horsed messengers, the relatively short distances that had to be traversed made this less important. It is not surprising therefore that it was this period that saw the birth of the genuine resident embassy, that is to say, a resident mission headed by a citizen of the prince or republic whose interests it served (Mattingly). This Italian system, the spirit and methods of which are captured so well in the despatches of Machiavelli (Detmold), evolved shortly into the French system that in the middle of the twentieth century was praised so highly by the British scholar-diplomat, Harold Nicolson (Nicolson, 1954). This was the first fully developed system of diplomacy and the basis of the modern – essentially bilateral – system (see Chapter 7).

In the early twentieth century the French system was modified but not – as some hoped and others feared – transformed. The 'open diplomacy' of ad hoc and permanent conferences (notably the League of Nations) was simply grafted onto the existing network of bilateral communications. As for the anti-diplomacy of the Communist regimes in Soviet Russia and subsequently in China, this was relatively short-lived. Why did diplomacy survive these assaults and continue to develop to such a degree and in such an inventive manner that at the beginning of the twenty-first century we can speak with some confidence of a world diplomatic system of unprecedented strength? The reason is that the conditions that first encouraged the development of diplomacy have for some decades obtained perhaps more fully than ever before. These are a balance of power between a plurality of states, mutually impinging interests of an unusually urgent kind, relative cultural (including religious and ideological) toleration, and efficient and secure international communication.

As already noted, diplomacy is an important means by which states pursue their foreign policies, and these policies are still framed in significant degree in many states in a ministry of foreign affairs. Such ministries also have the major responsibility for a state's diplomats serving abroad and for dealing (formally, at any rate) with foreign diplomats at home. It is for this reason that this book begins with a detailed examination of the origins and current position of the ministry of foreign affairs. Following this, it is divided into two parts. The first is devoted to a consideration of the art of negotiation, the most important activity undertaken in the world diplomatic system as whole. The second part of the book is devoted to an examination of the different channels through which negotiations, together with the other functions of diplomacy, are conducted.

Note

1 There are as many views on the concept of diplomacy as there are writers on the subject (Berridge and James, pp. 62–3). There is an especially instructive discussion in Smith Simpson (1980, ch. 1).

Further reading

Adcock, F. and D. J. Mosley, *Diplomacy in Ancient Greece* (Thames and Hudson: London, 1975), Part Two.
Anderson, M. S., *The Rise of Modern Diplomacy* (Longman: London, 1993).
Bozeman, Adda B., *Politics and Culture in International History*, 2nd edn (Transaction: New Brunswick and London, 1994), pp. 324–56, 457–504.
Bull, H., *The Anarchical Society: A Study of Order in World Politics* (Macmillan – now Palgrave: London, 1977), ch. 7.
Cohen, Raymond, and Raymond Westbrook (eds), *Amarna Diplomacy: The Beginnings of International Relations* (Johns Hopkins University Press: Baltimore and London, 2000).

Hamilton, Keith and Richard Langhorne, *The Practice of Diplomacy* (Routledge: London, 1995), chs 1–4.

Liverani, Mario, *International Relations in the Ancient Near East* (Palgrave: Basingstoke, 2001), Intro. and ch. 10.

Mattingly, G., *Renaissance Diplomacy* (Penguin: Harmondsworth, 1965).

Meier, S. A., *The Messenger in the Ancient Semitic World* (Scholars Press: Atlanta, Georgia, 1988).

Munn-Rankin, J. M., 'Diplomacy in Western Asia in the early second millennium B.C.', *Iraq* 18 (1956).

Queller, D. E., *The Office of Ambassador in the Middle Ages* (Princeton University Press: Princeton, New Jersey, 1967).

1
The Ministry of Foreign Affairs

In addition to a diplomatic service, most states today have a ministry dedicated to directing and administering it. This is usually known as the Ministry of Foreign Affairs (MFA). However, it is easy to forget that this was not always the case and that the MFA came relatively late onto the scene. In fact, its general appearance post-dated the arrival of the resident diplomatic mission by almost three centuries. This chapter will begin by looking at the origins and development of the MFA. It will then examine its different roles. These include staffing and supporting missions abroad, policy advice and implementation, policy coordination, dealing with foreign diplomats at home, public diplomacy, and building domestic support.

The origins and growth of the MFA

Until the seventeenth century, responsibility for diplomacy in the states of Europe was routinely allocated between different bureaucracies ('secretaries of state') on a geographical basis. Some of these offices were also responsible for certain domestic matters (Hamilton and Langhorne, pp. 72–3). It was in France that this picture began to change, when in 1626 the first foreign ministry, or 'Ministry of Foreign Affairs' as it is usually known today, was created by Cardinal Richelieu, the legendary chief minister of the French King, Louis XIII. This development was the inevitable corollary of his view that maintenance of an equilibrium between Europe's states was an essential principle of foreign policy, that this required the relations between them to be continuously nurtured, and that this in turn required resident ambassadors in all important capitals. More diplomacy multiplied the possibilities of inconsistency in both the formulation and execution of foreign policy; as a result, it demanded more unified direction and better preserved archives. As for the fact that diplomacy was increasingly conducted by representatives resident for long periods abroad, this demanded at least some degree of organized communications with them, with the attendant needs for ciphering and deciphering instructions and despatches. In sum, continuous negotiation abroad required not only continuous bureaucracy at home but also one rather than several competing bureaucracies.

It was not, however, until the eighteenth century that provision of advice on foreign policy and the administration of diplomacy by a single ministry of foreign affairs headed by a 'foreign minister' became the general rule in Europe (Horn, p. 1). Britain came late, having to wait until 1782 for the creation of the Foreign Office.[1] The US State Department was established shortly after this, in 1789 (Box 1.1). It was the middle of the nineteenth century before China, Japan, and Turkey followed suit.

Box 1.1 'Department of Foreign Affairs' to 'Department of State'

A 'Department of Foreign Affairs' was established by the Continental Congress on 10 January 1781. This title was also initially employed for the foreign ministry of the United States itself under legislation approved by the House and Senate on 21 July 1789 and signed into law by President Washington six days later. However, in September the Department was given certain *domestic* duties as well, which subsequently came to include management of the Mint, keeper of the Great Seal of the United States, and the taking of the census. No longer charged solely with *foreign* tasks, it was for this reason that at the same juncture the department's name was changed to 'Department of State'. Despite surrendering most of these domestic duties in the nineteenth century, the name stuck.

Source: http://www.state.gov/www/about-state/history/dephis.html

---

Even in Europe, however, it was well into the nineteenth century before the average foreign ministry, which remained small, had become bureaucratically sophisticated.[2] By this time, ministries were divided into different administrative units ('departments' or '*bureaux*') on the basis either of specialization in a particular function, for example protocol or treaties, or a particular geographical region. In addition to the foreign minister, who was the transient political head of the ministry, the typical foreign office had also acquired a permanent senior official to serve immediately under him and provide continuity. The powers of this official (in Britain the 'permanent under-secretary', elsewhere more commonly the secretary-general or director-general)[3] were greater in some states than others. Entry into the foreign ministry increasingly demanded suitable educational qualifications, even from the members of families that retained a strong position in recruitment until well into the twentieth century. (The diplomatic family may be inegalitarian but at least it provides an excellent education in the practical – as distinct from the technical – knowledge of diplomacy at no cost to the state.)[4]

The ministry of foreign affairs still had rivals for influence over the formulation and execution of foreign policy in the nineteenth century. Among these were the monarchs and presidents, chancellors and prime ministers, who felt that their positions gave them special prerogatives to dabble in this area; and war offices with their nascent intelligence services. Nevertheless, if the MFA had a golden age of influence and prestige, this was probably it. It did not last long. A distaste for both commerce and popular meddling in foreign policy was entrenched in most foreign ministries, which were essentially aristocratic in ethos, and this soon put them on the defensive in the following century. The First World War itself was also, of course, a tremendous blow to their prestige because it seemed to prove that the old diplomacy had failed in most spectacular fashion. Much of the burgeoning dissatisfaction with the way ministries such as these were staffed and organized, as well as with the manner in which they conducted their affairs, focused on the administrative (and in some instances social) divisions within the bureaucracy of diplomacy.

A major reason for the creation of a ministry of foreign affairs was, of course, to recruit, brief, despatch, finance, and maintain secure and regular communications with the state's diplomatic representatives abroad. (It should not be forgotten, though, that the ministry also acquired the task of maintaining communication with the diplomatic corps resident in its own capital.) However, despite this intimate link, work at home and work abroad were very different, with different advantages and different problems. Persons attracted to one sort were not as a rule attracted to the other, and it was not unusual for mutual sympathy to be at a discount. The result was that, except in small states, it became the norm for the two branches of diplomacy – the foreign ministry and its representatives abroad – to be organized separately and have distinctive career ladders. Between the two branches there was little transfer. It was also usual for the representatives abroad to be themselves divided into separate services, the diplomatic and the consular – and sometimes the commercial as well. Diplomats worked in the embassy or legation located in the capital city and concentrated on the more prestigious political work, while consuls were scattered around the major ports and industrial centres and dealt more with commercial matters. Conditions and rewards in the consular service were far inferior to those in the diplomatic service and it is not surprising that its recruits came from the lower reaches of the social hierarchy.[5]

These traditional bureaucratic divisions reinforced the prejudices of those involved in the different departments of overseas work and impeded not only mobility but also cooperation between them. The result was that, as European rivalry increased in the years before the First World War and manufacturing exporters (whose political influence had increased over the century) became more anxious for government support, pressure for a unified service began to mount. However, resistance remained strong and change came only slowly. Significant steps were taken towards the integration of all services in France in the decades before the First World War, but it was 1922 before they were merged in Norway, and 1927 before the diplomatic and consular services were merged in Italy. In Britain the staffs of the Foreign Office and the Diplomatic Service were merged immediately after the First World War, though they retained their separate 'identities' until 1943. The British Consular Service had to wait until the same year to become part of the new, unified 'Foreign Service' (restyled 'Diplomatic Service' in 1964). In the United States, separate diplomatic and consular services were merged into a unified service – the US Foreign Service – when the Rogers Act, also significant for putting American diplomacy for the first time on a secure professional basis, became law in 1924. However, it was not until the 1950s that, following the Wriston Report of 1954, the US Foreign Service absorbed the personnel of the hitherto separate Department of State. The Swedish services were not integrated until 1976, and the Dutch remain separate to this day.[6]

In some small part no doubt because of the advance in the cohesiveness of the bureaucracy of diplomacy, the ministry of foreign affairs remains a very visible department of central government in almost all states. However, while its tasks bear a strong family resemblance in whatever national capital it is located, its influence over the content of policy varies rather more from one to another. In states with long-established MFAs and a constitutional mode of government, as in Britain and France, the ministry tends to remain highly influential. In others, however, it is much weaker. These include states with shorter diplomatic traditions and highly personalized and arbitrary political leadership, as in much of the Third World.[7] The situation also tends to

Box 1.2   Formal titles and popular names

Some MFAs are referred to more commonly by the names of the buildings they occupy or the street or square on which they are located, even though today they may also have important offices elsewhere. The following list shows some of the better known among these, and also illustrates the variety of formal titles employed by the MFA.

Australia: *Department of Foreign Affairs and Trade*
Austria: *Federal Ministry for Foreign Affairs ('Ballhausplatz')*
Barbados: *Ministry of Foreign Affairs and Foreign Trade*
Brazil: *Ministry of Foreign Relations ('Itamaraty')*
Canada: *Department of Foreign Affairs and International Trade*
China, People's Republic of: *Ministry of Foreign Affairs*
France: *Ministry of Foreign Affairs ('Quai d'Orsay')*
India: *Ministry of External Affairs ('South Block')*
Italy: *Ministry of Foreign Affairs ('Farnesina')*
Korea, Republic of: *Ministry of Foreign Affairs and Trade*
Malaysia: *Ministry of Foreign Affairs ('Wisma Putra')*
Russia: *Ministry of Foreign Affairs*
Senegal: *Ministry of Foreign Affairs and Senegalese Abroad*
United Kingdom: *Foreign and Commonwealth Office ('Foreign Office' or 'FO')*
United States of America: *Department of State ('Foggy Bottom')*

be the same in any state where anxiety over military security has always generated acute neurosis and thus given great influence to the defence ministry, as in Israel and to a lesser degree in the United States. In all states, however, the influence of the ministry of foreign affairs fluctuates over time, tending to rise or dip for any number of reasons. Among the most important, though, is the personality and level of interest in foreign affairs of the head of government, which is usually great because of the growth of summitry (see Chapter 10). If a leader suspects political hostility in the MFA, or just regards it as spineless in the face of tough foreign opposition, the ministry's position will tend to be worse still. The Foreign and Commonwealth Office during Mrs Thatcher's period as prime minister in Britain in the 1980s is a case in point (Urban, pp. 9–10). The Malaysian MFA suffered even more when the even more autocratic Dr Mahatir became prime minister shortly afterwards (Ahmad, pp. 121–2).

Whether influential or not, the staff of most MFAs is now significantly larger relative to that of their missions abroad than it was in the nineteenth century. Furthermore, it is widely held that the tasks of MFAs are now so considerable that 'for every two diplomats posted abroad, there should be at least one official at Headquarters' (Rana, p. 255). In fact, at least in the MFAs of the European Union and G8 countries, the personnel ratio generally favours the ministry more than this. Five have ratios of 1:1 (as in China), while a further five actually have a ratio of staff of 2:1 in favour of the MFA.[8] What are these tasks that now demand such relatively large numbers at headquarters?

Staffing and supporting missions abroad

As already indicated, an important task for the MFA is, of course, providing the personnel for and physical fabric of the state's diplomatic and consular missions abroad. Under this head falls the business of recruitment, training, and selection for particular posts. It also includes finding, maintaining and providing security for buildings abroad, and supporting the diplomats (and their families), especially when they find themselves in 'hardship posts' or in the midst of an emergency. Thus most MFAs have departments dealing with personnel ('human resources'), training,[9] budgeting, real estate ('property abroad'), communications, and security. (These are commonly described as *administrative* departments or occasionally as 'corporate services', though others fall under this particular head as we shall see below.) These tasks are particularly important in the MFAs of states where the diplomatic career has tended to lose its glitter and where, as a result, morale has suffered and there is a significant loss of experienced staff in mid-career. Because of the murderous attacks on its embassies in recent years, the US State Department has had to devote considerable energy and resources to giving them greater protection, and now even has to have an Office of Casualty Assistance as well (Bergin; Loeffler; Montgomery). Achieving this protection without compromising their diplomatic objectives has not proved easy.

A less popular task now undertaken by many MFAs as part of their general support for missions abroad is their regular inspection. Permanent inspection units are usually briefed to advise on best practice and no doubt help to encourage it. Nevertheless, the fact that they are usually required to recommend methods by which costs might be reduced as well, often leads them to be seen by missions as tending more to undermine than support their work. When morale in the diplomatic service is already low, it is clearly important that this work is handled with sensitivity and conducted by persons who command professional respect. The *Semiannual Reports* of the US State Department's Office of Inspector General are available on the world wide web. These are unclassified summaries of detailed individual reports of inspections. However, some of the latter are also available. The 70-page *Report of Inspection on Embassy Bucharest, Romania*, conducted by an eight-person team in 1999 and producing 66 recommendations for changes in embassy practice, reveals just how carefully and sensitively this work needs to be carried out – and also how necessary it is.[10]

Policy advice and implementation

Once it has installed its diplomats and consuls abroad, the MFA has the task of making them work, as well as digesting the fruits of their labour. This is where the other departments come in, and most of these are arranged partly along geographical and partly along functional lines. *Geographical* departments normally concentrate on regions or occasionally individual states of particular importance to the country concerned, while *functional* departments deal typically with general issues such as arms control, drugs, human rights, and trade. Historically, the geographical departments came first and thus until relatively recently had more prestige. The attempt in the 1950s and 1960s to give more prominence to functional departments in the US State Department was made more difficult by personnel distinctions remaining from the pre-Wriston reform era. The functional departments were staffed by civil servants, while the geographical departments were staffed by diplomatic officers (Simpson, 1967, p. 19). Nevertheless, in the British Foreign and Commonwealth Office (FCO) the functional departments, which are more in harmony with the concept of 'globalization', now themselves tend to be the more prestigious, and this is probably typical of other MFAs. Functional departments focus expertise and advertise the fact that the MFA is seized with the current problems of greatest concern.[11] Nevertheless, it is unlikely that they will replace the geographical departments completely and – except in poor states with limited foreign interests (Box 1.3) – it would be a serious mistake to seek this end. Apart from the fact that, given the existence of duplicate international departments in the line ministries, it would weaken the case for a separate MFA, states remain the principal units of political organization in the world, and they are themselves located in regions with marked political, economic and cultural differences. If the conduct of relations with states were to be left entirely in the hands of functional departments, unmediated by expert regional knowledge, it is highly unlikely that it would be successful. With the rise in importance of international organizations, most MFAs now have *multilateral* departments as well.[12]

Box 1.3 MFA structure in less developed countries

The ministries of very poor states, especially micro-states, which by and large have extremely limited networks of diplomats abroad, tend to have few if any geographical departments. For example, in 2001 the Ministry of Foreign Affairs and Foreign Trade of Barbados only had eight departments in addition to those supporting the minister and permanent secretary. These were ones dealing with administration, protocol and conference coordination, foreign trade, international relations, consular affairs, information and communication, treaties, and the facilitation of the return of Barbados nationals. Even the MFA of the much larger – though certainly not richer – state of Senegal, in West Africa, had only two geographical departments, one for Africa and Asia, and another for Europe, the Americas, and the Pacific.

Many MFAs also have departments variously known as 'intelligence and research' or 'research and analysis'. These specialize in general background research and in assessing the significance of information obtained by the means which in many states challenged the diplomatic service so massively in this field in the second half of the twentieth century, namely, secret intelligence (Herman, 1998). The MFA is chiefly a consumer of the product of the intelligence service, or of the various specialized members of the 'intelligence community' where, as in the larger developed states, such a community exists. However, it sometimes plays a key role in the assessment and distribution throughout government of intelligence from all sources. Until 1985, the Joint Intelligence Committee, which plays this role in the British system, fell under the authority of the Foreign and Commonwealth Office (Urban, ch. 1, pp. 145–6; Herman, 1996, pp. 30–5, 260, 275).

If policy advice and implementation is to be carried out properly, the MFA's institutional memory, that is to say its archives, must be in good order. This applies especially to the details of promises made and received in the past and potential promises that have been long gestating in negotiations still not complete. This is why such an important section of even the earliest foreign ministries was their archive of correspondence and treaties.[13]

Since foreign policy must also be lawful and since in addition the MFA must sometimes seek to implement it by legal means, legal advice and support is always necessary as well. In some states it has been traditional to provide this from a law ministry (or 'ministry of justice') serving all government departments (Merillat, p. 4). Nevertheless, the predominant pattern is now for the MFA of even the average least developed country to have its own legal, or 'legal and treaties' division, headed by an officer usually known as 'the Legal Adviser' or, in French-speaking states, *Directeur des Affaires Juridiques*.[14] It is also now more usual for the members of this division to be lawyers specializing in this work and not diplomats with a legal education who are rotated between the legal division and general diplomatic work in posts abroad (Merillat, pp. 1–4, 6–8).

It is interesting, and perhaps hopeful for the strengthening of international law, that since the end of the 1980s informal meetings of the legal advisers of the MFAs of UN member states have been held on a regular basis at UN headquarters in New York. The MFAs of the developed states, and a few others, also have a policy-planning department. Very much a product of the period since the Second World War, this is a response to the criticism of unpreparedness and was inspired in part by the planning staffs long employed by military establishments.[15] Planning units appear in practice to be chiefly concerned with trying to anticipate future problems and thinking through how they might be met – and, in the process, challenging conventional mind-sets.[16] The planners in the British Foreign and Commonwealth Office appear not to try to look much beyond the medium term of about five years (Coles, pp. 87–8). More ambitiously, those in the Ministry of Foreign Affairs and Trade of the Republic of Korea are explicitly charged with considering 'mid- and long-term foreign policy'. To be able to do this the planners are given freedom from current operational preoccupations but are not left so remote from them that they become 'too academic' (Coles, p. 71).[17] With such a strategic brief and supposed to provide judgements independent of any consensus in a geographical or functional department, it is not surprising that the policy planners are usually permitted to work directly under the executive head of the MFA. However, it is often difficult to get busy foreign ministers, who must inevitably give priority to today's events, to focus on discussions of even the medium term, while the operational departments may well be obstructive (Rothstein, pp. 30–3). As a result, the policy planners sometimes feel that they are wasting their time.[18] This may well be true, though the political protection they afford to the MFA – which at least in states with a free and lively press has to be *seen* to be looking ahead – should not be overlooked.

However the MFA's departments are organized and whatever particular titles they are given, they collect reports and opinions from their missions abroad as well from outside bodies, including NGOs. In light of this information they advise their political masters on policy and issue instructions to missions consistent with the policy that is agreed. In an acute crisis, this work may be given to a special section within the ministry.[19] With the benefit of the constant stream of new information, the functional and geographical departments are (or should be) constantly re-examining the advice that they pass upwards.

It is inevitable that the policy advice and implementation function should lead MFA officials to adopt more or less pronounced 'departmental' attitudes on certain issues, even entrenched prejudices. For example, the British FCO was for long associated with pro-Arab sentiment, though when the issue of 'departmental attitudes' is raised today it is normally its pro-European reflexes that are mentioned. The South African Department of External Affairs inherited by the National Party from General Smuts in the fateful election of 1948 was regarded by the new government as hopelessly pro-British, while in the last years of the *apartheid* regime its successor came to be seen as *verligte* (enlightened on race). The Progressive Conservative leader, John Diefenbaker, who defeated the Liberal government of Canada in elections in 1957–8, was so convinced that officials in the Department of External Affairs were card-carrying supporters of Lester Pearson, who had been secretary of state since 1948, that he referred to them as 'Pearsonalities'.

Policy coordination

Despite the MFA's continuing role in foreign policy advice and implementation, it is rare for it now to have the same authority in the conduct of foreign relations relative to other ministries that it once had. The United States is perhaps unusual in having so many other agencies in addition to the State Department that are devoted chiefly to foreign affairs that they are referred to collectively as the 'foreign affairs community'. Nevertheless, it is a commonplace of discussion of this subject that in all states the 'line ministries' – trade, finance, defence, transport, environment, and so on, not forgetting the central bank – now engage in direct communication not only with their foreign counterparts but also with quite different agencies abroad. When that most eloquent scourge of the US State Department, Smith Simpson, wrote in praise of 'military diplomacy' in the 1960s, he did not have in mind simply military–military diplomacy. 'The very employment of foreign nationals at its far-ranging installations', he pointed out, 'obliges the military to negotiate not only with them but their labour organizations, with local communities, and with national ministries of labor, welfare, finance, and sometimes foreign affairs' (Simpson, 1967, p. 89). The extent of 'direct-dial diplomacy', as it is appropriately called, is now so great that the line ministries commonly have their own international departments (Rozental, pp. 139–40). As a result, it is no longer practical for the

MFA to insist that all calls to and from abroad be routed through its portals in order to ensure consistency in foreign policy and prevent foreigners from playing off one ministry against another. In short, the MFA can no longer aspire to be the state's 'gatekeeper' or 'international operator'.

The development of direct-dial diplomacy was, of course, a result of the growing complexity and range of international problems during the twentieth century, the diminishing ability of the generalists in the MFA to master them, and the increasing ease with which domestic ministries could make contact with ministries abroad. This development does not mean to say, however, that the MFA has relinquished the task of promoting consistency in the general design and implementation of foreign policy. On the contrary, it has used this trend, together with others,[20] to emphasize the importance of this task and seek to accomplish it in a different and more modest way, that is, by *coordinating* the foreign activities of the line ministries (Hocking, pp. 4, 9–10). It is right to do this because, as has been pointed out, coordination is 'the outstanding function of diplomacy and foreign ministries at this stage of development' (Langhorne and Wallace, p. 21).

Different MFAs seek to promote coordination in a variety of ways, and the bigger ones,[21] at least, do this first of all by retaining a strong emphasis on the geographical principle in the organization of their own departments. To take an example, it is obvious that if a major market for a state's arms exports overlaps with a region of great concern over human rights, it helps to ensure the coordination of policy on these subjects if there is a department exclusively concerned with this region. How does the MFA promote coordination beyond its own doors? A standard device is to insist on retaining control of all external diplomatic and consular missions and to require that officials from other ministries attached to them report home via the ambassador. A second common strategy is to ensure that senior MFA personnel are placed in key positions on any special foreign affairs committee attached to the office of a head of government, such as the Cabinet Office in Britain or the Prime Minister's External Affairs office in Japan.[22] A third option, employed in Mexico, is for the MFA to enjoy the legal prerogative of vetting all international treaties – however informally embodied – entered into by agencies of the government. A fourth, which is also employed in Mexico, is a requirement that the MFA must be given prior notice of any proposed official trip abroad by a senior government employee. A fifth is the interdepartmental (in the USA, 'inter-agency') committee, composed usually of senior officials of the departments with an interest in a particular aspect of foreign policy, and preferably chaired by an MFA representative.[23] A sixth is the temporary exchange of staff between the MFA and other ministries. And finally, the most radical solution is to house key functions under the same ministerial roof. The favoured, though still minority, option here is to merge the MFA with the ministry dealing with trade,[24] though this obviously does not solve the problem of coordinating the foreign activities of the remaining line ministries. This particular variant has not yet been favoured in the United States. However, in 1999 the Clinton administration oversaw the integration of three previously separate foreign affairs agencies into the 'lead foreign affairs agency', the State Department: the Arms Control and Disarmament Agency, the US Information Agency, and the US Agency for International Development.[25]

Dealing with foreign diplomats at home

Senior officials of the MFA periodically find themselves having to respond to a *démarche* on a particular subject made by the head of a foreign mission in the capital, and occasionally the foreign minister will summon a head of mission to listen to a protest of his own. When this sort of thing occurs the MFA is, of course, engaged in a function that has already been discussed – policy implementation. It should not be forgotten, however, that the MFA has other responsibilities relative to the resident diplomatic corps, though the scope of these and the energy expended in carrying them out varies with the ministry's nervousness about the activities (including life-style) of its members. Well aware of their information-gathering role and capacity for intrigue, as a rule governments have, since the inception of resident missions in the late fifteenth century, been more keen on sending than receiving them. (Although there were always monarchs who were flattered by the attentions of ambassadors and inclined to regard as an insult the departure of one before his replacement had arrived.) In some states, as in China in the second half of the nineteenth century, foreign missions were confined to a particular quarter, the better to keep their activities under close scrutiny. Today, though this custom is not entirely dead,[26] the vast majority of states are more relaxed about the political activities, at least, of the diplomatic corps in their capital cities.

Nevertheless, states have grown more concerned about the abuse of diplomatic immunities from the criminal and civil law, not least because the size of the diplomatic corps has grown considerably since the 1950s, chiefly because of the increase in the number of states. Partly for the same reason and partly because of the much greater ease of international travel, the number of visiting dignitaries has also increased vastly. It is not surprising, therefore, that all MFAs should have either a separate protocol department or one that embraces protocol together with a closely related function. Such departments contain experts in diplomatic and consular law and ceremonial. Among other things, they oversee the arrangements for visiting dignitaries and serve, in effect, as mediators between the diplomatic corps and the local community.[27] The Chinese government still takes a particularly close interest in the activities of the diplomatic corps, with a 'Diplomatic Personnel Service Bureau' affiliated to the MFA, as well as a Protocol Department. Among other things, the Bureau provides service staff for the diplomatic and consular missions in Beijing. Old habits also die hard in Russia, where an analogous organization – the Main Administration for Service to the Diplomatic Corps (*GlavUpDK*) – still survives.[28] In some states, too – the United States for example – the MFA itself is charged with assisting in both the physical protection of certain visiting dignitaries and foreign missions.[29]

Public diplomacy

Public diplomacy is foreign propaganda conducted or orchestrated by diplomats, and, as we shall see later (section on 'Propaganda' in Chapter 7), it is now a major task for diplomatic missions. This being so, it is an important function of the MFA to support them in this work with the supply of approved information on both foreign and domestic developments. The section responsible is usually known as the Information Department. However, since a state's image is also influenced by the reports of the foreign media correspondents who work in or out of its own capital, the MFA must also give careful attention to these individuals. It does so by means of a Press Department, though this may be merged with the former in a 'Press *and* Information' Department.[30] Whatever its precise title, the chief task here is to give 'breaking news' the best possible 'spin'; not surprisingly, this relatively new black art is known as 'news management'. The department or departments charged with public diplomacy are also increasingly required to devote resources to the electronic and online supply of information directly to the outside world, particularly via the MFA's web site. In the ministries of the larger states, they also have responsibility for directing, or agreeing priorities and measurements of performance with, the administrative arms of their cultural diplomacy (where separate) and those external radio and television broadcasting stations which are either directly or indirectly controlled by the state.[31] The US State Department now regards public diplomacy as so important that the previously separate US Information Agency was integrated into the Department in 1999. As a result, 'public diplomacy officers' are now attached to every regional and functional bureau.

Building support at home

Over recent decades, official commissions of inquiry have increasingly hounded some MFAs and their diplomatic services, and it is not difficult to see why. They had acquired a reputation for both social exclusiveness in recruitment and high living abroad, and faced a growing challenge to their very *raison d'être* not only from the 'direct-dial diplomacy' already mentioned but also from the more general implications for resident missions abroad of advanced telecommunications. It was thus an acute weakness that they had no domestic political base. Education ministries had teachers, agriculture ministries farmers, defence ministries the armed forces – but foreign ministries had only foreigners. As a result, over recent years many MFAs have begun to devote more resources to changing this situation, to building at least a modest degree of domestic support. They now do this by handling the national media at least as carefully as the foreign media. Thus Desk I of the Italian MFA's Press and Information Service handles the Italian media, while Desk II handles the foreign media. The State Department has one major bureau, the Bureau of Public Affairs, devoted almost exclusively to the domestic audience. Many MFAs also cultivate popular approval by providing up-to-date information on foreign destinations – not least via their recently created web sites – to intending travellers, including advice on personal safety. They also advertise the consular services which are available to their nationals should they find themselves in need of assistance once they are abroad, and a logical bureaucratic extension of this is now quite common: a department devoted to the welfare of nationals permanently resident abroad (see Box 1.4). MFAs also take every opportunity to impress on exporters and agencies seeking inward investment the value of the commercial diplomacy of their overseas missions. And in the small number of cases where they have actually merged with trade ministries they have not only promoted coordination but also moved directly to capture a key political constituency, namely, exporters. Finally, some MFAs have actually been opening their doors to NGOs,[32] academics, and others, not only in order to benefit from their specialist

---

Box 1.4 Emphasizing concern for nationals permanently resident abroad

Support for a state's 'nationals' or 'co-religionists' who are permanently resident abroad, whether they are passport-holders or not, is usually administered through the consular and/or geographical departments of the MFA, for good practical reasons. However, concern for them is advertised and energy on their behalf galvanized by creation of functional departments. The MFAs of at least the following states had such departments in 2001: Albania, Armenia ('Diaspora Department'), Czech Republic, Indonesia, Italy, Japan, Philippines, Portugal, Senegal, Slovenia, and Turkey. In the case of Senegal the MFA itself is actually called *Ministère des Affaires Etrangères et des Sénégalais de l'Extérieur*. The Chinese MFA does not have a department for overseas Chinese because there is a special agency for them under the State Council. Also noteworthy is the fact that one of the ten departments of the Barbados MFA is a 'Facilitation Unit for Returning Nationals'.

Source: MFA web sites, where available.

---

advice but also to recruit domestic allies. In short, it is now widely recognized that it is as important for the MFA to engage in 'outreach' at home as it is for its missions to engage in this abroad.

Summary

In most states today the ministry of foreign affairs must formally share influence over the making of foreign policy with other ministries and executive agencies. Nevertheless, in many of them it retains significant influence via its geographical expertise, control of the diplomatic service abroad, investment in public diplomacy, cultivation of domestic alliances, and growing acceptance that it is uniquely well positioned to coordinate the state's multidimensional international relationships. Most of these, from time to time, issue in the activity of negotiation, which – even narrowly conceived – represents the most important function of diplomacy. It is thus appropriate to turn next to this subject. Cardinal Richelieu, with whom this chapter began, would, I am certain, have approved of this decision.

Notes

Quotations not sourced in a footnote are from the web site of the MFA concerned.

1   Foreign affairs had previously been divided between two departments, namely, the Northern and Southern Departments, whose areas of competence lay roughly – very roughly – either side of the division between northern and southern Europe. However, each also had domestic responsibilities. The Northern Department became the Foreign Office and Charles James Fox was appointed the first Secretary of State for Foreign Affairs. The Southern Department became the Home Office (Cecil, pp. 541–2).

2   For the remainder of the historical introduction to this chapter, I have drawn heavily on the Introduction to Steiner (ed.) (1982).

3   Not to be confused with the 'political director', who is 'a special animal, usually directly below the civil service head of the MFA, masterminding the political work' (Kishan Rana to the author). Following Britain's entry into the European Community in the 1970s, the FCO also acquired a political director in order to facilitate British participation in European Political Co-operation. Since that time the permanent under-secretary has steadily become more and more of a departmental manager and enjoyed correspondingly less time to devote to policy.

4   Making the distinction between knowledge of technique, which can be taught and learned from a book, and practical knowledge, which can only be imparted and acquired through apprenticeship to a master, Michael Oakeshott reminds us of this in his famous essay, 'Rationalism in Politics' (p. 34).

5   It is not for nothing that Platt called his excellent book on the history of the British consular service *The Cinderella Service*.

6   It is important to add that while there may have been a considerable degree of administrative unification, the distinction between diplomatic and consular work is still widely acknowledged and is reflected in international law. Indeed, diplomatic and consular agents operate under different legal regimes, the former under the Vienna Convention on Diplomatic Relations 1961 and the latter under the Vienna Convention on Consular Relations 1963.

7   However, the plight of the MFA in developing countries (including 'emerging market economies') appears now not to be so uniformly hopeless as it was at least as late as the middle of the 1970s. Compare Robertson's article (pp. 4–9), published in 1998 with the sections on 'The decision making process' in Clapham, published twenty years earlier.

8   I am grateful to Stefano Baldi for supplying the information on which I have made these rough calculations.

9   Sometimes a fully-fledged 'Diplomatic Academy' or 'Diplomatic Institute' such as the Rio Branco Institute in Brazil.

10   The security level of this remarkable document, which attacks the management style of the ambassador quite remorselessly, was originally 'Sensitive but Unclassified'. It was then changed to 'Unclassified', only a few paragraphs having been whited out. It can be found at http://oig.state.gov/pdf/ bucharest.pdf For the work of the Office of Inspector General and its various publications, start at the home page, http://oig.state.gov/

11   Hiving off a function from the MFA and creating a completely separate ministry is an even better way of doing this. Thus whenever the Labour Party comes to power in Britain the overseas aid programme tends to be taken away from the FCO and given its own ministry. This not only advertises Labour's concern for this issue but also provides a defence against the

ingrained suspicion that aid is never distributed where it is most needed but where instead it best serves Britain's political interests. The aid programme is reabsorbed into the Foreign and Commonwealth Office (FCO) when the less squeamish Conservatives return (Dickie, pp. 60–1; Kampfner, pp. 166–7).

12 In the FCO, some important functional departments are now part of an 'International Organizations' command.

13 Before separate foreign ministries were created, such archives were kept by other secretaries of state or palace officials. They even existed in the palaces of the 'great kings' of the ancient Near East (Meier, p. 212).

14 A Legal Adviser, defined as a short form for 'Head of the Office responsible for International Legal Services', was listed for over 160 states by the UN's Legal Adviser, Hans Corell, in a circular letter of 15 November 2000. Of these, between 120 and 130 are recognizable as specialist legal advisers within an MFA. I am grateful to the Mongolian MFA for copy of this (public) document.

15 It is no accident that the US State Department was given its first planning staff when a former military man, General George C. Marshall, became Secretary of State after World War II (Simpson, 1967, pp. 23, 79, 85).

16 This glorified 'contingency planning' is not what Rothstein had in mind when in 1972 he argued for a long-range planning staff to be established *outside* the State Department. Planning undertaken within the Department by persons recruited from its 'operators' would be incapable of examining fundamental assumptions and thus not be genuine planning at all. See especially ch. 2.

17 This problem has been recognized for a long time. In a spurt of reform in the US State Department in the early 1960s, 'planning advisers were assigned to the operating bureaus in a fresh effort to reduce the fatal gap between planning and doing' (Simpson, 1967, p. 214).

18 The experience of George Kennan is still instructive. The first director of the State Department's planning staff, he resigned after Acheson, who had replaced Marshall as Secretary of State, began to make him feel like a 'court jester' and the operational units began to insist on policy recommendations going up through the 'line of command' (Kennan, pp. 426–7, 465–6).

19 Practice varies in this regard. Thus it is not surprising that the Israeli MFA should have a 'situation room' and the US State Department an 'operations center' that are continuously operational, though in Britain the FCO has 'emergency rooms' which are only opened and staffed when a crisis breaks.

20 Pursuit of the same or related negotiations through multilateral as well as bilateral channels, back-channels as well as front ones, and unofficial as well as official channels.

21 Of course, in states where the MFA is completely marginalized, as for example in certain developing countries where economic and financial problems completely dominate their international relations, coordination via the MFA is a forlorn hope (Akokpari).

22 Of course, such bodies are themselves usually charged with a coordinating role. Another case in point is the National Security Council (NSC) in the United States. However, it is impossible for the US State Department to exert predominant influence on the NSC, since this has its own powerful staff and

also, at the minimum, equal representation of the Department of Defense, the CIA, and the Joint Chiefs of Staff. The Vice-President is also a member of the NSC.

23   In Britain, a de facto version of this that is in permanent being is the network of private offices of ministers in Whitehall (Henderson, 1984, p. 113).

24   At the time of writing, and as far as I can detect, this has happened only in the cases of Australia, Barbados, Belgium, Canada, South Korea, Swaziland, and Sweden. In the Australian Department of Foreign Affairs and Trade (DFAT), there remain separate foreign and trade ministers and both sit in the Cabinet; nevertheless, the foreign minister is normally the senior minister (Harris, p. 33).

25   However, in the cases of arms control and aid, this was done less out of a desire for better coordination than a wish to downgrade these issue areas in American foreign policy by curbing their administrative autonomy. (I am grateful to David H. Dunn for this qualification.)

26   The Saudi MFA is keen to advertise its own 'Diplomatic Quarter', which was created as recently as the mid-1980s and is located five miles from the centre of the political capital, Riyadh, but quite close to Diriyah, the ancestral home of the Saudi royal family. Until this time, the embassies were located in Jeddah, the commercial capital of the kingdom and main port of entry for pilgrims en route to the holy cities.

27   There is a full and interesting description of the varied responsibilities of the State Department's Office of Protocol (which has tasks abroad as well) in *State Magazine*, Jan. 1999, which can be found at http://www.state.gov/www/publications/statemag_jan99/bom.html

28   This traces its roots back to 1921, that is to say, to the heroic aftermath of the Bolshevik revolution (http:www.mid.ru/mid/eng/glavupdk.htm).

29   The State Department's Bureau of Diplomatic Security Service has an 'Office of Foreign Missions'.

30   In the US State Department it is known as the Office of International Information Programs. However, the Bureau of Public Affairs (targeted at the domestic audience) and the Bureau of Educational and Cultural Affairs also fall under the direction of the Under Secretary for Public Diplomacy and Public Affairs, a post first created in late 1999. In the British Foreign and Commonwealth Office this department is known as 'News Department'.

31   In Britain's case, these are, respectively, the British Council and the BBC World Service.

32   In some adventurous ministries it is now also not unusual for NGOs even to be permitted membership of national delegations to certain major conferences.

Further reading

Boyce, Peter J., *Foreign Affairs for New States* (St. Martin's Press – now Palgrave: New York, 1977), chs 6–8.

Bullen, Roger (ed.), *The Foreign Office, 1782–1982* (University Publications of America: Frederick, Maryland, 1984).

Clapham, Christopher (ed.), *Foreign Policy Making in Developing States: A Comparative Approach* (Saxon House: Farnborough, Hampshire, 1978) [sections on 'The decision making process'].

Coles, John, *Making Foreign Policy: A Certain Idea of Britain* (John Murray: London, 2000).

Dickie, John, *Inside the Foreign Office* (Chapman & Hall: London, 1992).

Hennessy, Peter, *Whitehall* (Fontana: London, 1990).

Herman, Michael, *Intelligence Power in Peace and War* (Cambridge University Press: Cambridge, 1996).

Herman, Michael, 'Diplomacy and intelligence', *Diplomacy & Statecraft*, vol. 9, no. 2, July 1998, pp. 1–22.

Hocking, Brian (ed.), *Foreign Ministries: Change and Adaptation* (Macmillan – now Palgrave: Basingstoke, 1999).

International Insights, vol. 14, summer 1998. Special Issue on 'The Foreign Ministry in Developing Countries and Emerging Market Economies', ed. Justin Robertson.

Jones, Ray, *The Nineteenth-Century Foreign Office: An Administrative History* (Weidenfeld & Nicolson: London, 1971).

Kennan, George F., *Memoirs, 1925–1950* (Hutchinson: London, 1967), pp. 325–7, 426–7, 465–6 [on formation of policy planning staff in the State Department].

Kennan, George F., 'Diplomacy without Diplomats?', *Foreign Affairs*, 76(5), 1997.

Loeffler, Jane C., *The Architecture of Diplomacy: Building America's Embassies* (Princeton Architectural Press: New York, 1998).

Merillat, H. C. L. (ed.), *Legal Advisers and Foreign Affairs* (Oceana: Dobbs Ferry, New York, 1964).

Middleton, Charles Ronald, *The Administration of British Foreign Policy, 1782–1846* (Duke University Press: Durham, North Carolina, 1977).

Prados, John, *Keepers of the Keys: A History of the National Security Council from Truman to Bush* (Morrow: New York, 1991).

Rana, Kishan S., *Inside Diplomacy* (Manas: New Delhi, 2000), ch. 11 [on the Indian MFA].

Rothstein, Robert L., *Planning, Prediction, and Policymaking in Foreign Affairs: Theory and Practice* (Little, Brown: Boston, 1972).

Simpson, Smith, *Anatomy of the State Department* (Houghton Mifflin: Boston, 1967).

Steiner, Zara, *The Foreign Office and Foreign Policy, 1898–1914* (Cambridge University Press: Cambridge, 1969).

Steiner, Zara (ed.), *The Times Survey of Foreign Ministries of the World* (Times Books: London, 1982).

Theakston, Kevin, 'New Labour and the Foreign Office', in R. Little and M. Wickham-Jones (eds), *New Labour's Foreign Policy* (Manchester University Press: Manchester and New York, 2000).

Urban, Mark, *UK Eyes Alpha: The Inside Story of British Intelligence* (Faber and Faber: London and Boston, 1996).

Ward, Sir A. W. and G. P. Gooch (eds), *The Cambridge History of British Foreign Policy 1783–1919*, vol. III 1866–1919 (Cambridge University Press: Cambridge, 1923), ch. VIII, 'The Foreign Office', by Algernon Cecil.

Many ministries of foreign affairs have their own web sites, and these are steadily becoming more numerous and improving in quality. Most provide at least a list of the different departments (sometimes even an 'organigram'), while a few go so far as to give a detailed history of the ministry. In the last regard, the web site of the Canadian MFA is outstanding. The back copies of *State Magazine*, available via the US State Department's web site, are also extremely useful. The easiest way to locate these sites is to use the Mediterranean Diplomatic Academy's excellent *Diplo Directory*, the URL of which is http://diplo.diplomacy.edu/directory/

For additional references on the role of the legal adviser in the MFA, see the very useful bibliography compiled and updated by Hans Corell, the UN's own legal adviser: 'The Role of the Legal Adviser: List of Literature', http://www.un.org/law/counsel/litlist.htm

Part I
The Art of Negotiation

Introduction to Part I

In international politics, negotiation, narrowly conceived, consists of discussion between officially designated representatives designed to achieve the formal agreement of their governments to the way forward on an issue that is either of shared concern or in dispute between them. Negotiation, as noted in the Introduction to this book, is only one of the functions of diplomacy and in some situations not the most urgent; this might be issuing a warning or seeking clarification of a statement. In traditional diplomacy via resident missions, it is also true that negotiation is not the activity to which most time is generally devoted. (Although when diplomats 'lobby' some agency of the state to which they are accredited, as they have always spent much of their time doing, the only differences from negotiation are that the dialogue is configured differently and any successes are not formally registered.) Negotiation even conceived narrowly remains nevertheless the most important function of diplomacy when itself conceived broadly. This is in part because the diplomatic system now encompasses considerably more than the work of resident missions. And negotiation becomes more and more its operational focus as we move into the realms of multilateral diplomacy, summitry, and above all into that other growth sector of the world diplomatic system – mediation. Furthermore, it hardly needs labouring that it is the process of negotiation that grapples directly with the most threatening problems, whether they are economic dislocation, environmental catastrophe, or war. It is because negotiation narrowly conceived is the most important function of diplomacy broadly conceived that it is to this that the first Part of this book is devoted.

Students of negotiations, notably Zartman and Berman, divide them into three distinct stages: those concerned with prenegotiations, formula, and details. The first two chapters of Part I hinge on these distinctions,

Chapter 2 dealing with prenegotiations and Chapter 3 with the formula and details stages together – 'around-the-table' negotiations. The characteristics of each stage are analysed, including their characteristic difficulties. However, two cautions must at once be registered. First, the concept of sequential stages of negotiation is an analytical construct. In reality, not only do the stages usually overlap but sometimes the difficulties of a particular stage are so acute that 'back-tracking' (return to an earlier stage) is unavoidable. Secondly, the notion of three-stage negotiations has developed principally out of analysis of talks on issues where the stakes are high, typically between previously or still warring parties. In negotiations between friendly states on matters of relatively low importance the prenegotiations stage will present few problems and may barely be noticeable at all. Since negotiations of the high stakes kind, however, are clearly the most important, it is they that are principally in mind in Chapter 2. This will also concentrate on bilateral rather than multilateral negotiations, though the latter – while presenting some different problems and possibilities – proceed through the same stages (Touval 1989). Following discussion of the stages of negotiations, Chapter 4 considers the various devices whereby their momentum may be preserved or – if lost – regained. In Chapter 5, the final chapter in Part I, an examination will be found of the different ways in which negotiated agreements might be presented to the world and why different situations demand that agreements be differently 'packaged'.

2
Prenegotiations

At first glance, the term 'prenegotiations' is a terrible misnomer, in fact a contradiction in terms. It seems, that is to say, clearly illogical to describe the first stage of negotiations as '*pre*negotiations'. Indeed, a great deal of negotiation is conducted in this stage, even though it may not be as stylized as that in the later stages; furthermore, some of this negotiation, albeit disguised, concerns substantive issues. Nevertheless, it is common to find states continuing to place great emphasis on instruments of conflict during this period as well, so perhaps it is not so misleading after all. Prenegotiation, then, is the whole range of activity conducted prior to the first stage of formal substantive, or 'around-the-table', negotiation (Saunders). It is directed at achieving agreement on three matters. The first of these is agreement on the possibility that negotiation may prove advantageous to all parties concerned. The second is agreement on an agenda for talks. And the third is agreement on the manner in which the talks should be conducted – questions of procedure. This chapter will consider each of these subjects in turn.

Agreeing the need to negotiate

It is an unusual situation in which the parties to a conflict, whether it is principally military, economic, or waged by means of propaganda, are *equally* convinced that a stalemate exists or, in other words, that each has a veto over the outcome preferred by the other. It is also an unusual situation in which, even if there is widespread acceptance of a stalemate, all are *equally* agreed that negotiation is the only way forward. One party may believe that time is on its side. This may be because of some anticipated technical or scientific development that it hopes will alter the balance of military power, or because of a possible change of leadership

29

on the part of a major power that will change the diplomatic context in its favour. And even if there is widespread agreement that the time is ripe for a negotiated settlement, it is also an unusual situation in which all are *equally* prepared to acknowledge this – suing for peace, after all, is usually a sign of weakness.

It should not be surprising, therefore, that establishing the need for negotiations is often a complicated and delicate matter, 'in many cases … more complicated, time-consuming, and difficult than reaching agreement once negotiations [*sic*] have begun' (Saunders, p. 249). For one thing, because establishing the need for negotiations rests funda-mentally on gaining acceptance of the fact that a stalemate exists, any party to whom suspicions of weakness attach may feel that it actually has to raise the temperature of the conflict while simultaneously putting out feelers for negotiations. Third parties may be calling instead for 'gestures of goodwill' but stepping up the pressure will safeguard the balance and offer protection against domestic hard-liners. If on the other hand powerful third parties are positioning themselves to act as mediators, they may be able, for example by regulating the flow of arms to the rivals, to engineer a stalemate themselves (see Chapter 11).

In bitter conflicts where the stakes are high, for example in the Middle East and until the beginning of the 1990s in South Africa, acceptance of a stalemate nearly always takes a long time. When the issues concern core values and perhaps even survival itself, it is obvious that there will be enormous reluctance to accept that another party has the ability to block achievement of one's aspirations or permanently threaten an otherwise satisfactory status quo. Acceptance of a stalemate in such circumstances requires repeated demonstration of power and resolve by both parties. In the Arab–Israeli conflict it took four wars (five in-cluding the War of Attrition from 1967 until 1970) before Egypt made peace with Israel, in 1979, and then it required the assistance of sus-tained top-level American mediation and the application of heavy pres-sure to both sides. It was a further 14 years before the PLO and Israel reached out for the olive branch. Acceptance of a stalemate may also require each party to lobby the allies of the other, for if these powers concede that there is a stalemate this is more likely to be accepted by the parties themselves.

If in the end existence of a stalemate is accepted, the parties next have to acknowledge the possibility that a negotiated settlement (though not of course *any* negotiated settlement) may be better for all concerned than continuing with things as they are. This is perhaps the true begin-ning of prenegotiations. Through direct or indirect contacts between rivals and through propaganda directed at allies and domestic constituencies, this generally means conveying three messages. The first is that the parties have important common interests as well as interests that divide them.[1] The second is that disaster will be inescapable if negotiations are not grasped. The third is that there is a possible solution. This may involve the suggestion that negotiation of the dispute in question be 'linked' to another in which the parties are also on opposite sides, thus increasing the scope for trade-offs.

Indeed, encouraging the belief that negotiations are at any rate worth a try means floating a 'formula' or 'framework' for a settlement. This will have to give something to both sides, and at the least suggest that enlisting intelligence, imagination, and empathy, that is to say, diplomacy, may be able to produce a solution. It will, however, also have to be fairly vague because a vague formula avoids giving hostages to fortune in a world in which circumstances are constantly changing. Such a formula is also meat and drink to that ubiquitous individual, the wishful thinker, and at this early stage, when nothing that will help to launch the negotiations can be spurned, the wishful thinker is the negotiator's ally.

When parties to a conflict start to explore the possibility of a negotiated settlement they do not, of course, do this in a political vacuum. A variety of circumstances, at home and abroad, will affect the likelihood that negotiations will be launched successfully. To begin with, it is obviously necessary for the leadership on both sides to be domestically secure. This will give them the confidence that they will be able to ride out any charge that they are proposing to 'sell out' to the enemy. In democracies, this consideration argues for rapid movement after elections, when a new government has the opportunity to take unpopular action in the reasonable expectation that the voters will either have forgotten or secured compensating blessings by the time they are next able to express a view. Thus the American president, Jimmy Carter, moved as fast as possible on the Arab–Israeli front after his inauguration in January 1977 because he knew that the kind of settlement that he had in mind would cause some anguish to the powerful Jewish lobby in the United States (Quandt, ch. 2). In autocracies domestic hard-line opponents have to be dealt with in some other way before negotiations, at any rate substantive negotiations, can be launched. Lin Piao, the pro-Soviet minister of defence in Communist China who opposed any rapprochement between Peking and Washington, died in a mysterious air crash in early 1972.

If the leaderships of the parties contemplating negotiations should be domestically secure, it is a commonplace – but worth repeating for all that – that it is a further advantage for them to have a record of hostility to the other side. With such a curriculum vitae they are invulnerable to the charge that their disposition to negotiate is prompted by secret sympathies for the enemy or an inadequate grasp of their own national or ideological priorities; and they are the best placed to hold their own conservatives in line. Thus it was that the reputation for fierce anti-Communism of US President Richard Nixon, was a great asset to him in the early 1970s. This was because he had come to the conclusion that it was necessary to restore normal relations with Communist China, improve relations with the Soviet Union, return Okinawa to Japan, and dump South Vietnam – all policies that were anathema to American conservatives (Safire, pp. 366–7). Another leader whose 'superhawk' reputation stood him in good stead when it came to making peace with his enemy was the Israeli prime minister, Menachem Begin. Begin, who headed the Likud coalition that triumphed in the elections in mid-1977, was a former leader of the Jewish underground movement, the Irgun, and currently leader of its political successor, the Herut Party. Herut had a reputation for extremism and Begin's name itself was trad-itionally linked to the policy of absolute refusal to surrender territory to the Arabs – 'not one inch' (Weizman, pp. 36–7). This reputation helped him to carry the Knesset through protracted and difficult negotiations from 1977 to early 1979. These talks produced the surrender of Sinai to Egypt and an agreement on the West Bank that to many Israeli hardliners looked like the thin end of the wedge of a future Palestinian state.

Finally, it is perhaps worth noting that prenegotiations are most likely to make progress if incidents that cause public alarm are avoided. Of course, this is true of all stages of negotiations, as the Hebron massacre in March 1993, which occurred while Israel and the PLO were trying to settle the details of their 'framework agreement' of the previous Septem-ber, so tragically demonstrated. However, it is particularly true of the prenegotiations stage because this is the most fragile. In this stage, relatively little prestige will have been tied to a successful outcome, and retreat from negotiations will not, therefore, generally carry a high price (Stein, pp. 482–3). A high premium attaches, therefore, to the avoidance of incidents such as exchanges of fire along a ceasefire line, hostile popular demonstrations, or virulent press attacks on one side or the other. And the reasons for this are obvious: they put pressure on leaders to increase their demands; they also give them a pretext, if they want one, to avoid or break off initial contacts with the other party.

Agreeing the agenda

If the need for negotiations is recognized and conditions are propitious, it becomes possible to discuss an agenda for talks. This means not only agreeing what will be discussed but also the order in which the agreed items will be taken. Unless one of the parties is indifferent to these points on the complacent grounds that it is merely entering a 'dialogue' rather than a negotiation (De Soto, p. 362), this often creates more difficulties than might be imagined. Why?

There are three main reasons why agenda *content* might be controversial. The first is that the language of a proposed agenda may indicate that one party has already conceded a vital point. A perfect example of this is provided by the argument over the agenda when the government of El Salvador and the coalition of insurgent groups (FMLN) with which it was faced began to edge towards negotiations at the end of the 1980s. Not surprisingly, the FMLN wanted El Salvador's existing armed forces abolished. As a result, the wording it proposed for the armed forces item on the agenda was 'the future' of the armed forces. By contrast, the government insisted on discussing their 'restructuring' or, even better, 'modernization'. Acceptance of the latter wording by the FMLN clearly indicated their acceptance that the armed forces could not be abolished, and had provoked 'serious controversy' (De Soto, p. 363).

A proposed agenda may even imply a proposed deal. As a result, accept the agenda and, in principle, one accepts the deal. This is why the United States resisted the suggestion of Saddam Hussein that the Palestinian question as well as Iraqi occupation of Kuwait should be on the agenda of talks to avert the reversal of this occupation by force in late 1990 and early 1991. Had this proposal been accepted, Washington would have conceded that it was reasonable to give Baghdad something for the Palestinians *in return for* withdrawal from Kuwait. But it had no intention of doing this, since it would have rewarded Saddam's aggression with a major propaganda victory and compromised utterly the American policy of persuading Israel to maintain a low profile in the crisis. Sometimes, nevertheless, proposed agendas containing implicit deals are accepted, especially if the deal has been floated earlier as a possible 'formula' or 'framework for agreement' and eventually been accepted as at least a basis for negotiation. Such was the case with the American proposal, first made in the early 1980s, that the issues of South African withdrawal from Namibia and Cuban (plus ANC) withdrawal from Angola should be 'linked'. This meant that the parties should discuss them simultaneously, the assumption being that the withdrawal of the one would be the price of withdrawal by the other. (Linkage is discussed further in the section below dealing with the formula stage.)

The second reason why serious difficulties can be caused by agenda content is that agendas are sometimes used as weapons of propaganda. This is possible because while it is a proper inheritance of the French system of diplomacy that the cut and thrust of negotiations should remain secret, it is normally accepted that the subjects of discussion, that is, the agenda, should – at least in broad outline – be public knowledge. This being so, the parties to a potential negotiation can suggest agenda items that they know will never produce concessions from the other side merely in order to advertise their own priorities. If for some reason the victims of this treatment feel bound to permit their inclusion on the agenda, they will not only have handed a propaganda victory to the opposition but perhaps created all manner of trouble for themselves with friends and allies. It was for reasons such as these that the South African foreign minister, Eric Louw, wanted items such as the arming of blacks and Asian immigration into East Africa on the agenda of a white man's conference in 1955 (Berridge, 1992a, pp. 133–7) and that Chou En-lai insisted that Taiwan should be on the agenda of the Nixon visit to China in February 1972. Louw was only thwarted with difficulty, while Chou was not thwarted at all – the stakes for the Americans were too high to be jeopardized by a refusal to concede on this issue.

The third common source of argument over the content of the agenda concerns its generality or vagueness. It is certainly true, as already indicated, that this might with advantage be a feature of any formula floated in the early days of prenegotiations. However, when the agenda itself is being constructed a party that knows that it will never get the other to agree to inscription of a specific item may strive to secure a vague agenda. This will enable it to bring up the issue in which it is interested once the real talks get under way (De Soto, p. 363; Webster, p. 62).

As for the *order* of the agenda, this can also create difficulties. This is because the parties to any negotiation generally approach them in the expectation that they will have to give concessions on some items and receive them on others. It is also natural for them to demand that the latter should be taken first. There are two reasons for this. First, the side that has to wait until later for the items on which it needs concessions may be induced to be generous on the early items in order to increase the likelihood of reciprocal treatment when its turn comes round. Secondly, the side that gets early concessions avoids an impression of weakness and so avoids encouraging the opposition and – if there are leaks – trouble at home. Calculations of this sort were evident during important negotiations between the South African government and the shipping companies in the Europe–South Africa trade in late 1965 and early 1966. Until the very end of three series of negotiations covering thirty-three formal meetings, the government managed to delay discussion of the issue of an increase in freight rates, which was the item on which it expected to have to make concessions to the companies. In the meanwhile, the government won concession after concession on other items, such as the shipment of arms in national flag vessels (Berridge, 1987, pp. 102–8). In a more recent example, Syria demanded that the return of the Golan Heights (seized from them in 1967) should be settled in negotiations with Israel before any other matters could be considered. In this case, though, the other party refused to go along and – despite the best efforts of President Clinton in his last days before leaving office – the negotiations failed to make progress (*The Guardian*, 18 Jan. 2000).

Of course, the significance of the order in which agenda items are taken is reduced if it is possible to make the grant of early concessions conditional on receipt of later ones; and this often happens. On the other hand, conditionality cannot obscure the fact that the party concerned is willing in principle to make these concessions, or entirely erase the image of weakness created by their early granting. Indeed, the party that agrees to permit early consideration of items on which it expects to have to give most concessions has already conceded a point – or missed a trick. Furthermore, since the principal beneficiary of negotiations on the first items will generally maintain that it has made some concessions on these points as well, it may not always be easy to secure payment later – and if conditionality is evoked too forcefully may lead to a charge of bad faith. In general, then, the order or sequence in which agenda items are taken is unlikely to be a matter of indifference.

Agreeing procedure

With the agenda agreed[2] the final task of the prenegotiations stage is agreement on procedure. Here there are four main questions to resolve: format, venue, level and composition of delegations, and timing.

Format

As to the format of the negotiations, will they be direct (face-to-face) or indirect? Direct talks between enemies have many practical advantages, and are discussed in more detail later (see end of Chapter 11). If, because of problems of 'face' or legal recognition, the talks nevertheless need an intermediary, who will this be? Will it have to be a genuine mediator or will provision of good offices by a third party be sufficient? (On mediation and good offices, see Chapter 11.) Whatever the role of the third party, can the negotiations be made somewhat easier by taking the form of proximity talks, as in the case of the UN-mediated talks between the Afghan Communist government and the Pakistanis that were held in Geneva in the mid-1980s (Berridge, 1991, p. 64)? In such talks an intermediary is employed but the delegations of the principal parties are prepared to base themselves in close proximity to each other, typically in the same hotel or conference centre.[3] This obviously makes the mediator's job easier.

If more than two parties are to be involved in the talks, as is often the case, will they be conducted by a series of parallel bilateral discussions, a multilateral conference, or some combination of both? Bilateral discussions have in their favour maximum flexibility, speed and secrecy. On the other hand, they are likely to inspire suspicion among allies that one or other among their number is seeking a separate deal with the enemy; they also lack the propaganda value of a big conference. If a combination of bilateral discussion and multilateral conference is preferred, what powers shall the multilateral 'plenary' conference have, relative to decisions made in its bilateral subcommittees? Do the latter merely report to the former as a matter of courtesy, or do they give it a veto? If a key player fears it may be in a minority in the plenary it is highly unlikely that it will agree to the latter course. Apart from established conventions, choice of format is thus influenced by the degree of urgency attending a negotiation, the state of relations among allies, and the determination of the most powerful or most resolute among the parties as to which format will suit its own interests best. Weaker states generally prefer to negotiate with more powerful ones in a multilateral forum since this maximizes their chances of forming coalitions with like-minded and similarly vulnerable parties; hence 'the pro-supranational inclinations of most of the small member states of the European Union' (Meerts, p. 82).

Not surprisingly, the question of format was a serious and complicated problem in the case of Jimmy Carter's Middle East diplomacy in the late 1970s. With the drastic decline in Soviet influence in Egypt which had preceded the Yom Kippur War, the United States was firmly in the driving seat as far as negotiations to resolve the Arab–Israeli conflict were concerned. And Washington's view was that, while secret bilateral diplomacy was the only format that would be likely to achieve any real

---

Box 2.1   The Geneva Conference format for Middle East peace negotiations

This had its immediate origins in the aftermath of the Yom Kippur War, when the UN Security Council called (in Resolution 338) for immediate talks between the Arabs and the Israelis 'aimed at establishing a just and durable peace in the Middle East'. A conference was duly held in Geneva in late December 1973. It had six signal features. First, it was held under UN auspices.[4] Secondly, it was effectively co-chaired by the superpowers, the United States and the Soviet Union. Thirdly, all immediately interested parties were invited, which meant the Israelis sitting down with the Arabs. Fourthly, it consisted chiefly of 'a battery of public speeches' rather than serious secret negotiation (Kissinger, 1982, ch. 17). Fifthly, neither superpower would be present in negotiations at the sub-committee level (Quandt, p. 143). Sixthly, the plenary conference was to have no right of veto over decisions taken in any subsequent bilateral negotiations.[5]

---

breakthrough, this would only happen if the 'Geneva Conference' format (Box 2.1) was to be employed in some way. Among other things, this would 'symbolize trends toward making peace' and thus put pressure on the radicals, minimize the chances of the Soviet Union disrupting the process out of pique at being excluded and, above all, legitimize direct Arab–Israeli contact. In each of these regards the Geneva Conference had had some degree of success. However, by the time that Carter inherited the mantle of Middle East brokerage in 1977 circumstances had changed.

Carter's reasons for initially supporting a reconvening of Geneva, albeit after significant progress had been made in bilateral talks (Quandt, pp. 61, 76), were essentially the same as those of Kissinger. These reasons were protecting the flank of the moderate Arab states on the Palestinian question (there would be 'Palestinian' representation of some kind at Geneva as well as representation of all Arab states), advertising the peace process, and limiting the potential of the Soviet Union for trouble-making (Quandt, pp. 118–21, 137–43). However, Egypt had moved much further away from the Soviet Union by 1977 and was worried about the influence that the Geneva format might give it over a settlement. This format, especially if it involved a unified Arab delegation, would also reduce its flexibility in negotiations with Israel. These considerations were now the more important for Egypt since the relatively easy steps of military disengagement had by now been achieved, and what was left were the big questions: sovereignty over Sinai and the future of the West Bank, in that order. Geneva might help Egypt but, as it was shaping up, it was more likely to prove a trap. In the event, the delay in reconvening

Geneva, caused in part by the enormous difficulty of agreeing on how the Palestinians should be represented, gave Sadat the pretext for sabotaging this route by making his spectacular journey to Jerusalem in November 1977. After this, the Geneva format was a dead letter, despite the fact that much of the top-level and time-consuming diplomacy of 1977 had been concerned with preparing for it.

Venue

Choice of the format of a negotiation sometimes goes a long way towards dictating where they will take place, their venue. For example, had the Arab–Israeli talks of the Carter years in fact followed the Geneva Conference format, it is likely that they would have taken place in Geneva. Indeed, the American proposal was that, as in 1973, the UN secretary-general should once more issue the invitations, and there is no suggestion in the public record of the discussions at the time that an alternative venue was ever seriously considered. It was likely, then, that the talks would have taken place in Geneva – but not inevitable. When the next international conference on the Middle East, co-chaired by the super-powers and in most essentials resembling the 1973 Geneva Conference,[6] actually took place, in the aftermath of the Gulf War in November 1991, it did not take place in Geneva but in Madrid. This was *not* because the Swiss city had been destroyed by fire or was suffering from a strike by air-traffic controllers. Why is venue often an important matter in prenegotiations and why does it, as a result, often cause considerable difficulties?

The venue of negotiations is important because if a state is able to persuade its rival to send a delegation to its own shores, this will be of great practical convenience to it. For this reason it will also suggest very strongly that it is the more powerful. In consequence, the travellers will have suffered a loss of face. It is hardly surprising, therefore, in light of the speed and efficiency with which images and other kinds of information can be flashed across the world, that this happens only rarely, and that alternative solutions are the subject of discussion in the pre-negotiations stage. In fact, there are three common strategies for getting over this problem: neutral ground, meeting 'halfway', and alternating (rotating, if there are more than two parties) home venues.

Some venues are chosen for negotiations because either by convention or law they are neutral ground. This, of course, explains the popularity of venues in Switzerland and Austria, both permanently neutral states in international law. Vienna, the capital of Austria, has the added advantage of unique historical association with the development of modern diplomacy, from the Congress of 1815 to the Conference on

Diplomatic Intercourse and Immunities in 1961 (see Chapter 7). The Hague, which was chosen as the site of the Iran–United States Claims Tribunal in 1981, provides another example. Although the Netherlands is a NATO member, The Hague is home to the International Court of Justice and also the Permanent Court of Arbitration, which, indeed, provided the Iran–United States Claims Tribunal with its first quarters in the city (Berridge, 1994, p. 124).

Another traditional device for saving face is to choose a venue for negotiations which is roughly equidistant between the capitals of the rival states. Since compromise is of the essence of diplomacy, it is appropriate as well as face-saving if the parties agree to meet somewhere that is geographically 'halfway' between their own countries. This, of course, was yet another ingredient of the appeal of Vienna during the Cold War, since it is roughly equidistant between Moscow and the capitals of the European members of NATO. And it was the whole of the appeal of Wake Island in the Pacific Ocean as the venue for the highly sensitive and subsequently controversial talks in October 1950 between President Truman and Douglas MacArthur, a particularly troublesome general. MacArthur was virtually the American 'emperor' of Japan. He had not visited the United States since 1938 and Truman had never met him.[7] What is particularly interesting about the convention of 'meeting halfway', however, is that its appeal is so great that a state may even be content to forgo neutral ground and meet a rival on the territory of the latter's ally – provided it is 'halfway' between them. Thus when in 1986 the Soviet leader, Mikhail Gorbachev, proposed a US–Soviet summit preparatory to the one already arranged in Washington, he mentioned as possibilities either London or Reykjavik, though both Britain and Iceland were NATO members. However, both were consistent with his other suggestion, which was that he and President Reagan should meet 'somewhere halfway' (Adelman, p. 25). In the event, they settled on Reykjavik.

Finally, states can avoid any loss of prestige over the issue of venue by agreeing – should there be a need for lengthy negotiations – to alternate between their respective capitals. Since someone has to be the first to travel, however, taking it in turns is a solution that is generally acceptable only after some diplomatic breakthrough and general improvement in relations. There has to be, in other words, reasonable confidence that a sequence will be established, that each will share the benefits of negotiating at home. For example, after the initial superpower summits in the 1950s and early 1960s, which were held on neutral ground (Geneva and Vienna), a rough pattern of alternation was established in the early 1970s. At about the same time, the Americans and the Chinese Communists agreed to meet alternately in their embassies in Warsaw (Berridge, 1994, p. 88). Following the settlement of the Angola/Namibia conflicts in 1988, the venue of the regular meetings of the joint commission created to consolidate the agreement rotated between the capitals of the full members (Berridge, 1994, Box 7.1, p. 121). And this is the procedure adopted for summit meetings of the member states of the EU, the European Council, as noted in Chapter 10.

Venue, however, is not only of symbolic importance because of its implications for prestige; it may also be of symbolic significance because of the ability of a particular venue to assist one or other of the parties in making some propaganda point. For example, Israel has generally wanted talks with the Arabs to take place in the Middle East itself rather than outside, as was the case with some of the negotiations with Egypt after 1977 and some with the PLO after 1993. One of the reasons for this is that it emphasizes the point that Israel is a legitimate member state of the region rather than a temporary foreign implant. For the same kind of reason, among others, South Africa was much more enthusiastic about holding the 1988 talks on Angola and Namibia in Africa rather than in Europe or North America.[8] And to return to the Middle East, it seems likely that one of the reasons why Madrid rather than Geneva was chosen for the 1991 conference on the Middle East was the need to underline for the benefit of Israel that this would be in no sense a UN-driven conference.[9] Israel, of course, had a general aversion to the UN, which went back to the General Assembly's 'Zionism is a form of racism' resolution of the mid-1970s. But it also disliked the UN's identification with the version of the 'international conference' proposal associated with Saddam Hussein and the PLO at the time of the Gulf War.

Practical considerations, as hinted earlier, are also of first-class importance in influencing preferences for the venue of negotiations. It is generally for these reasons, as well as reasons of prestige, that states prefer their rivals to come to them. In true Middle Kingdom tradition, 'the Chinese', as Binnendijk points out, 'unquestionably prefer to negotiate on their own territory as it facilitates their internal communications and decision-making procedures and maximizes their control over the ambiance of a negotiation' (Binnendijk, p. 9). If states nevertheless have to send delegations abroad to negotiate, it is thus generally an advantage if they do not have to send them too far. Proximity usually makes communication with home easier and also makes it easier to respond quickly to any sudden developments by flying in more senior personnel or recalling negotiators for consultation. If the venue has to be more remote, it is an advantage if it is in a country where they have a sizeable embassy. This will provide them with local back-up and reliable communication facilities with home. The force of this point was brought home to the American delegation that accompanied President Reagan to the summit with Gorbachev in the Icelandic capital of Reykjavik in October 1986. The secure 'bubble'[10] in the US embassy was the smallest ever built and could seat only eight people. At one point this maximum had already been reached when the President himself turned up. Being closest to the door, the US Arms Control Director, Kenneth Adelman, at once surrendered his chair to his chief. 'I then plopped down on the only square foot of unoccupied floor space,' he reports, 'leaning solidly against the President's legs and with nearly everyone's shoes touching my legs' (Adelman, p. 46).

Some venues also have air services, conference facilities, hotels, entertainment, and security that are vastly superior to those available to others. Some also have better climates. The Mozambique capital of Lourenço Marques (now Maputo) was quite rightly rejected as the venue for a major conference on southern African transport in the early 1950s partly on the grounds that the weather in the chosen month, February, was intolerably hot and humid.

Delegations

The third procedural point requiring agreement is the nature of the delegations, which embraces level, composition, and size. The last aspect is not normally controversial, unless a state proposes to send a delegation that is so small that it implies lack of seriousness of purpose or so large[11] that difficult problems of accommodation and security are raised. Level and composition of delegations is, however, another matter altogether.

Whether or not talks should be held at ministerial or merely official level has always been an issue in prenegotiations, since the higher the level the more priority might reasonably be assumed and the more rapid progress reasonably expected. (This now generally subsumes the question of whether or not the delegation has 'full powers'.) For example, in the 1950s, the South African government, ever anxious to persuade the British government to signal high priority to defence talks on Africa, was constantly urging London to conduct negotiations at senior ministerial level. By contrast, Britain, which did not share the enthusiasm of Pretoria for this subject and was anxious to avoid over-identification with its racial policies, was generally adamant that they should be 'written down' to the level of officials. In some regimes, of course, the line between 'officials' and 'ministers' never had any meaning, and even in those where it did it now seems more blurred. Nevertheless, it remains fairly obvious who is important and who is not. The greater ease of foreign travel has also made it more difficult for states to resist the notion that their most senior people – including those at the 'summit' – cannot take part in a negotiation abroad on grounds of practical impossibility. One answer to this problem is mixed delegations, which seem increasingly common, including delegations in which ministers participate for short periods. This is often the case with negotiations that it is formally agreed should be held at 'foreign minister' level. Of course, if there is a huge disparity in status between the states in question, the issue of level of delegations is less likely to be troublesome. Micro-states know that, as a general rule, matters to which they are happy to have their president attend cannot command the personal attention of the leader of a superpower.

The level of a delegation obviously has an intimate bearing on its composition. Nevertheless, level might be agreed but problems of composition remain. This is especially the case where a multilateral negotiation is proposed but there is hostility to participation by certain parties *at any level*. This is typically because of the non-recognition of one potential participant by another, for example the non-recognition of Communist China by the United States at the time of the Geneva Conference on South-East Asia in 1954. To take another example, the refusal of Israel to have anything whatever to do with the PLO, together with the Arab insistence that talks on the future of the West Bank and Gaza would be meaningless without it, led to a horrendous wrangle in 1977. As in the case of the issue of the agenda, this illustrated that prenegotiations can in fact disguise the most vital points of substance. For had the Israelis conceded separate Palestinian representation (whether by the PLO or in some other manner), they would have conceded a separate Palestinian identity – and thus, on grounds of national self-determination, the right of the Palestinians to their own state. It was much better from the Israeli point of view, therefore, that, if the so-called 'Palestinians' were to be represented at all, it should be as part of a Jordanian delegation, since it was a widely held view in Israel that the Palestinians were 'really' Jordanians.[12]

Timing

The final procedural question is timing. The issue of whether or not there should be a deadline for concluding the talks and, if so, what sort it should be, is so important to the question of diplomatic momentum that it is better to leave this discussion until Chapter 4. But when should the negotiations commence? The possibility that favourable circumstances are unlikely to last for ever argues for a prompt start, but pressing for this may suggest weakness. Other commitments on the part of key negotiators have to be considered as well, practical arrangements made, and time allowed for the preparation of papers and appropriate consultations. The more parties are involved and the more sensitive the issues at stake, the longer all of this is likely to take. However, it is unusual today for the timing of the opening of a negotiation to be as difficult as it was for the Congress of Münster and Osnabrück that was summoned to end the Thirty Years War. This was originally called for 25 March 1642, then put back to the start of July 1643, and did not officially open until 4 December 1644 (Satow, vol. II, pp. 5–6).

The practical difficulties of finding a mutually convenient date for the start of negotiations nevertheless remain considerable in the modern world, even for those that are part of a regular pattern. For example, the General Council of the World Trade Organization (WTO) agreed in January 2001 to accept the invitation of the government of Qatar to hold its next ministerial conference at its capital, Doha, in early November. However, it found subsequently that these dates clashed with a summit meeting in Rome of the Food and Agriculture Organization. The government of Qatar then pointed out that it could not host the meeting after 9 November due the commencement of Ramadan, which would not end until about 16 December, rather close to Christmas. As for bringing it forward, there was the problem of the summit of the Asia-Pacific Economic Cooperation forum expected to be held in mid-October in China (Raghavan). Because of practical difficulties such as this, it may not be normal practice to want good omens before commencing a negotiation as well. (Though it would be surprising if this was not the case in those parts of the world where astrology, which penetrated the White House itself during the Reagan years, is influential.) However, dates on the calendar that evoke particularly bitter memories are naturally regarded as inauspicious. 'Bloody Sundays' are avoided with great care – and with good reason. For any attempt to relaunch negotiations between Palestinians and Israelis, the anniversary of the creation of the state of Israel, 14 May 1948, falls into the same category.

Summary

It should never be forgotten that states sometimes engage in prenegotiations, and even substantive negotiations for that matter, merely in order to buy time or obtain the propaganda advantages that may attach to being seen to be seeking a 'peaceful solution'. Procrastinating or, as the British government used to call it, 'playing it long', has an extended history in diplomacy. In prenegotiations, then, and bearing this in mind, states first have to agree that it may be in their mutual interests to negotiate at all. Having agreed that negotiating may be better than not negotiating, they then have to agree an agenda and all of the multifarious questions that come up under the heading of 'procedure'. This being so, it may be thought surprising that states ever get round to substantive negotiations at all. That they do is testimony not only to the remorseless logic of circumstance but to the fact that diplomacy is a professionalized activity.

Notes

1 For example, in the prenegotiations phase of the Soviet–American arms control negotiations that followed the Cuban missile crisis in 1962, this meant emphasizing the mutual interest in avoiding nuclear war.

2 Failure to iron out every last detail of the agenda does not – surprisingly enough – necessarily prevent progress into the negotiation proper (Stein, p. 490). However, it seems probable that the likelihood of this occurring will vary according to the nature of the negotiation and the degree of trust existing between the parties.

3 The term 'proximity talks' is also sometimes applied to mediated talks in which the parties are physically more remote, though this hardly seems good usage.

4 The venue was the UN's European headquarters, and the UN secretary-general issued the invitations and presided in the conference's opening phase.

5 This conference was itself, of course, in direct line of descent from earlier multilateral conferences on regional questions chaired by major powers from opposite sides of the Cold War, and for that matter also held in Geneva. These included the Geneva Conference on South-East Asia (1954), which was co-chaired by Britain and the Soviet Union, and reconvened in 1961–2 in order to discuss Laos.

6 It was co-chaired by the United States and the Soviet Union and consisted of all interested parties, including the PLO (though this was included in a 'joint delegation' with Jordan). However, the UN, at Israeli insistence, was only present in an observer capacity.

7 On this intriguing episode, see M. Miller, *Plain Speaking: An Oral Biography of Harry S Truman* (Coronet: London, 1976) pp. 314–20; D. Acheson, *Present at the Creation: My Years in the State Department* (Norton: New York and London, 1987) pp. 456–7; and P. Lowe, *The Origins of the Korean War* (Longman: London and New York, 1986) p. 194. Although in *Plain Speaking* Truman claims that Wake Island was a 'halfway point', Merle Miller points out that the president had to fly 4700 miles from San Francisco while the general only had to fly 1900 miles from Tokyo.

8 In the event, Brazzaville and Cairo were the settings for some rounds of the negotiations.

9 Madrid was also conveniently placed for the PLO, which was headquartered in Tunis, while the Spanish government was currently enjoying a rapprochement with Israel following the establishment of diplomatic relations in 1986 and the constitutional recognition of Judaism in 1990. Interestingly enough, Spain was one of three foreign venues that came up in a conversation between Brzezinski and Carter in July 1978 as possibilities for the Middle East summit which was, in the event, held at Camp David in the subsequent September. The other two were Portugal and Morocco (Brzezinski, 1983, p. 250).

10 All US embassies contain a 'bubble': 'a square, transparent plastic room specially coated to assure that it cannot be bugged' (Adelman, p. 45).

11 American presidential parties, for example, typically number between six and eight hundred people (Kissinger, 1979, p. 75), though these are obviously not all diplomats.

12 On the various options for getting over this problem that were considered by the Americans, see Quandt, pp. 74–5.

Further reading

Cohen, R., *Negotiating across Cultures*, 2nd edn (US Institute of Peace Press: Washington, 1997), pp. 67–82.

Cradock, P., *Experiences of China* (John Murray: London, 1994), chs 16–18.

Gross-Stein, J. (ed.), *Getting to the Table: The Process of International Pre-negotiation* (Johns Hopkins University Press: Baltimore, 1989).

Quandt, W. B., *Camp David: Peacemaking and Politics* (Brookings Institution: Washington, 1986), chs 3–7.

Saunders, H., 'We need a larger theory of negotiation: the importance of pre-negotiating phases', *Negotiation Journal*, vol. 1, 1985.

Zartman, I. W. and M. Berman, *The Practical Negotiator* (Yale University Press: New Haven and London, 1982), ch. 3.

3
'Around-the-Table' Negotiations

If prenegotiations are successfully concluded, the next task for the negotiators is to move into 'around-the-table' mode.[1] This is generally more formal and there is usually more public awareness of what, in broad terms, is going on. First comes the task of trying to agree on the basic principles of a settlement: the 'formula stage'. If this is achieved, the details then have to be added. This chapter will begin by looking at the formula stage and conclude with an examination of the 'details stage'. This is often more difficult, not least because it is the moment of truth for the negotiators.

The formula stage

For the broad principles of a settlement there are many deliberately anodyne synonyms, among the more common of which are 'guidelines' and 'framework for agreement'. The UN, which has a legendary reputation for fertile imagination in this department, currently seems to favour the term 'set of ideas'. Zartman and Berman prefer 'formula' and, since it is short and clear, so do I. Among classic examples of formulas agreed in negotiations in recent years and at the time of writing (May 2001) still a 'basis for negotiations', are those on Cyprus and the Arab–Israeli conflict. The 'high-level agreements' on Cyprus of 1977 and 1979 provided for a deal in which the Greeks would admit a federation[2] in return for surrender by the Turks of some of the territory seized in the invasion of 1974. As for the Middle East, in UN Security Council Resolution 242 of November 1967, passed following the Six Day War, it was agreed that Israeli forces would withdraw 'from territories [not, famously, from *the* territories] occupied in the recent conflict'. In return for this the Arab states would recognize the state of Israel and end the condition of belligerency with it: the 'land for peace' formula.

The chief characteristics of a good formula are fairly obvious: comprehensiveness, balance, and flexibility. Clearly, the best one will offer solutions to all major points of dispute between the parties. However, this is often not practical politics and a formula is not vitiated if this is impossible (Zartman and Berman, pp. 109–14). Some issues may be registered but postponed for later consideration, as was the case with Taiwan in the Shanghai Communiqué in February 1972. Others may be fudged, as with the question of a state for the Palestinian Arabs in the Camp David Accords of September 1978. And others may be omitted altogether, as with multiple independently targetable re-entry vehicles (MIRVs) in the interim agreement on the limitation of offensive arms produced at the end of SALT I in May 1972. Whichever strategy is employed will depend on the priorities of the moment and the nature of the external pressure on the parties. It was, for example, unnecessary for the United States and the Soviet Union to fudge, or pretend to have made progress, on MIRVs in SALT I since neither party was under overwhelming pressure on this particular score. By contrast, Egyptian leadership of the Arab world turned on whether or not there appeared to be something for the Palestinians in the Camp David Accords; in the event, of course, it was not enough. Secondly, something has to be given to both sides in an exchange that is generally thought to be roughly balanced. And, although the formula must not be as vague as the kind floated in the prenegotiations stage, it must still contain sufficient flexibility to permit each side to believe that it might be improved in the details stage of the negotiations. So much is fairly obvious. What is sometimes less obvious is the best way to obtain this formula.

The nettle of general principle may be grasped immediately by the negotiators in the formula stage. This is sometimes described as the 'deductive approach' (Zartman and Berman, p. 89) and requires no further comment. It is the logical way to proceed. Alternatively, the nettle of principle may be approached with caution, by stealth, perhaps from its flank, and always slowly. Sometimes described as the 'inductive approach', this is more commonly known as 'step-by-step' diplomacy. One of the most advertised cases of the latter approach in recent years was the Middle East diplomacy of Henry Kissinger in the years following the Yom Kippur War of October 1973 (Golan). However, this has also been essentially the approach of the 'functionalists' to European integration since the end of the Second World War. This does require further comment.

The step-by-step approach is usually considered appropriate to the negotiation of a dispute characterized by great complexity and pathological mistrust. In such circumstances it normally makes sense to begin the negotiations on an agenda limited in scope and restricted to items that are relatively uncontroversial. This makes the negotiation more manageable, which is especially important if the diplomatic resources of the parties are also limited. It also permits mistrust to be gradually broken down, builds faith in the efficacy of diplomacy by making early successes more likely, and familiarizes the parties with the procedures involved in dealing with each other ('learning to walk before trying to run'). The idea, of course, is that, as confidence builds, the more difficult questions can gradually be broached with more prospect of success; they may even turn out to have been implicitly broken down already (Zartman and Berman, p. 90). If the initial negotiation is predicated on the hope that more recalcitrant parties will be drawn in later, the step-by-step approach also has the advantage of establishing precedents. Thus it was Kissinger's hope, in the event justified, that having negotiated a limited disengagement agreement between Israel and Egypt, the Syrians would be emboldened to risk a similar step themselves.

The step-by-step approach, however, is not without its problems. It can mislead by suggesting a relative lack of concern over the bigger questions; it carries the danger of 'paying the whole wallet' for just one item (Zartman and Berman, p. 178); above all, it takes time. Because it takes time, the favourable circumstances that made launching the negotiations possible may change for the worse and the moment may be lost. Of course, there may have been no alternative to employing the step-by-step approach but this is the risk that it always carries.

If and when a formula for a settlement is agreed, it is commonly announced to the world, sometimes in a huge blaze of publicity. Such was the case with the Camp David Accords. However, if the formula is based on 'linkage', that is, the trading of concessions in unrelated, or only remotely connected, issue areas, the negotiations may at this point run into difficulties. (This might have happened earlier if the deal was suspected from the nature of the agreed agenda.) The reason for this is that linkage, or 'negotiating on a broad front', is more likely to break an impasse by increasing the scope for imaginative solutions. However, it is deeply offensive to those who believe that issues should be treated on their merits, especially if their interests are harmed in the process without any *quid pro quo* on their own issue. As Hoffmann points out, 'on each issue, a separate constituency develops, which objects to being treated as a pawn in a global log-rolling game' (Hoffmann, p. 61). This is why Kissinger's problems with members of the anti-defence spending lobby were magnified when it became clear early in the first Nixon administration that he was contemplating trading US concessions in arms control negotiations for Soviet help in places such as Damascus and Hanoi. The issue of nuclear weapons, they believed, should be dealt with on its merits. It is also why many members of the OAU were enraged when it became clear that the Americans and the South Africans were insisting on Cuba's departure from Angola as the price for South Africa's withdrawal from Namibia. Cuban troops were in Angola at the invitation of the recognized government, it was argued, whereas the occupation of Namibia was illegal and South Africa was obliged to get out anyway. Nevertheless, in a formula based on linkage, there are winners as well as losers; this helps.

The details stage

If a formula is agreed by the parties to a negotiation, whether by imme-diate, head-on talks following prenegotiations or by the more oblique step-by-step approach, and whether based on linkage or not, the final stage involves fleshing it out – agreeing the details. This is by no means as simple as it sounds. Indeed, insofar as it is possible to generalize about negotiations, the details stage is a strong candidate for the dubious honour of being called the most difficult stage of all.

One aspect of the formula agreed on Cyprus in the late 1970s was that the island should have a new constitution. This would be a bi-communal, bi-zonal federation. 'Bi-communal' meant that the composition of the central government and its agencies would have to reflect the division of the population between Turkish Cypriots and Greek Cypriots, which was roughly 2:8. As for 'bi-zonality', this meant that the island itself (effectively partitioned following the Turkish invasion of 1974) would become a federal state based on two geographical zones, a Turkish zone in the north and a Greek one in the south. So far so good. But this left a myriad of sensitive details to be agreed, as might be imagined. Not the least among these was where *exactly* the line would be drawn on the ground between the two zones.

A further example of the difficulties of the details stage is provided by the agreement in mid-1988 that South Africa would withdraw its forces from Namibia and permit the country to become independent in return for the withdrawal of Cuban troops from Angola. For this left a large number of vital issues of detail to resolve on which the interests of the parties were clearly divergent. In the case of the Cuban troops alone, these included the following. When exactly would the departure commence? When would it terminate? Would the withdrawal be front-loaded, end-loaded, or consist of a uniform stream (the same number of troops leaving in each month)? From which areas of Angola would the first troops be withdrawn? And so on. Why is the details stage often so difficult and why, as a result, do talks often founder here?

Difficulties

The first reason for difficulty in the details stage is that it is, by definition, complicated. It may not be more complicated than prenegotiations (though it usually is); but it is invariably more complicated than the formula stage. In addition to providing a difficulty in itself, complexity also means as a rule that bigger teams of negotiators are required in the details stage; and this brings in its train much greater scope for disagreement *within* the negotiating teams. It is, for example, a commonplace of American commentary on the detailed arms control negotiations between the United States and the Soviet Union in the 1970s that the really tough negotiations took place not in Vienna or Helsinki but between the various agencies of the administration in Washington.

Secondly, it is in the details stage that careful thought has to be given to the definition of terms, or to establishing a common language. This is obviously necessary to avoid misunderstanding but can be extremely problematical because some definitions serve the interests of some parties better than others. Definitions proved to be a nightmare in the US–Soviet arms control negotiations, where wrangles over some terms – chiefly concerning categories of weapon – lasted for years. It was, for example, not until 1986 – sixteen years after SALT I began in 1969 – that Soviet negotiators abandoned their view that 'strategic' weapons were those capable of reaching the territory of a potential adversary irrespective of their location (Adelman, p. 52). On such a definition, US 'forward-based systems' such as those in Western Europe would be included in any regime to limit 'strategic weapons', while Soviet missiles targeted at Western Europe but unable to reach the United States would not.

Thirdly, because the details stage of negotiation is complicated and time-consuming, and usually requires the participation of specialists (Vance, p. 232), the negotiating teams are normally composed of individuals of lower authority than those involved – or at any rate leading – in the negotiations during the formula stage. This may well cause delays as they will need to refer back for guidance to their political masters or mistresses. The stickiness of the details stage caused by this situation may well be compounded further, since, having returned home, their principals will be under less pressure from the other side and more from their own constituencies. This may lead to a reversion to a tougher attitude and cause hard-line instructions to be issued to the negotiators saddled with fleshing out the formula. This is precisely what happened after the Camp David formulas had been agreed in the rarified atmosphere of the American presidential retreat in September 1978. 'Isolating the leaders from the press and their own public opinion', as Quandt notes, 'had no doubt been a prime ingredient in reaching the two framework agreements. Now, however, each leader would have to return to the real world in which domestic constituencies would have their say. As each of the Camp David participants felt compelled to justify what he had done at the summit,' Quandt continues, 'the gap separating them began to widen again' (Quandt, p. 259; also pp. 262, 270, 271, 275). Indeed, it was only after the resumption of top-level participation in the talks, not least by President Carter himself, that at least an Egypt–Israel peace treaty – if not an agreement on the Palestinian question – was finally produced five months after the 'framework' had been agreed.

A fourth reason why the details stage is often particularly difficult is that it may well present an opportunity to one or both sides to load the balance of advantage in the agreed formula in their favour. In light of the complexity of this stage, this may occur in a manner not necessarily easy to detect (Zartman and Berman, pp. 149–52). In other words, and especially if trust between the parties is minimal, the atmosphere in the details stage is likely to suffer simply because of the fear that each side may be trying to redraft the formula by massaging the small print.

Finally, what often makes the details stage the toughest of all is the simple fact that it is the last stage: *the moment of truth*. What is agreed here has to be acted on, so if the negotiators get it wrong they will suffer. When the details stage is concluded, it may mean soldiers surrendering positions in defence of which they have lost brothers, settlers giving up land in which they have sunk roots, exporters losing prized markets, or workers losing their livelihoods. There should thus be no vagueness and no inconsistencies – and the deal should be defensible at home. Magnanimity is thus generally at a discount in the details stage of negotiations.

Negotiating strategies

Detailed agreements are negotiated by one or other of two means, or – more usually – by some combination of both. The first method is to compromise on individual issues, for example by splitting the difference between the opening demands of the parties on the timetable for a troop withdrawal. This is what happened in regard to the Cuban troops in Angola during the American-brokered negotiations in 1988. The South Africans, of course, wanted them out as soon as possible and had in mind a timetable of months. By contrast, the Marxist government of Angola, anxious to retain the protection afforded by Castro's 'internationalist military contingent' for as long as possible, was thinking of a timetable for its withdrawal in terms of three or four years. In the end, they compromised on a year and half.[3]

The second method for making concessions is to give the other side more or less what it wants on one issue in return for satisfaction on a separate one.[4] Described by Zartman and Berman as 'exchanging points', this works best when each party is able to acquire from the other something worth more to it than what it has had to surrender in return. This was elaborated by the sociologist George Homans in a work published in 1961, and is thus sometimes known as 'Homans's theorem' (Zartman and Berman, pp. 13–14, 66, 175–6). A simple example would be the exchange of a packet of rich biscuits for a piece of lean steak, where the former was held initially by a meat-loving weight-watcher and the latter by a vegetarian with a sweet tooth.

A variant on Homans's theorem is a deal in which one party trades something which it values highly but which it knows it is going to have to surrender anyway, irrespective of whether or not it gets a quid pro quo from the other side. In principle, both parties can do this as well. The trick here, of course, is to make sure that the other side does not share the same information. This is where liberal democracies are at a severe disadvantage compared to authoritarian regimes, which was a constant lament of Henry Kissinger in the 1970s. Thus in seeking to trade a US freeze in the deployment of Anti-Ballistic Missiles (ABMs) in return for Soviet limitations on offensive nuclear forces, Kissinger was seriously hampered by the obvious determination of Congress to kill off the ABM programme anyway (Kissinger, 1979, pp. 194–210, 534–51). Nor did it help him in his negotiations with the North Vietnamese in Paris that, under even more fierce Congressional pressure, his major trump card – US military power in South Vietnam – was slipping remorselessly from his grasp with every fresh public announcement of further troop withdrawals. When the other party knows that history is on its side, it has little incentive to pay for 'concessions'.

Whichever strategy for making and seeking concessions, or whichever combination of them, is adopted will depend on circumstances and the established style of the negotiators. In the last regard, there are significant variations between different national cultures. Where the negotiators come from different cultural traditions, this can naturally cause problems (Cohen, 1997). There remains, however, the issue of the general attitude to strike in negotiations, whether, that is, the negotiators should be accommodating or tough. Each has obvious advantages and disadvantages, and since the circumstances of different negotiations vary so enormously generalization in this area is a risky business. Nevertheless, at the price of inviting the charge of banality, the following might be hazarded. First, extremes of flexibility and rigidity are both inconsistent with the logic of negotiation. Secondly, since this involves concessions by both sides (by definition), it is usually believed best to make them in one fell swoop in order to avoid the impression given by making small concessions incrementally, that there are always more for the asking (Zartman and Berman, p. 171).[5] Thirdly, if concessions are, nevertheless, extracted incrementally, the impression of weakness may be reduced by exploitation of various tactical expedients. Among these are making the concessions contingent on a final 'package deal', periodically suspending the talks in order to remind the other party that too much pressure might lead to their collapse, and raising the question of the formula again. Fourthly, a tough attitude in negotiations is most appropriate to parties that are confident that they can walk away without major damage to their position, which helps to explain the attitude of the Begin government during the Camp David negotiations. It is equally appropriate to regimes based on religious fanaticism or police terror that are indifferent to the costs imposed by diplomatic failure on their own people.

Summary

Negotiation is thus generally a lengthy and laborious process, proceeding through 'prenegotiations' and a formula to the details phase. In each stage there is a risk of breakdown, though this is probably most acute in the first and last – in the first not least because the 'exit costs' (Stein, p. 482) are low, while in the last because this is the negotiators' moment of truth. The momentum of the negotiations may thus falter even if both parties in a bilateral negotiation, or a majority of parties in a multilateral negotiation, are serious about making them a success. How diplomatic momentum might be sustained is thus a serious question, and it is to this that we must next turn.

Notes

1   I owe this phrase to Saunders (1985).
2   This would give the Turks sovereignty over some of their affairs; the independence constitution of the island was a unitary one.
3   The timetable was spelled out in detail in an Annex to the agreements; see Berridge, 1991, pp. 159–60, where this is reproduced.
4   This is in principle the same as 'linkage', discussed earlier. The difference is that here the issues, while separate, are of the same species.
5   Kissinger somewhere describes the incremental approach as 'salami tactics'.

Further reading

Berridge, G. R., 'Diplomacy and the Angola/Namibia accords, December 1988', *International Affairs*, vol. 65, no. 3, 1989.

Binnendijk, H. (ed.), *National Negotiating Styles* (Center for the Study of Foreign Affairs, Foreign Service Institute, US Department of State: Washington, 1987).

Cohen, R., *Negotiating across Cultures*, 2nd edn (US Institute of Peace Press: Washington, 1997).

Crocker, C. A., *High Noon in Southern Africa: Making Peace in a Rough Neighbourhood* (Norton: New York and London, 1992).

Faure, G. O. and J. Z. Rubin (eds), *Culture and Negotiation: the Resolution of Water Disputes* (Sage: Newbury Park, Calif., London and New Delhi, 1993).

Golan, M., *The Secret Conversations of Henry Kissinger: Step-by-Step Diplomacy in the Middle East* (Quadrangle: New York, 1976).

Kremenyuk, V. A. (ed.), *International Negotiation* (Jossey-Bass: San Francisco and Oxford, 1991).

Lee, D., *Middle Powers and Commercial Diplomacy: British Influence at the Kennedy Trade Round* (Macmillan – now Palgrave: Basingstoke, 1999).

Meerts, P., 'The changing nature of diplomatic negotiation', in J. Melissen (ed.), *Innovation in Diplomatic Practice* (Macmillan – now Palgrave: Basingstoke, 1999).

Quandt, W. B., *Camp David: Peacemaking and Politics* (Brookings: Washington, 1986), chs. 8–12.

Touval, S., 'Multilateral negotiation: an analytic approach', *Negotiation Journal*, vol. 5, no. 2, 1989.

Vance, C., *Hard Choices: Critical Years in America's Foreign Policy* (Simon & Schuster: New York, 1983).

Webster, Sir C., *The Art and Practice of Diplomacy* (Chatto & Windus: London, 1961).

Zartman, I. W. (ed.), *International Multilateral Negotiation* (Jossey-Bass: San Francisco, 1997).

Zartman, I. W. and M. Berman, *The Practical Negotiator* (Yale University Press: New Haven and London, 1982), chs 4–6.

4
Diplomatic Momentum

The momentum of a negotiation may falter even if the parties are serious about proceeding. This was a recurring problem with the Uruguay Round of GATT negotiations, which started in September 1986 and was not finally completed until April 1994. Why might momentum falter? Why is it serious? And what might be done to prevent it? The first two questions are not especially problematical and have in any case already been touched upon. As a result, the greater part of this chapter will be concerned with the practical stratagems that fall under the heading of the third, other than inducements such as side payments and guarantees offered by a mediator, which will be dealt with in Chapter 11.

Three reasons why momentum might be lost, especially in the details stage of negotiations, have already been mentioned but will bear recapitulation here. First, there is the characteristic withdrawal of senior ministers or officials following conclusion of the formula stage, which may well lead to a slackening in pace because of the greater need for reference home for instructions when difficulties occur. Secondly, there is the deliberate delay caused by a party feeling on the defensive in order to impress the other side with the difficulty it is having in granting certain concessions. Thirdly, there is the effect of the sheer complexity of much contemporary international negotiation, especially multilateral negotiation. So much we already know.

Talks may also be slowed down or even temporarily interrupted, however, by a host of other factors. Key personnel may be drawn away from any stage of negotiations by the need to attend to even more urgent matters. These include time-consuming commitments in annual national and international calendars such as party congresses, the opening of new parliamentary sessions, regular summit meetings, the start of the new session of the UN General Assembly in September, and so on. They may be delayed by disputes within delegations, which was notoriously the case with the EC delegation in the GATT negotiations. They may be delayed by the serious possibility of a change in government of one or more of the parties. This is likely if it is feared that any agreement negotiated will be disavowed or in practice circumvented by the new government, or alternatively if it is anticipated that the new government will agree to better terms. Final term American presidents in their third and fourth years have notorious difficulty in being taken seriously as negotiators. (Of course, if one party expects worse terms from a new government the talks may gain rather than lose momentum; see below.) The talks may be delayed by the genuine illness of a key player. They may also be interrupted, as the Israel–PLO negotiations on the withdrawal of Israeli forces from Gaza and Jericho were interrupted for over a month, by an incident such as the Hebron mosque massacre on 25 February 1994. Such an occurrence makes it unseemly for one or other party to be seen pursuing negotiations for the time being.[1]

If there is a lull in the talks for any reason, the great danger is that it will drag on and become permanent. There are four main reasons why this may be a real danger. First, an absence of progress may demoralize the negotiators and, just as important, demoralize their supporters. Secondly, such a development will provide the enemies of negotiations with a fresh opportunity for sabotage and provide them with further ammunition as well: 'we told you so!' Thirdly, both parties are still likely to be on their best behaviour. As a result, one or other may be led to draw the false conclusion that perhaps the status quo is not so bad after all, and that the price of a deal is too high. Finally, and perhaps most fatally of all, a lull in negotiations permits the attention of key personnel to be drawn to other items on the crowded international agenda. This at one time seemed to be the likely fate of the Uruguay Round in early 1991, when the Gulf War literally blew up at just the point when a pre-Christmas crisis left the talks drifting aimlessly and urgently in need of top-level attention. In such circumstances, what can be done to sustain momentum, and to regain it if lost?

One way to maintain high momentum is, of course, for one side to give in to the other on every item on the agenda; but this would be a capitulation rather than a negotiation. Nevertheless, an important method of sustaining momentum in a genuine negotiation is to employ the step-by-step approach discussed in the previous chapter. This minimizes the risk of stalemate by proceeding in piecemeal fashion, usually from the less to the more difficult issues; and by building up a list of tangible achievements over a relatively long period demonstrates the value of diplomacy. A good example of such an achievement used to this end was the Cairo Accords on security, signed between the PLO and Israel in early February 1994, which broke months of deadlock in the details stage of this negotiation but left other issues for later. If ratification of the initial achievements is contingent on a package deal, the step-by-step approach also gives the negotiators a vested interest in driving the talks towards a final conclusion. After all, they will not normally wish to see their achievements thrown away and have to admit that their time has been wasted. The step-by-step approach, however, is rarely able to maintain momentum unaided, not least because it has a down side, too. Its unavoidable slowness, together with the impression that it generally gives of 'ducking' the main issues, can generate exasperation. It is, then, perhaps the step-by-step approach that is the strategy of negotiation most in need of special assistance in the maintaining of momentum. How can this be provided?

Deadlines

A traditional device regularly employed by negotiators in order to keep up the momentum of their talks is to employ deadlines, that is, calendar dates by which either some partial, interim, or final agreement must be reached. Effective deadlines, however, must meet two clear conditions: they must be real but they must also be realistic.

To begin with, then, real penalties must flow from failure to reach agreement by the specified date. If a deadline is missed, there must be a clear risk that the opportunity for a settlement will slip away. Alternatively, there must be an equally clear risk that, while a settlement itself may not be seriously jeopardized, one or more of the parties concerned will have to pay a higher price for it.

Artificial deadlines[2]

Deadlines that are determined by best estimates of the time required for a negotiation but are in other respects arbitrary, do not usually carry penalties of the kind just mentioned, unless, that is, one of the parties feels that it has much the stronger hand (Box 4.1). Such artificial deadlines are sometimes described as 'target dates' and are 'not meant to be more than a psychological device to egg negotiations on'; in sum, 'not really deadlines at all', though those who fail to spot the difference may be forgiven (De Soto, pp. 363–4). Such deadlines may have some small, positive impact on the momentum of talks, especially if they are

---

Box 4.1   The Chinese 'deadline' on Hong Kong

A party to a negotiation confident that it has much the stronger hand can announce a deadline without any discussion and accompany it with the threat that it will take unilateral action on the issue if a settlement is not reached by this date. In effect, this is virtually an ultimatum, and the weaker party may well conclude that if it wishes to retain some influence over events it has no alternative but to adapt to the timetable that has been dictated to it. An example is provided by the Sino-British negotiations over the transfer of Hong Kong back to China. In September 1983, a few months after the start of the negotiations, the Chinese Communist government announced that if a settlement was not achieved within a year, that is, by September 1984, it would simply make known its own decisions on the future of the island. The British fell in with this timetable and the Joint Declaration on Hong Kong was initialled in this same month. A 'practical deadline' also stimulated progress in these talks: the expiry of the 99-year lease on the so-called 'New Territories' (which composed 92 per cent of the territory of the colony of Hong Kong) on 30 June 1997 (Cradock, pp. 162, 189–90, 196–7).

---

publicly announced; after all, failure to meet them will be a minor blow to the professional reputations of the negotiators. On the other hand, they can usually gain more than compensating marks from their supporters by maintaining – which may well be true – that they would have been failing in their duty to settle by the agreed date since the terms achieved remained unsatisfactory. Missing the deadline was evidence of a 'tough' stand rather than incompetence, sloth, or lack of seriousness of purpose. The best deadlines are thus those that are either deliberately pegged by the negotiators (or their masters) to some date that has significance more or less independent of the negotiations, or which are forced on the negotiators by circumstance. In the first case, the symbolic deadline, professional competence will be at issue (as with the artificial deadline) but so will the negotiators' respect for the event commemorated. In the second, the practical deadline, reputation for professional competence may be less at stake but another kind of penalty could be far more serious.

Symbolic deadlines

Symbolic deadlines are much favoured by negotiators anxious to bring negotiations to a conclusion. Such deadlines are often dates that would have symbolic significance for the subject of the negotiations whether the negotiations were taking place or not. Good examples in peace negotiations are the anniversaries of the outbreak of a war, a ceasefire resolution, or – especially suitable – some spectacular, grisly and altogether gratuitous massacre. The birthday or anniversary of the death of a great leader may, however, serve equally well, as may the date of the founding of some major international organization. And, such is the media-inspired fascination with multiples of ten, that the most prized anniversaries are half-centenaries, centenaries, and bi-centenaries; even mere tenth anniversaries are eagerly commandeered. Dates in the calendars of the great religions are also useful – in the Christian tradition especially, of course, Christmas itself.

The importance of symbolic deadlines is not difficult to understand. Dates of symbolic significance have long been exploited for propaganda purposes by lobbyists for whom they are important and, partly for this reason and partly because they are ideal pegs on which to hang articles and broadcasts, they have long been the stock in trade of the mass media. In the modern world, therefore, it is highly unlikely that any date of symbolic importance for some group or other will go unnoticed. In early 1994 the story of the Bosnian conflict was on more than one occasion pushed from the headline news in Britain. This was achieved by coverage of wrangles over the best way to commemorate the 50th anniversary of the Normandy landings of 6 June 1944, which presaged the defeat of Hitler in the Second World War.

The pressure exerted by a symbolic deadline, therefore, is this: with unusual media attention focused on the negotiations in the weeks immediately preceding it, the negotiators can expect unusually high marks for meeting the deadline and unusually low ones for letting it slip by. For this is an important date, and concluding by this time will show proper respect for the event which it commemorates, while letting it slip away will imply – whatever the protests to the contrary – at best indifference to and at worst contempt for its significance. The penalty is a propaganda penalty. A good example of such a deadline was the proposal of the Cuban government in May 1988, endorsed by both Washington and Moscow, that the Angola/Namibia negotiations should be completed by 29 September (Crocker, 1999, p. 229). The appeal of this was that it was the tenth anniversary of the passing of UN Security Council Resolution 435 on the arrangements for the independence of South African-controlled Namibia. Not taking this deadline seriously, therefore, would imply not taking seriously the question of Namibian independence – a 'motherhood' issue (Berridge, 1989, pp. 475–6). A more recent example is provided by the 'target date' of 9 April established for a settlement of the internal conflict in Northern Ireland in 1998. It was probably no coincidence that this was actually achieved at about 5.30pm on the following day – Good Friday, the traditional start of the Easter festival. Not surprisingly, this settlement has been known ever since as 'the Good Friday Agreement'.

The usefulness of a symbolic date as a deadline will obviously vary with the importance attached to the event which it commemorates, and will be significantly reduced if it is forced by mediators on parties whose own estimation of the event varies. This was the case with the proposed deadline used as the first illustration in the previous paragraph. This is because South Africa itself – a key player in these negotiations – could hardly have been expected to be unduly worried by the prospect of appearing indifferent to the celebration of the passage of what was a transparently anti-South African resolution. In the event, at South Africa's suggestion, the deadline for the Angola/Namibia negotiations was brought forward to 1 September (Berridge, 1989, p. 476). Nevertheless, the regularity with which symbolic deadlines are employed in negotiations is testimony to the value attached to them.

Practical deadlines

There is little doubt, however, that, as the name for them that comes most readily to mind suggests, practical deadlines are usually the most valuable when it comes to sustaining momentum in negotiations (De Soto, pp. 377–8, 382). These are deadlines imposed by events that are either completely beyond the control of the negotiating party or only cancelled at considerable cost. Into the last category fall deadlines imposed by summit meetings, which will be discussed in Chapter 10. Into the former fall deadlines imposed by any number of events. These include scheduled elections, the opening of other conferences where the subject at issue may be high on the agenda, the expiry of the negotiating authority of a key party, and the expiry of a ceasefire agreement. They also include the expiry of the mandate of a peacekeeping force, and previously announced dates for the commencement and completion of military withdrawals where the details remain to be negotiated. It is true that practical deadlines may leave insufficient time to perfect an agreement (De Soto, p. 379) but an imperfect agreement is usually better than no agreement at all.

In *Camp David: Peacemaking and Politics*, William Quandt gives a brilliant exposition of the practical deadlines imposed by the US electoral cycle on American diplomacy, particularly on important negotiations in which the president plays a personal role (Quandt, ch. 2). Only in the first year of the president's maximum of two four-year terms is he relatively free of the pressure of electoral deadlines, and in this first year the emphasis is in any case usually on prenegotiations. In the second year he begins to look for diplomatic breakthroughs in advance of the mid-term elections for Congress in November. In the third year it is not long before he is worrying about the effects of his diplomacy on the notoriously protracted nominating process for presidential candidates. And in the fourth year, unless it is his second term, he is obviously worrying about the general election in November itself.

It is not altogether accidental that it was just two months before the mid-term elections in 1978 that President Carter devoted 13 days to summit diplomacy on the Middle East at Camp David. Nor is it accidental that his 'clear priority after Camp David was to conclude the [detailed] treaty negotiations as quickly as possible, literally within days' (Quandt, p. 260). It is, however, interesting that his sense of urgency was also heightened by an even tighter practical deadline: the ninth Arab League summit that was scheduled to meet in Baghdad in late October. For it was feared that the 'moderate' states of Jordan and Saudi Arabia would both come under intense pressure at this event from the 'radical' Arab states[3] to denounce the Camp David Accords, and that this would cause Sadat to lose his nerve (Quandt, p. 260; Vance, p. 229; Carter, pp. 404–9). By the beginning of 1979, at which point the details stage of the Egypt–Israel negotiations had still not been completed, Carter was of course in his third year. It is also worth adding here that the presidential election in November 1988, together with the imminent arrival of a new administration in the following January, put pressure on all the parties to make tangible progress in the Angola/ Namibia negotiations. It increased the pressure on the American mediator, Chester Crocker, because although Ronald Reagan was retiring, the Republican candidate, Vice-President George Bush, was obviously anxious to highlight as many foreign policy achievements for the administration as possible in his own election campaign. As for Crocker, who had led the negotiations for such a long time, it was also natural that he would want a personal success before probably leaving office himself.

Of course, the prospect of a presidential election in the United States can also put considerable pressure for a settlement on America's negoti-ating partners. This will happen if they expect to get a worse deal from the rival presidential candidate than from the incumbent, and if there is a real possibility that the former might win. This was the calculus that was at work on the Iranians in the Iran hostages negotiations at the beginning of 1981. Apprehensive of the attitude of the new conservative Republican administration of Ronald Reagan but at the same time determined to complete their humiliation of Jimmy Carter, they finally settled on the very day of the new president's inauguration, 20 January 1981.

Fear of the attitude of a rival presidential candidate was also the calculus that was at work on the South Africans in the Angola/Namibia negotiations in 1988. They knew that they were unlikely ever to get a better deal from the Americans than under Ronald Reagan, and certainly not from the liberal Democrat, Michael Dukakis, who was running against Vice-President Bush. The prospect of a new administration in January – albeit still a Republican one since Bush had won – also put pressure on *all* the parties to these negotiations to clear final hurdles that appeared in early December. This was because the Americans 'openly' advertised the fact that this would 'likely mean a change of personnel and a basic policy review' (Crocker, 1999, p. 229).

Another good example of a practical deadline working to keep a negotiation in motion was the Brussels ministerial meeting in GATT's Uruguay Round in the first week of December 1990. The deadline injected urgency into these talks because the US delegation's Congressional mandate was due to run out on 1 March 1991, and there was a real fear that because of hostility in the United States to the direction of the negotiations this would not be renewed. Since any package negotiated would have to be submitted to Congress by this date, Carla Hills, the US trade representative, insisted that she would need the time between December and the end of February in order to prepare the necessary legislation. Hence the effective deadline on the negotiations was the December ministerial meeting.

Finally, the practical deadlines imposed on the details stage of the Israel–PLO negotiations by the dates agreed in the Declaration of Principles of September 1993 for the withdrawal of Israeli forces from Gaza and Jericho might be mentioned. On this occasion it was announced that the withdrawal would commence on 13 December 1993 and be completed by 13 April 1994. These dates were of particular importance to the PLO leader, Yasser Arafat, who was under intense pressure to deliver tangible progress from his own supporters as well as from more radical Palestinian elements. It is true that the Israeli prime minister, Yitzak Rabin, subsequently declared that 'there are no sacred dates' (*The Independent*, 11 February 1994). Nevertheless, it was clear that failure by Israel to take the agreed withdrawal dates seriously would lead to intense international criticism, not least from the United States, and might destroy the man who remained Israel's most promising negotiating partner – Yasser Arafat. The Palestinian self-rule agreement was finally signed on 4 May under the equally intense pressure generated in the previous week by the public announcement on 28 April of a 'pre-signing summit' between Arafat and Rabin in Cairo. To this, more than 2500 guests and 40 foreign ministers were invited – another practical deadline.

If the first condition of an effective deadline is that real penalties must be expected to flow from failure to meet it,[4] the second is that they must not be too tight. They must, in other words, and with the proviso that this will not apply to some practical deadlines (which are in any case often beyond the control of the negotiators), allow sufficient time for the negotiations to be concluded. In short, effective deadlines must be realistic as well as real.

It often happens, of course, that 'effective' deadlines, whether symbolic or practical, are missed: they slip by with the negotiations still incomplete. The Angola/Namibia negotiations were not concluded by 1 September 1988 (Crocker, 1999, p. 229). The Egypt–Israel Peace Treaty was still unsigned at the time of the American mid-term elections and the Arab League Summit in early November 1978.[5] And the Uruguay Round plodded on for over three years following December 1990. Nevertheless, it is reasonable to conclude that, in light of the urgency that these deadlines visibly injected into these negotiations, they would have taken even longer in their absence and might not have been concluded at all.

Metaphors of movement

Our conceptual system mediates the manner in which we both think and act, and it is now uncontroversial that this system is 'fundamentally metaphorical in nature'.[6] Metaphors, which are representations of one thing in terms of another (for example, 'time is money'), have their effect by highlighting and organizing certain aspects of our experience while hiding those that are inconsistent with it. Moreover, although most of the metaphors that shape the lives of peoples and governments alike do so unconsciously, they can be deliberately chosen and manipulated – not least by those same governments. 'War' and 'battle' are common metaphors employed by governments to encourage their citizens to 'close ranks' and make exceptional 'sacrifices' in situations that bear no resemblance to real warfare. The 'war on want' and the 'battle against inflation', are familiar metaphors which come to mind here. It is hardly surprising, therefore, that metaphors should also be deliberately employed by those seeking to preserve the momentum of negotiations, and that these metaphors should chiefly be metaphors of *movement*.

A common instance of such a metaphor used in negotiations is that of the automobile. Negotiations are often said to be 'driven forward' and thus by implication to be capable, like a car, of high speeds and versatility in manoeuvring around 'obstacles in the road'. If they come to a stop despite a 'green light', this is because they have 'stalled', a condition usually caused by the sort of embarrassing incompetence that is best corrected as soon as possible. In case the drivers of the talks are in any doubt about the direction in which they are headed, a 'road map' of the sequence in which agreed points should be implemented is sometimes provided. The Americans did this in their negotiations over the normalization of relations with the Vietnamese in the early 1990s (Berridge, 1994, pp. 57–8).

Even more common in the language of negotiations than the automobile metaphor is the metaphor of the train, perhaps because trains have far fewer opportunities to make detours. If the negotiation is like a 'train', it will be perilous for all concerned if it does not stay 'on the track' – if, that is to say, it is 'derailed' – in any case a very rare occurrence. It will also be dangerous for anyone 'to get off' before it 'pulls into the station'. And general exasperation will ensue if the talks get 'shunted into a siding'. The train metaphor is particularly useful because it can cope with lulls in a negotiation: trains, after all, stop in stations – but only briefly. Trains also run to timetables, so the metaphor reinforces the use of deadlines. And only rare and terrible disasters prevent them from arriving at their terminus eventually. Complicated negotiations are also commonly described as 'dual track' or 'multi-track', and negotiations by unofficial bodies and individuals as 'track two' diplomacy (see Chapter 11). 'Back-tracking' is the worst of all sins in negotiations. The popularity of the train metaphor is not difficult to understand. In the Angola/Namibia negotiations the Americans used it repeatedly (Berridge, 1989, p. 477; see also the section on 'Publicity' below). And so they appear to have done again in setting up the conference on the Middle East at Madrid in 1991.[7]

Metaphors of movement of the kind just described help to prevent loss of momentum in negotiations by stimulating all of the participants, together with their supporters, to believe that they are on something that is condemned to forward motion. In consequence, they are also encouraged to resign themselves to helping it reach its destination. At this point it will be clear, and needs to be emphasized, that implicit in the metaphor of movement is a further metaphor – the *metaphor of the journey* – and that both are at the same time *metaphors of collaboration*. A metaphor of movement sometimes used by negotiators that brings out the collaborative aspect particularly well is the 'race against time'. This is a race against one or other of the sort of 'deadlines' – themselves now revealed as an instance of this metaphor – that were discussed in the previous section. This kind of race is a race in which the parties collaborate against their common enemy, time, rather than one in which they compete against each other. In the negotiation that is like a 'race against time' there are no prizes for 'not finishing' or 'dropping out early'. Obstacles that are met in the negotiation are 'hurdles', and it is the duty of everyone, including those for whom an early shower might in reality be the best option, to 'clear' them. Negotiators of countries on the verge of war, as in the case of the United States and Iraq in early 1991, are now generally expected to go 'the extra mile' for peace.

If the collaborative element is particularly apparent in the 'race against time' metaphor used in negotiations, the metaphor of the *journey* – which has a starting point and proceeds through stages to its goal – is more obvious in other familiar language. And it is extremely interesting that in their stimulating book, Lakoff and Johnson (pp. 89–91) themselves stress the importance of the journey metaphor. It is true that they use it as an example of a metaphor of argument rather than negotiation, but negotiation is no more than a special variant of this. The production by the US State Department's metaphor machine of the 'road map' metaphor, an obvious instance of the metaphor of the journey, has already been noted. There is, however, another instance – one that is far more important, as demonstrated by the fact that it is the commanding concept of Part I of this book and so far has been taken for granted. This, of course, is the concept of 'stages of negotiation', and the related metaphor – also noted by Lakoff and Johnson (p. 90) – of 'step-by-step' diplomacy.

In sum, metaphors of movement, especially those that imply the need for collaboration on a shared journey, are a common device employed by those anxious to preserve the momentum of a negotiation. Of course, the degree of their effectiveness in different situations must remain largely speculative. Nevertheless, in the light of both the revelations of linguistic philosophy and the evidence of the repeated use of these metaphors in negotiations, two conclusions seem reasonable. The first is that the influence of these metaphors will often be considerable, and the second is that it will be most significant for the behaviour of those for whom continued negotiation is risky and for whom, therefore, metaphors of movement are a treacherous guide. The potency of such metaphors, especially if picked up, embellished and repeated by the mass media, must be difficult to resist. This brings us naturally to publicity.

Publicity

It is a cliché of studies of diplomacy that publicity is the enemy of negotiation, and this is substantially true. However, employed judiciously, publicity about a negotiation can also help to drive it forward. In addition to implanting and constantly emphasizing appropriate metaphors, it can do this in at least three other ways: first, by flying kites to see how the other side will react; secondly, by mobilizing popular support for a negotiated solution; and thirdly, by 'talking up the talks'. Propaganda and diplomacy are thus not necessarily antithetical; it all depends on the nature of the propaganda. This is one of the reasons why the press office is such an important department of heads of government and their foreign ministries, as noted in the section on public diplomacy in Chapter 1.

Floating formulas or flying kites, both publicly and privately, is obviously of special importance in prenegotiations, as already remarked, but it is not confined to this stage. For example, during the fourteen weeks of substantive negotiations held on Rhodesia at Lancaster House in London in 1979, the Head of News Department at the Foreign Office, Sir Nicholas Fenn, often aired suggestions for the press to report (Dickie, p. 249). Flying kites openly can expedite negotiations by preparing the public for an eventual settlement. It can perhaps do this even more effectively by permitting negotiators to gain greater insight into the ambitions and anxieties of their interlocutors by noting their reactions when the kites sail up. An idea *publicly* accepted, or at least not dismissed outright, will be regarded as a serious basis for negotiation because this will be an indication that the party concerned believes it could sell this at home. According to John Dickie's well-informed account of the Lancaster House talks, 'it was of great interest to Sir Anthony Duff, as head of the British negotiating team, to gauge the public and private reactions of the other delegations to what appeared as a result [of News Department's briefings] in the Press' (Dickie, p. 249).

Even authoritarian regimes ignore their own popular opinion at their peril, as the Shah of Iran discovered, and they are in any case almost always anxious to influence foreign opinion. As a result, mobilizing the public in support of important negotiations will be a priority for any government committed to them, especially if they appear to be flagging. This was why the Egyptian leader, Anwar Sadat, took the dramatic step of journeying to Jerusalem itself in November 1977 to address the Israeli people over the heads of their government. It was also why the Carter administration decided shortly afterwards to 'mount a public campaign' directed at both American and Israeli opinion to bring pressure to bear on the government of Menachem Begin (Quandt, p. 162).

Another important way of sustaining momentum in negotiations is to give the public the impression that they are nearer to success than is in reality the case. 'Talking up the talks' cannot be done repeatedly or in circumstances when it is manifestly obvious that success is nowhere in sight. This will result in a loss of public credibility. It may also rebound by angering the delegation of the more recalcitrant party, which may find itself – unfairly – in hot water with its own supporters. Nevertheless, used sparingly and when clear progress in one or other stage of the negotiations has been made, talking up the talks can prove very useful indeed. It was employed by the British Foreign Secretary, Lord Carrington, at the Lancaster House talks on Rhodesia (Dickie, p. 250), by the UN mediator in the Afghanistan talks in the 1980s (Harrison, p. 35), and also by Chester Crocker in the Angola/Namibia negotiations. Crocker's tactic, as in the case of the other two negotiators, was to sound optimistic at press briefings once it was clear that there was a genuine chance of a breakthrough. Any party that then deserted the talks or behaved in an obstructive manner would be the target of attack from the many influential quarters that, in the current atmosphere of superpower rapprochement and war-weariness in southern Africa, favoured a settlement. A report written a few days after the final breakthrough at Geneva, in November 1988, summed up this particular ploy very neatly, as well as highlighting the use of the train metaphor in these negotiations:

Once a little momentum was achieved, Mr Crocker would drive the talks train faster and faster, briefing journalists on how well negotiations were going and how close to agreement they were. If the participants tried to stop the train or get off they would be seen as wreckers. It failed a few times, but each time Mr Crocker put the train back on the tracks and started again. 'If anyone had got off the train when they arrived in Geneva they would have sprained a wrist,' one US official said after agreement was reached on Tuesday night. 'If anyone tries to get off now they will break both legs.'

(*The Independent*, 17 November 1988)

Raising the level of the talks

A negotiation may lose its momentum because of the inadequate authority of the teams employed in it rather than because of any interruption. In this event, the obvious solution is to raise the level of the talks, that is, to insert or reinsert more senior personnel – if they can be spared. This actually has more than one advantage. First, and most obviously, it injects into the negotiations people who are more likely to have the authority to make the difficult decisions entailed in granting concessions. Secondly, it brings these decision-makers once more face to face with the realities of the negotiation and dilutes to some extent the influence on them of their home constituencies. Thirdly, it may also provide an opportunity to bring *different* people into the process, with fresh ideas. And fourthly, providing it is done publicly, it will be symbolically significant: raising the level of the talks, in other words, will indicate that the parties to the negotiation continue to attach high priority to progress. This will generally raise public expectations of success and thus increase the pressure for a settlement.

There are at least four different ways of raising the level of negotiations. The most obvious but not necessarily the most common is to do this in set-piece fashion. For example, following confirmation at the Leeds Castle conference in July 1978 that no further progress in the Egypt–Israel negotiations could be made at foreign minister level, Jimmy Carter decided to propose a summit at Camp David (Quandt, pp. 165, 199). The same tactic was employed, as already noted, in the Israel–PLO negotiations in May 1994. A more common method is to inject senior personnel into a negotiation in a more ad hoc manner. Thus, in order 'to speed up the talks', Jimmy Carter briefly joined the foreign minister-level negotiations that were held at Blair House in Washington in October 1978 in order to flesh out the details of the Camp David Accords agreed the previous month (Quandt, p. 272). A third method is to create a second channel at a higher level and often in a different place, while leaving the lower-level channel untouched. This has the advantage of achieving a division of labour on the agenda while retaining the lower-level channel as an all-purpose fall-back in the event of difficulties. For example, US–North Korea talks began to take place at ministerial level in New York following admission of Pyongyang to the UN in September 1991 but counsellor-level talks continued in Beijing.

Finally, it is important to stress a variation on the latter strategy: the creation of a higher-level channel that on important issues short-circuits the lower-level channel and concerning the activities of which the latter is kept in complete ignorance. This is what Henry Kissinger called a 'backchannel' (Kissinger, 1979, pp. 138–40, 722–3), and was illustrated notably by his Washington discussions on arms control with Soviet Ambassador to the United States Anatoly Dobrynin. This subject was under formal negotiation alternately in Helsinki and Vienna (Kissinger, 1979, pp. 805–23). The advantages of backchannels are secrecy, speed, and the avoidance of internal bureaucratic battles, and are a tactic notoriously favoured by Yasser Arafat.[8] The disadvantages of backchannels, however, are also numerous. They include the possibility of overlooking key points, damaging the morale of the 'front-channel' negotiators when they find out what is going on, and the related difficulty of getting those who have been excluded from the decision-making to support the implementation of any agreement that emerges.

Summary

The momentum of negotiations may falter for any number of reasons, even though the parties remain committed to progress. This is serious because a slow-down can turn into a lull, and a lull can become a full stop. In order to prevent this, negotiators characteristically resort to both artificial and symbolic deadlines, and lean on such practical ones as are to hand. They also employ publicity and metaphors of movement, and they raise the level of the talks as a last resort. If an agreement is eventually reached, with or without the assistance of these devices (and it will be the rare agreement that needs none of them), it will still need to be packaged. It is to this final question of Part I which we now turn.

Notes

1 On 19 March, the Middle East Editor of *The Independent* noted: 'it is unlikely that the PLO will return to talks until after the traditional 40-day period of mourning and the celebration of the Muslim feast of Eid al-Adha next month.'
2 In the earlier edition of this book I employed the term 'notional deadline'. However I think that 'artificial deadline' is clearer. It is the term used by De Soto (De Soto, p. 378).
3 Algeria, Libya, South Yemen, Syria and the PLO had already held a summit of their Anti-Sadat 'Steadfastness and Confrontation Front' in Damascus on 23 September (Lukacs, pp. 469–70).

4   Whether in the event they do or not is not the point.
5   Although Quandt reports that this summit was scheduled for 'late October', it
    actually took place between 2 and 5 November.
6   The introduction to this section follows the analysis very closely in the stimu-
    lating and accessible work by Lakoff and Johnson (1980), especially pp. 3, 10,
    156–8.
7   In his chapter on this in *Herding Cats*, called (inevitably) 'The Road to Madrid',
    James Baker, US Secretary of State at the time, reports that 'I told them [the
    Palestinians] the train was moving and they'd better not miss it' (Crocker et
    al., p. 200).
8   'Only three others are said to have been fully aware of the secret Norway
    negotiations with Israel. When Dr Haidar Abdel Shafi, the widely respected
    leader of the Palestinian team during 10 rounds of talks with Israel, arrived in
    Tunis last August for further instructions, it was to be told a deal had already
    been struck behind his back,' *Financial Times*, 26/27 February 1994.

Further reading

Berridge, G. R., 'Diplomacy and the Angola/Namibia Accords, December 1988',
    International Affairs, vol. 65, no. 3, 1989.
Carter, J., *Keeping Faith: Memoirs of a President* (Bantam Books: New York, 1982),
    pp. 267–429 (on the Egypt–Israel negotiations).
Cradock, P., *Experiences of China* (John Murray: London, 1994), chs 16–20, 23 (on
    the negotiations in 1983–4 for the transfer of Hong Kong from British to
    Chinese sovereignty).
De Soto, A., 'Ending violent conflict in El Salvador', in C. A. Crocker, F. A.
    Hampson, and P. Aall (eds), *Herding Cats: Multiparty Mediation in a Complex
    World* (United States Institute of Peace Press: Washington DC, 1999).
Harrison, S., 'Inside the Afghan talks', *Foreign Policy*, 1988.
Lakoff, G. and M. Johnson, *Metaphors We Live By* (University of Chicago Press:
    Chicago and London, 1980), esp. chs 1–3, 11, 16 and 23.
Quandt, W. B., *Camp David: Peacemaking and Politics* (Brookings Institution:
    Washington, DC, 1986).
Sullivan, J. G., 'How peace came to El Salvador', *Orbis* (winter 1994), pp. 83–98.

5
Packaging Agreements

Diplomatic agreements vary in form to an almost bewildering degree. They vary most obviously in title or style: 'treaties', 'final acts', 'protocols', 'exchanges of notes' – even 'agreements', for example. However, they also vary significantly in textual structure, language, and whether or not they are accompanied by 'side letters'. They also vary (though since Woodrow Wilson's campaign for open diplomacy at the time of the First World War there has become entrenched a presumption that they should not) in whether they are publicized or kept secret. The purpose of this chapter is to explain this variation and to indicate what form an agreement might take depending on its subject matter and the political needs of its authors.

There are four main reasons, aside from accident and changing linguistic preferences, which help to explain the multiplicity of forms taken by international agreements. The first is that some create international legal obligations while others do not. The second is that some forms of agreement are better at signalling the importance of the subject matter, while others are better at disguising its significance. The third is that some are simply more convenient to use than others; they are easier to draw up and avoid the need for ratification. And the fourth is that some are better than others at saving the face of parties who have been obliged to make potentially embarrassing concessions in order to achieve a settlement.

The form taken by any particular agreement will depend on what premium is attached to each of these considerations by the parties to the negotiation. It will also depend on the degree of harmony between them on these questions, and – in the absence of harmony – the degree to which concessions on form can be traded for concessions on substance.

International legal obligations at a premium

The parties to a negotiation may agree that the subject of their agreement is not appropriate to regulation by international law. This may be because it is obvious that it is more appropriately governed by municipal law, as are a great many commercial accords. Alternatively, it may be because the agreement merely amounts to a statement of commonly held principles or objectives. Such was the case with the Atlantic Charter of 1941 and the Helsinki Final Act of 1975, which was the product of the 35-nation Conference on Security and Cooperation in Europe (Gore-Booth, 1979, pp. 238–9; Shaw, p. 562). If, however, the parties to a negotiation concur that their agreement should create obligations enforceable in *international* law, then they must put it in the form of a treaty (Box 5.1).

In view of the widespread cynicism about the effectiveness of international law, why might the parties to a negotiation want to create an agreement entailing international legal obligations? They do this because they know that such obligations are, in fact, honoured far more often than not, even by states with unsavoury reputations (Henkin, p. 47). Among other reasons, this is mainly because the obligations derive from consent, because natural inhibitions to law-breaking exist in the relations between states that do not obtain in the relations between individuals, and because a reputation for failing to keep agreements will make it extremely difficult to promote policy by means of negotiation in the future (Berridge, 1992b, pp. 157–62; Bull, ch. 6).

Box 5.1   What is a 'treaty'?

The term 'treaty' derives from the French word *traiter*, to negotiate. It was defined by the Vienna Convention on the Law of Treaties (1969), which came into force in 1980. This stated that a treaty is 'an international agreement concluded between States in written form and governed by international law, whether embodied in a single instrument or in two or more related instruments and whatever its particular designation'. It is important to add to this that in order to be 'governed by international law', an agreement must (under Article 102 of the UN Charter) 'as soon as possible be registered with the Secretariat and published by it'. This is because unregistered agreements cannot be invoked before 'any organ of the United Nations', which includes the International Court of Justice (Ware, p. 1). In short, parties who want their agreement to create international legal obligations must write it out and give a copy to the UN; in so doing, they have created a 'treaty'.

Signalling importance at a premium

Creating a treaty is one thing; calling a treaty a 'treaty' is another. In fact, treaties are more often than not called something quite different. A few of these alternative titles were mentioned at the beginning of this chapter; others include 'act', 'charter', 'concordat', 'convention', 'covenant', 'declaration', 'exchange of correspondence', 'general agreement', *modus vivendi*, 'pact', 'understanding', and even 'agreed minutes'.[1] Some treaties are nevertheless still called 'treaties' and there is a consensus that this style is adopted when there is a desire to underline the importance of an agreement.[2] This is because of the term's historical association with the international deliberations of princes or their plenipotentiaries, and because the treaty so-called is presented in an imposing manner, complete with seals as well as signatures (Box 5.2). Agreements on matters of special international significance that have, accordingly, been styled 'treaties' include the North Atlantic Treaty of 4 April 1949 which created the West's Cold War alliance, the Treaties of Rome of 25 March 1957 which created the European Communities, and the various Treaties of Accession of new members to the EC (Gore-Booth, 1979, pp. 239–40). Agreements ending wars are, of course, commonly called 'peace treaties', as in the case of the Treaty of Peace between the Arab Republic of Egypt and the State of Israel of 26 March 1979. And agreements providing all-important guarantees of a territorial or constitutional settlement are invariably called 'treaties of guarantee'. In this case a good example is the Cyprus Guarantee Treaty of 16 August 1960. These, however, are not so common today as once they were.[3]

If an agreement is believed by its authors to be of great political importance but is not of such a character as to warrant creation of legal obligations, its importance cannot be signalled nor its binding character reinforced by calling it a 'treaty': it is not a treaty. However, precisely because the parties have rejected the possibility of clothing their agreement in international law but remain 'politically' bound by it as well as deeply attached to the agreement's propaganda value, it is doubly important to dress it in fine attire of a different kind. Hence the use of imposing titles such as Atlantic 'Charter' and Helsinki 'Final Act', as mentioned in the previous section.[4]

Convenience at a premium

Since states today negotiate on so many matters, an international agreement does not have to be of merely routine character for convenience to

---

Box 5.2 The treaty so-called

The 'treaty' so-called usually has the following characteristics:

- descriptive title
- preamble, including the names and titles of the High Contracting Parties (if in heads of state form), the general purpose of the agreement, the names and official designations of the plenipotentiaries, and an affirmation that the latter have produced their full powers, etc.
- substantive articles, which are numbered I, II, etc., commonly beginning with definitions, and usually leading from the general to the more specific
- final clauses, which deal with matters such as the extent of application of the treaty, signature, ratification, accession by other parties, entry into force, duration and provision for renewal
- clause stating 'in witness whereof' the undersigned plenipotentiaries have signed this treaty
- indication of the place where the treaty is signed, together with the authentic language or languages of the text, and date of signature
- seals and signatures of the plenipotentiaries

Source: Grenville and Wasserstein, p. 13; Gore-Booth, 1979, pp. 240–1.

---

be an important consideration in dictating its shape (Aurisch, p. 281). Convenience argues for informal agreements: treaties not styled as 'treaties', or agreements which, because they remain unpublished, are treaties in neither form nor substance. What inconveniences are avoided by packaging an agreement informally?

First of all, the complexities of formal treaty drafting and its attendant procedures, such as the production of documents certifying that the plenipotentiaries have 'full powers', are avoided. This is probably of special benefit to smaller and newer foreign ministries but is also likely to be regarded as an advantage by the overburdened ministries of the bigger powers as well. Not surprisingly, therefore, 'exchanges of notes' or 'exchanges of letters', which consist simply of a letter from one of the parties spelling out the terms of the agreement and a reply from the other indicating acceptance, are now the most common form of treaty. They require none of the elaborate construction of the treaty so-called; nor do they require the presentation of full powers (Gore-Booth, 1979, pp. 247–8).

The second inconvenience that may be avoided by informal packaging is ratification of the agreement, though it should first be stressed that ratification is still widely valued and provision for it is a feature of almost all written constitutions. It is also a feature of the unwritten constitution of the United Kingdom (Ware, p. 1; Shaw, pp. 568–9).

Ratification means confirmation on the part of the negotiators' political masters that they will honour an agreement negotiated and signed on their behalf. It became normal practice when poor communications made it difficult if not impossible for there to be any certainty that negotiators had not exceeded their powers – or that their masters had not changed their minds altogether since dispatching them on their diplomatic errand. The revolution in communications has, of course, virtually removed this problem, though governments still sometimes favour a form of agreement that requires ratification. This may be because they have certain anxieties about the agreement: perhaps it had to be negotiated under the lash of an over-tight practical deadline (see Chapter 4) and thus requires time for second thoughts. They may also insist on such an agreement because they know that its significance is such that it will be politically unsupportable at home, and thus unimpressive to their foreign interlocutors, in the absence of some expression of popular approval, typically by a special majority in a representative assembly. In a genuine democracy, the ultimate form of ratification is a referendum, such as that held by the Labour government in Britain in 1974 on the issue of whether or not the United Kingdom should remain a signatory of the Treaties of Rome.

There are, nevertheless, clearly many occasions when governments feel the need neither for an opportunity for second thoughts on an agreement nor for its popular endorsement. In these circumstances they are naturally keen to avoid the delay in the coming into force of an agreement caused by the need for its ratification; and they are especially anxious to avoid the risk of a demand for its renegotiation that this might entail. This was the notorious fate of the Treaty of Versailles, signed in June 1919 but in the following November and again in March 1920 refused the two-thirds majority by the US Senate needed for American ratification. The strain of campaigning for ratification, coming as it did on top of the mental and physical exertions of the peace negotiations themselves, had also caused the American president, Woodrow Wilson, to have a severe stroke from which he very nearly died (Dimbleby and Reynolds, pp. 70–3). Six decades later, President Jimmy Carter had an equally acute problem of ratification with the second Strategic Arms Limitation Treaty, though fortunately it did not have the same effect on his health.

An executive that feels no need for ratification is, then, unlikely to invite certain delay and possible trouble by casting its agreements in a form that requires ratification by a popular assembly. Since the American view is that treaties, by definition, require ratification (Shaw,

p. 569),[5] it is thus obvious that the United States executive branch will avoid this form of agreement in these circumstances, and will probably have little difficulty in persuading its negotiating partners to concur. In fact, as is well known, it is in order to avoid the possible embarrassments of the ratification process in the Senate, that there has been massive resort to the 'executive agreement' in place of treaties so-called by successive American administrations since Wilson's time. Technically, these are international agreements entered into by the president either after Congress has by law given him a *general* authorization in the field concerned (Bradshaw and Pring, pp. 407–8); or, in the case of 'pure' executive agreements, by virtue of certain unfettered plenary powers that the president possesses under the constitution, for example as Commander-in-Chief (Franck and Weisband, pp. 144, 149). In practice they are simply any international agreement entered into by the US executive branch that is not called a treaty and therefore does not require the 'advice and consent of the Senate' (Franck and Weisband, pp. 141–2). Since the Second World War, US presidents have entered into roughly seven times more executive agreements than treaties;[6] of the 1271 international agreements entered into by the second Reagan administration, only 47 were treaties (Ragsdale, pp. 76–7).

Another way of sidestepping the Senate is for the United States executive branch and its foreign negotiating partner each to issue a 'unilateral non-binding declaration', which in practice nevertheless is expected to be politically effective. The classic example here is provided by the separate but virtually simultaneous declarations of the United States and the Soviet Union immediately prior to the date of expiration of the Interim Agreement on Strategic Offensive Arms on 3 October 1977. Each indicated in its separate statement that, provided the other showed similar restraint, it would continue to honour the provisions of the technically dead Agreement (Glennon, pp. 267–9).

One of the titles common to a large proportion of the thousands of executive agreements to which the United States government is a party, as well as to a large proportion of the international agreements entered into by other states, is, as already mentioned, the exchange of notes or exchange of letters. This does not normally require ratification, and so comes into force immediately upon signature. As a result, it is popular for this reason as well as because it avoids the formal complexities of the treaty so-called. Informal agreements with other titles may, however, also be so framed in order to avoid pressure for ratification.

The final inconvenience that may be avoided by packaging agreements informally is the inconvenience of unwanted publicity, that is, publicity that may stir up political opponents at home or present intelligence gifts to unfriendly states. To avoid the former, agreements on sensitive matters may be published (and thus become binding) but in such informal style as to be unlikely to attract attention. Two examples might be cited here. The first is the so-called Simonstown Agreements between Britain and the Union of South Africa that were concluded in 1955. The British wanted to play these down because they entailed surrender to Afrikaner nationalist control of imperial facilities (the Simonstown naval base) and at the same time close military cooperation with racist South Africa. The agreements took the form of an 'exchange of letters' (Berridge, 1992a, ch. 5). The second good example is the Anglo-Argentine agreement on the Falkland Islands of 1971. The Argentinians were not anxious to advertise this because they had gained nothing on sovereignty. The British were not anxious to advertise it either because the practical schemes dealing with access and technical cooperation to which they had agreed could nevertheless have been interpreted as the thin end of the wedge of surrendering sovereignty. The agreement was in two parts. First, there was a 'joint statement' initialled (rather than signed) by delegation heads on 1 July, thus indicating only that negotiations were closed (Wood and Serres, p. 221). Secondly, there was an 'exchange of notes' on 5 August between the British Chargé d'Affaires in Buenos Aires and the Argentine Minister of Foreign Affairs, which referred to and qualified the joint statement (Grenville and Wasserstein, pp. 11, 433–6).

To avoid presenting intelligence gifts to unfriendly states, the parties to a successful negotiation may not only conclude an informal agreement but withhold publication. Of course, this means that it is not a treaty, that it is, in other words, not legally binding. But there are circumstances in which this is relatively unimportant, for example in the case of certain kinds of defence agreements between close allies, bound to each other by urgent common interest and perhaps by ties of sentiment as well. As Ware has noted, a good example of such an agreement is the UK–US Memorandum of Understanding on British participation in the Strategic Defence Initiative. This was signed in 1985 but, in Britain, revealed in its details only later, and in confidence, to the Defence Select Committee of the House of Commons (Ware, p. 3).

Saving face at a premium

In politically sensitive negotiations where publicity for any agreement achieved is unavoidable and even desirable, what excites special interest in the packaging of any agreement is the issue of 'face'. This means the necessity to save from excessive embarrassment those parties whose concessions would otherwise make them vulnerable to the wrath of their supporters. Face is a particularly important consideration in 'shame cultures' such as those of the Arab Middle East (Cohen, 1997, p. 183).

Where face is a vital issue, the composition and structure, as well as the title of any agreement, may not only be an important but also a controversial element in a negotiation. It will be important because some kinds of packaging will be better than others at disguising the concessions that have had to be made. It is also likely to be controversial because what one side wants to disguise the other will usually want to highlight. Settlement of the Iran hostages crisis was helped by using a form of agreement – a declaration by the Algerian mediators – which suggested that Ayatollah Khomeini had made his gesture to the third party rather than to 'the Great Satan' (see Chapter 11; Grenville and Wasserstein, p. 11). It is fortunate that this was of no great concern to the diabolical United States. In what other ways can agreements be packaged in order to save face and thus ease a settlement?

Both languages – or more

It should first be noted, even though it may seem obvious, that diplomatic agreements in the contemporary world must be sensitive to the issue of language – such is the latter's centrality to nationality. Of course, this has not always been the case. Until the seventeenth century most treaties were written in Latin, thereafter in French, and in the twentieth century chiefly in English (Grenville and Wasserstein, p. 10). However, since the end of the Second World War it has become much more common for copies of agreements made between parties speaking different languages to be translated into the language of each. Furthermore, as might be imagined and as was confirmed by the Vienna Convention on the Law of Treaties, each version is typically described as 'equally authentic' or 'equally authoritative'.

The diplomatic advantage of drafting agreements in the language of each party is that it fosters the impression – whether true or not – that negotiated agreements reflect relationships of equality and provide for an exchange of concessions on an equal basis. After 1945, to take some examples, agreements between the United States and the Soviet Union were written in English and Russian, and between the United States and South American countries in English and Spanish. The Paris Peace Accords of 1973, which ended the Vietnam War, were drawn up in English and Vietnamese. The agreement concluded between Cuba and Angola in 1988, which concerned the withdrawal of the forces of the former from the territory of the latter, was written in Spanish and Portuguese. In each of these cases there were good political reasons for doing everything possible to suggest equality of status.

It should be added, though, that while there may be a clear diplomatic advantage to having equally authoritative agreements in different languages, there is a clear diplomatic disadvantage as well. This is because an agreement might be vague or loose at certain points and, in the course of its implementation, it may transpire that one interpretation is favoured more by the language of one text than it is by the language of the other. Where there are only two languages, this is obviously a recipe for trouble. It is for this reason that states sometimes wisely agree to have the text also drawn up in a third language – usually English – and agree that this shall prevail in the event of a divergence of interpretation between the other two. This is what happened in the Geneva Accords on Afghanistan of 1988. The two accords which formally involved only the Pakistanis and the Afghans were drawn up in Urdu and Pashtu, while that which formally involved the Soviet Union as well was also written in Russian. In addition, all three agreements had an English version and it was agreed that this text would prevail in the event of 'any divergence of interpretation' (Berridge, 1991, App. 5). It is even more likely that this arrangement, provision for which was also made in the Vienna Convention on the Law of Treaties, will be employed in agreements where an English-speaking state has been employed as a mediator. A case in point is the Egypt–Israel Peace Treaty of March 1979. This was written in Arabic, Hebrew, and English, and provided that the master text would be the English one.

Many agreements, however, have no master text, thereby underlining the greater importance that is generally attached to saving face compared to avoiding possible future misunderstandings. To take but one example, the first of the two 'Angola/Namibia Accords', signed in December 1988, to which South Africa, Cuba, and Angola was each a party, was signed in English, Spanish, and Portuguese versions, 'each language being equally authentic'. No text was nominated as the one that would prevail in the event of disagreement.

Small print

Sensitivity to language only addresses the question of face in the most general way, of course, and negotiators must needs turn to other devices when they are confronted with the problem of disguising a sensitive concession in the text of an agreement. Perhaps the most common way of doing this is to say very little about it, tuck it away in some obscure recess, and ensure that the rest of the agreement is padded out with relatively trivial detail. A good example of this strategy can be found in the UN-brokered agreements of 1988 between the Soviet-backed Afghan Communist government and the American-backed Pakistanis, one of the most important provisions of which concerned the withdrawal of Soviet troops from Afghanistan. The Soviet Union, of course, was extremely sensitive to any suggestion that it was abandoning its clients in Kabul to the ferocious if disorganized *mujahedin*. The trouble was that the Soviet concession – troop withdrawals – was the sort of thing that was considerably more attractive to television news editors than the American quid pro quo that Moscow hoped would enable the Afghan Communist regime to survive, that is, the termination of material support to the *mujahedin*. As a result, in the three agreements and one declaration that made up what were popularly known as the 'Geneva Accords' on Afghanistan, only two short sentences were devoted to the Soviet troop withdrawal. Furthermore, they were tacked onto the end of a paragraph (number five) which gave no signpost at the beginning to what was to come at the end. And the agreement of which these two sentences were the most pregnant part was padded out, rather in the manner of a 'final act', with a resumé of the history of the negotiations, the titles of the other agreements reached, and general principles of international law (Berridge, 1991, pp. 148–51).

Another 'small print' technique for saving face is to place embarrassing concessions in documentary appendages to the main text. These take many forms: side letters, interpretive notes, appendices, additional protocols, and so on. Whatever their title, the point remains to make the concessions binding by putting them in a written, public agreement but to do so in such a way as to make them less likely to attract attention and easier to play down for those obliged to grant them. Numerous side letters – exchanges of correspondence which are figuratively speaking placed at the 'side' of the main documents – were published to accompany the two main agreements in the Camp David 'Accords' of September 1978 and the Egypt–Israel Peace Treaty of the following March. While most of these served purposes other than face-saving,[7] some existed for precisely this reason. These included the anodyne restatements of existing positions on the incendiary question of the status of Jerusalem. The Egyptians wanted the matter dealt with in side letters to obscure the fact that they had made no progress on the issue. As for the Israelis, they happily concurred in order to obscure the fact that they had been prepared to talk about it at all (Carter, pp. 395, 397–9; Vance, pp. 225–6). The Israelis even persuaded the Americans not to restate the substance of their own position on East Jerusalem, which was that it was occupied territory. Instead, they merely stated in their own letter that their position remained that outlined in statements by two former American ambassadors to the United Nations (Quandt, p. 252).

It should be added, though, that tucking sensitive matters away in documentary appendages to the main agreement has at least two disadvantages. First, in a complex and tense negotiation under great pressure of time, there is more chance of a slip-up. For example, in September 1978 the Americans failed to secure unambiguous written Israeli agreement to a freeze on new settlements in the West Bank and Gaza until the autonomy negotiations had been concluded, which proved to be a very serious oversight. It is inconceivable that this could have occurred had this issue been addressed in the general framework accord rather than by means of a side letter which, in the event, the Israelis never signed (Vance, p. 228). Secondly, it can subsequently be claimed that ancillary documents do not have 'the same value' as the main text of an agreement. This is what the Israeli premier, Menachem Begin, alleged of the side letter of 17 September 1978 from Sadat to Carter. This was the one in which the Egyptian president indicated his readiness to negotiate on the West Bank and Gaza on behalf of the Palestinians in the event of a refusal by Jordan to assume this responsibility (Quandt, pp. 299, 386–7).[8]

Euphemisms

It is notorious that politicians who live by the vote also live by the euphemism, and that the more difficult the position in which they find themselves the more inventive in this regard they become. This is rarely an edifying spectacle. In diplomacy, however, the use of euphemisms is more defensible. Indeed, in the description of concessions, the use of words or expressions more palatable to the party that has made them is another face-saving feature of almost all politically sensitive international agreements, though at some price in terms of accuracy.

A good example of the use of euphemisms is to be found in the Geneva Accords on Afghanistan referred to earlier, in which Soviet sensitivities on the issue of the withdrawal of their troops were so solicitously addressed by confining the relevant provisions to the small print. The risk of humiliating the Kremlin was reduced further by the complete absence of any reference whatever to the withdrawal of 'Soviet' troops. What were to be withdrawn instead were 'foreign' troops. It might be added, too, that the agreement containing the provisions on 'foreign' troop withdrawals was headed by a title which was itself a masterpiece of euphemistic obscurantism: 'Agreement on the Interrelationships for the Settlement of the Situation relating to Afghanistan' (Berridge, 1991, App. 5).

These examples illustrate the fact that euphemistic language can help states to sign agreements providing for the withdrawal of their military forces from situations where their prestige is at stake. Others can be found to demonstrate its usefulness where they are being bought off, that is, induced to surrender some principled position by cash or payment in kind. It is, for example, perfectly obvious that rich states negotiating with poorer ones often find it possible to smooth the road to an agreement by discreetly handing over extremely large amounts of money. Since, however, it would be humiliating to the poorer state if this were to be too obvious, and not present the richer one in an especially flattering light either, these large amounts of money are never called 'large amounts of money'. Instead, they are usually called 'reconstruction aid'. This is what the Americans called the large amounts of money repeatedly offered to the North Vietnamese, from as early as April 1965, to encourage them to negotiate an end to the Vietnam War. They were finally referred to – coyly and briefly – in Article 21 of the peace settlement of January 1973. The North Vietnamese, of course, wanted to call them 'reparations' (Kissinger, 1982, pp. 37–43).

'Separate but related' agreements

Where an agreement is based on linkage, it may be necessary to obscure this as much as possible, especially if one party has for years prior to the settlement insisted that it would have nothing to do with any such deal. This had been the position of the Angolans and their supporters (more the latter) in regard to the proposal that South Africa would withdraw from Namibia if, *in return*, Cuba would withdraw from Angola. Linkage is deeply offensive to those who believe that issues should be resolved 'on their merits'. It is thus significant that when a settlement of the south-west African imbroglio was achieved at the end of 1988 (which was, of course, based on this linkage), it was embodied not in one agreement but two. One dealt exclusively with Namibian independence and the other only with the withdrawal of Cuban troops from Angola. Moreover, South Africa was not even presented as a party to the latter and so, obviously, did not sign it (Berridge, 1989).

The same device had been employed in the Camp David Accords a decade earlier. The draft Egypt–Israel peace treaty was presented as one of two 'accords' published simultaneously, while the other was a much more general 'Framework for Peace in the Middle East', the nub of which dealt with the West Bank and Gaza. Having the two 'related' in this way satisfied the Egyptian president, who was anxious to preserve his position that progress on the Egypt–Israel front was linked to progress on the Palestinian question. Having them nevertheless 'separated' in the text satisfied the Israeli prime minister, who was even more anxious to avoid the suggestion that progress in bilateral relations was conditional on any such thing (Quandt, pp. 211, 230).

Summary

The form taken by diplomatic agreements, especially those giving expression to settlements of great political sensitivity, is often of considerable significance. When creating an international legal obligation is at a premium, the parties to an agreement will want to package it as a 'treaty', that is, write it out and give a copy to the UN. If they want to draw attention to it as well, they may go so far as to call it a 'treaty'. If the press of business is great and their agreement is not so important, they will readily settle for an informal agreement such as an exchange of notes, which may or may not be published and which, therefore, may or may not be a treaty. If saving face is at a premium, the parties to an agreement can resort to any number of expedients, the tactical purposes of which are to obscure and minimize the most sensitive concessions. This is not disreputable; it is a significant part of the art of negotiation.

Notes

1   For detailed treatment of these generally, see Gore-Booth, 1979, Book IV.
2   However, it should be noted that, as the Foreign Relations Committee of the US Senate has complained, 'trivial agreements' are sometimes sent to the Senate as treaties while much more important ones are classified as 'executive agreements' and thus withheld. A trivial agreement sent as a treaty was one to regulate shrimp-fishing off the coast of Brazil (Franck and Weisband, p. 145). The executive branch presumably does this sort of thing to make the Senate feel that its constitutional prerogatives in foreign policy-making have not been entirely ignored; see the discussion of executive agreements below.
3   It is no doubt in part because they did not intend to provide genuine guarantees of the Geneva Accords on Afghanistan of 14 April 1988 that the United States and the Soviet Union styled their agreement of the same date on this subject as a '*Declaration* on International Guarantees' (Berridge, 1991, pp. 65, 66, 146).

4   Generally speaking, 'Final Acts' consist of summaries of the proceedings of an international conference (Gore-Booth, 1979, pp. 260–2). This means, incidentally, that a conference will often produce a treaty or other form of agreement *in addition* to a 'Final Act'. For example, the 1961 Vienna Conference which is dealt with in Chapter 7 of this book produced not only the 'Vienna Convention on Diplomatic Relations', together with two optional 'protocols', but also a 'Final Act'. As well as summarizing the proceedings, this contained the texts of four 'Resolutions Adopted by the Conference', one of which was on special missions.

5   The British view, by contrast, is that a treaty only requires ratification if it is clear that this is the intention of the parties (Shaw, p. 569), which means that British governments can be more relaxed about using treaties. It should be added, however, that British governments can afford to be more relaxed about this than American governments anyway, since the former exist only to the extent that they command a majority in the ratifying body, namely the House of Commons.

6   Compare Johnson, ch. 1.

7   Most were designed to reinforce observance of the agreements either by recording key commitments by the main parties (together and singly) in the shape of promises to the American president, or by recording undertakings to one or both of the main parties by the American president. An example of the latter was the US promise to Israel to fund construction of new airfields in the Negev in order to compensate it for surrender of those in Sinai. Since these agreements all involved the United States, which did not wish to be seen as a main party to either the Camp David Accords or the subsequent peace treaty, side letters were clearly appropriate.

8   Begin hoped to persuade the Americans that there was no point in discussing the West Bank at all if the Jordanians refused to take part.

Further reading

Barston, R. P., *Modern Diplomacy*, 2nd edn (Longman: London, 1997) ch. 10.

Cohen, R., *Negotiating Across Cultures*, rev. edn (US Institute of Peace Press: Washington, 1997) ch. 9.

Cradock, P., *Experiences of China* (John Murray: London, 1994), chs 19, 20, 23.

Franck, T. M. and E. Weisband, *Foreign Policy by Congress* (Oxford University Press: New York and Oxford, 1979).

Glennon, M. J., 'The Senate role in treaty ratification', *American Journal of International Law*, vol. 77, 1983.

Gore-Booth, Lord (ed.), *Satow's Guide to Diplomatic Practice*, 5th edn (Longman: London, 1979).

Grenville, J. A. S. and B. Wasserstein, *The Major International Treaties since 1945: A history and guide with texts* (Methuen: London and New York, 1987).

Johnson, L. K., *The Making of International Agreements: Congress confronts the Executive* (New York University Press: New York and London, 1984).

Shaw, M. N., *International Law*, 4th edn (Grotius: Cambridge, 1997).

Wood, J. R. and J. Serres, *Diplomatic Ceremonial and Protocol: Principles, Procedures and Practices* (Macmillan – now Palgrave: London, 1970), ch. 13.

Part II
The Modes of Diplomacy

Introduction to Part II

It has been argued in Part I that the most important function of diplomacy is negotiation. It has also been stressed, however, that this is certainly not always the function to which those professionally involved in this activity devote most of their time, and that diplomacy has other important functions as well. These include information gathering, lobbying, clarifying intentions, supporting commercial and financial activities, assisting nationals abroad, and promoting popular sympathy for the state's foreign policy – at home as well as abroad. Part II expands its focus in order to embrace these other functions, while employing as its organizing principle the *different modes* or *channels* through which all of the functions of diplomacy are pursued. These include direct telecommunications, bilateral diplomacy (conventional and unconventional), multilateral diplomacy, summitry, and mediation.

Direct telecommunication between states, which is the subject of the chapter that follows, could be dealt with in the one on bilateral diplomacy. To the extent that 'conference telephone calls' are exchanged between officials of three or more ministries, it could also be considered in the chapter on multilateral diplomacy. Since heads of state or government are now constantly telephoning each other, it could without awkwardness be brought under the heading of summitry as well. However, telecommunication is now such an important means of direct communication between states, with similar advantages and disadvantages in whatever context it is employed, that it seems appropriate to devote a special chapter to this subject. A prior examination of its limitations also provides a justification for devoting the remainder of Part II to face-to-face diplomacy, albeit a face-to-face diplomacy itself vitally supported by advanced telecommunications.

6
Telecommunications

From ancient times until well into the nineteenth century, all messages, including diplomatic messages, were carried by hand. Even at the beginning of the twenty-first century diplomatic couriers are still sometimes employed for the delivery of certain top-secret packages.[1] But none of this, of course, represents 'telecommunication', and it is telecommunication that has had such a profound impact on diplomacy over the past 150 years. This chapter will not examine the impact that this has had on traditional, bilateral diplomacy, which will be reserved for the next. Instead, the focus here will be on the implications of telecommunications for direct dealings between governments, especially heads of government and their ministers, which either completely ignore or belatedly inform the resident mission. The chapter will concentrate on crisis diplomacy but also look at the significance of telecommunications in routine diplomacy; and it will conclude with a consideration of its limitations. First of all, however, what is telecommunication?

Telecommunication is any mode of communication over a long distance (*tele* is Greek for 'far') that requires human agency only in the sending and reception of the message that it contains and not, as with a diplomatic courier, in its conveyance. The communication by drums and smoke-signals which originated in ancient times, and the optical telegraph or 'semaphore' systems introduced in Europe in the late eighteenth century, therefore, were forms of telecommunication just as much as the telegrams, radio and television broadcasts, faxes, and e-mails of today. Nevertheless, it is not surprising that telecommunication did not make a major impact on diplomacy until the introduction of the electric telegraph towards the middle of the nineteenth century. Soon using submarine as well as land cables, written messages sent by telegraph cut delivery times over some routes from weeks to hours; they were also more reliable. In the early twentieth century, a further radical development occurred in telecommunication when it became possible to deliver the spoken word over vast distances by telephone (available in the late nineteenth century over only short distances) and short wave radio. Since the Second World War further well-known refinements have been added, notably fax, electronic mail, and multi-media video-conferencing. Recent and imminent increases in cheap bandwidth, the wire and cable 'pipes' through which all this information flows, and even more the prospect of 'wireless' communications via an increase in the number of satellites, will add even more to the efficiency and sophistication of communication. This latest development in information and communications technologies (ICTs) will also vastly enhance the extent and mobility of the points from which messages may be transmitted and received, as well as their speed.

Worries over security, in particular, have traditionally caused governments to employ the latest technological developments in telecommunications in the exchange of classified messages only with great caution and after considerable hesitation.[2] Nevertheless, in the end the appeal of these various means of communication has generally won the day, and the appeal of none has been greater than that of the telephone – especially in a crisis.

Crisis diplomacy

Telephone diplomacy

The appeal of a secure telephone connection as a means of making possible direct communication between governments over great distances is obvious. Other forms of telecommunication may be as fast as the telephone but in other important respects it is superior to them. For one thing, it is – at least in principle – easier to use. For another, it is more personal and therefore more flattering to the recipient; written messages, especially at the highest level, are usually drafted by someone else and recognized as such. The telephone also provides unrivalled certainty that a message has got through.[3] Furthermore, it can generally be assumed that a telephone call (unless recorded)[4] will generate no verbatim transcript and thus be deniable if this should prove expedient. It also makes possible the *immediate* correction of a misunderstanding or *immediate* adjustment of a statement that has given unintended offence, so that neither is allowed to fester. Finally, the telephone provides the opportunity to extract an *immediate* response from the party at the other end of the line. It is chiefly for these reasons that political leaders and senior officials attach such importance to using the telephone in maintaining their overseas communications.

Despite its obvious advantages, it is clear that telephone diplomacy is regarded as more appropriate in some circumstances, and in some relationships, than in others. Its advantages are particularly apparent during a major international crisis, though more for orchestrating the response of an alliance than for exploring the possibility of a settlement with an adversary.

A particularly vivid account of the effective use of the telephone in a crisis is provided in the memoirs of James Callaghan, British foreign secretary in the mid-1970s (Callaghan, pp. 342–6). Here he describes in some detail the many calls he exchanged in the hours immediately following the Turkish invasion of Cyprus on 20 July 1974, which led to an immediate threat of war between Greece and Turkey. This was a crisis in which Britain could not avoid playing a key role because not only was Cyprus a member of the Commonwealth but also Britain was one of the three guarantors of its constitution, independence and territorial integrity under the Treaty of Guarantee of 1960. The other two guarantors were fellow NATO allies Greece and Turkey. Callaghan wished to obtain an immediate ceasefire and get talks going between the Greeks and the Turks, for which, of course, he needed American assistance. In the course of a day of 'mad activity' on 21 July, Callaghan spoke on two occasions each to the Turkish president, the Greek foreign minister, and the French foreign minister (acting for the European Community). He also spoke to the Austrian chancellor, Bruno Kreisky, about the possibility of using Vienna as the venue for the talks. And he spoke to US secretary of state, Henry Kissinger, 'about nine or ten times'. By means of these 'almost continuous telephone exchanges', amplified massively by the fact that Kissinger was also calling both the Greeks and the Turks, shortly before midnight Callaghan learned that the Turks had finally accepted a ceasefire effective from 14.00 on the following day. Talks between the foreign ministers of the three guarantor powers began three days after that.

A further example of the use of the telephone in a crisis is provided by the calls exchanged in October 1983 on the White House–10 Downing Street 'hot line' (Box 6.1). The first call was made by the British prime minister, Margaret Thatcher, and was designed to underline the importance of a written message just dispatched imploring the American president, Ronald Reagan, not to invade the Commonwealth state of Grenada. (Only the previous day the British foreign secretary had publicly stated that he had no knowledge of any American intention to

---

Box 6.1   The White House–10 Downing Street 'hot line'

This telephone hot line was probably set up in the early 1960s. There is a reference to it in the FO file at the Public Record Office, dated 1966, dealing with the prime minister's wish to establish a similar line to Moscow (FO371/188931). It had both vocal and text facility, and presumably still does. In an interview enquiry in 1993 Mrs Thatcher was asked whether it was used very often. She replied: 'No, I don't think these things ought to be used very often. But I sometimes received a very welcome call at difficult times from Ronald Reagan, who was very, very thoughtful' (Thatcher, 1993, p. 10). This was consistent with the traditional Whitehall view that personal, top-level exchanges of this sort should be regarded as 'the diplomatic weapon of last resort' (PRO, PREM11/2869).

---

intervene in Grenada. A subsequent invasion of a Commonwealth state by Britain's closest ally, without consultation, would make Mrs Thatcher look weak and foolish – as, of course, it did.) As it turned out, her telephone diplomacy was ineffective – it was already too late. However, the story was different with the call that she received back from Ronald Reagan the following day. The president began with a gallant and disarming preamble, which was just as well because, on her own admission, the Iron Lady was 'not in the sunniest of moods' (Thatcher, 1995, p. 332). He then apologized for the embarrassment that had been caused and explained the practical considerations that had made full consultation impossible. This clearly had a soothing effect on Mrs Thatcher. 'There was not much I felt able to say', she records in her memoirs, 'and so I more or less held my peace, but I was glad to have received the telephone call' (Thatcher, 1995, pp. 331–3). This exchange over the hot line was the more effective because, despite the closeness of these two leaders, it was rarely used (see Box 6.1).

In the run-up to the Gulf War at the beginning of 1991, the US president, George Bush, famously used the telephone to contact the Malaysian prime minister in a Tokyo restaurant in order to secure his support for a vital Security Council resolution. Between the opening of this crisis in August 1990 and the end of the year, George Bush exchanged 40 telephone calls with another leader whose support was even more vital to him in this crisis, Turgut Ozal, the president of Turkey (Stearns, p. 11).

Personal messages exchanged over the telephone are also a common feature of the diplomacy between friendly states when the fate of governments or regimes is at stake. The telephone was an important means of top-level communication between the United States and two of its clients, Ferdinand Marcos of the Philippines and the Shah of Iran, when it became clear that their regimes were in imminent peril (Shultz, 1993, p. 637; Brzezinski, pp. 361, 365, 370). An avowedly similar case occurred shortly prior to Ronald Reagan's visit to Germany in 1985, in the course of which it was planned that, jointly with the West German Chancellor, Helmut Kohl, he would lay a wreath at the German military cemetery at Bitburg. When news of this was announced and it was learned that the cemetery contained the graves of members of the Waffen SS, the White House was engulfed in controversy. It seemed as if Reagan might be forced to cancel the visit to Bitburg; even his wife Nancy argued for cancellation (Reagan, p. 380). At this point, Kohl wrote a letter to Reagan, and a few days later followed this up with a telephone call in which he told the president that the West German government would fall if he cancelled the visit. George Shultz, Reagan's secretary of state, was astonished by this call but knew, he has since recorded, 'that the president could not ignore such an emotionally charged plea from Chancellor Kohl' (Shultz, 1993, p. 550).

In all these examples, what is apparent is that the telephone excelled as an instrument for achieving rapid personal exchanges between friendly states, sometimes to highlight the importance of a written message already dispatched, when urgent decisions were essential. The absence of language barriers, and confidence that any slips of the tongue or ill-considered statements would be treated charitably, also favoured use of the telephone. The last point is particularly important and is probably the main reason why, though it is not unknown (Keeley, p. 6; see also Box 6.2), the telephone is rarely a feature of diplomacy between hostile states (Solomon, p. 4). Telephone conversations cannot be entirely scripted: remarks made spontaneously may not convey exactly the meaning intended (even if simultaneous translation is not needed), and the issues that come up are not entirely predictable. Things said

---

Box 6.2   The Reagan–Assad exchange

In July 1985, President Reagan placed a telephone call to President Assad of Syria, a Soviet-backed state regarded in Washington as a sponsor of terrorism. He thanked him for his role in ending the crisis provoked by the hijacking to Beirut of a TWA airliner and urged him to use his influence to secure the release of the remaining American kidnap victims being held in Lebanon. The president added, however, that he wanted Assad to end his support for terrorism. Not surprisingly, the conversation was 'stiff and cold' (Shultz, pp. 667–8). 'He got a little feisty', the president subsequently recorded in his memoirs, 'and suggested I was threatening to attack Lebanon' (Reagan, p. 497). This perhaps illustrates why this sort of call is rare.

over the telephone cannot be unsaid, and there is no telling to what use an adversary might put a suitably edited tape-recording of a telephone conversation. Written messages that subsequently prove embarrassing may plausibly be dismissed as forgeries but this is more difficult with taped conversations, as President Nixon found to his cost during the Watergate affair. Furthermore, while there may be disadvantages to the recording of a telephone conversation, a disadvantage may also attach to its absence: a subsequent difference of opinion as to what was actually said (Shultz, 1997, p. 6). During the tense period in Sino-American relations in April 2001 provoked by the mid-air collision over the South China Sea between a United States EP-3 spy plane and a Chinese jet fighter, President Bush wisely decided not to try to resolve the matter by telephoning his Chinese opposite number, Jiang Zemin. He relied instead on traditional channels,[5] which in the event proved successful.

It is perhaps not surprising, therefore, that letters delivered via ambassadors, rather than telephone calls, were the normal medium of direct communication between the White House and the Kremlin during the Cold War. It is true that they also enjoyed a 'Direct Communications Link' but this was not a telephone line.[6] Installed following the alarm caused by the Cuban missile crisis of October 1962, this original 'hot line' was a direct telegraph link designed to help cope with the consequences of accidental or unauthorized use of nuclear weapons, though it was occasionally used in other urgent circumstances (Box 6.3). It

---

Box 6.3   Non-emergency uses of the US–Soviet 'hot line'

According to President Carter's National Security Adviser, Zbigniew Brzezinski, the first time this hot line was used in this way was when, on his suggestion, Carter sent a message on arms control to the Soviet leader, Leonid Brezhnev, on 4 March 1977. The idea – always close to Brzezinski's heart – was that this would obviate 'the need to go through our respective Foreign Ministries or Embassies' (Brzezinski, p. 161). Unfortunately, on the testimony of Georgy Kornienko, the principal Americanist in the Soviet Foreign Ministry at the time, the stratagem back-fired. This was because 'at the Moscow end of the "hot line", maintained by the KGB, translators were on duty who were far from highly qualified, and were moreover unfamiliar with the subject matter of the strategic arms negotiations. Therefore their translation of Carter's message was marred by many inaccuracies and rough spots, which did not exactly facilitate its good reception by Soviet leaders' (Kornienko, pp. 4–5). Nevertheless, this was not the last time the US–Soviet hot line was used in a non-emergency situation. It was used again, for example, once more on American initiative, in the Daniloff affair in September 1986, which was threatening to jeopardize a summit meeting (Shultz, p. 732).

consisted of a wire-telegraph circuit which was routed Washington–London–Copenhagen–Stockholm–Helsinki–Moscow, and a back-up radio-telegraph circuit routed Washington–Tangier–Moscow. At each end were teleprinter terminals through which encoded messages in the sender's language were received. It had proved its worth during the Arab–Israeli Six Day War in 1967 but had weaknesses, one of which became apparent when the landline link in Finland was put out of action by a farmer's plough. As a result, in 1971 the hot line was upgraded with satellite circuits and soon proved useful again, especially during the Arab–Israeli war in October 1973. The hot line continued to have no 'voice capability' on the grounds that oral exchanges, with their requirement for simultaneous translation, would have been less accurate than the written message (Smith, G., 1980, pp. 281, 292–3, 296, 521–7). It was given a fax facility in 1985, and in 1987 was supplemented by the creation of 'Nuclear Risk Reduction Centers', directly linked via satellite using high-speed computers and fax machines. The American Center was established in the State Department and its Soviet equivalent in the Ministry of Defence in Moscow. Their purpose is the rapid, accurate and secure transmission of information required under arms control agreements (Harahan, ch. 3). In July 1999 it was announced that a parallel hot line would link the US secretary of state with her Russian counterpart (*Augusta Chronicle Online*, p. 1).

Direct telecommunication, certainly by telephone, seems for good reasons, then, to be a rarity in the delicate diplomacy between hostile states. Nevertheless, it may be employed following a breakthrough secured by other means, for example, to arrange subsequent meetings or clarify the wording of an agreement. Following a breakdown in talks at the beginning of 1994 between Israel and the PLO on a textual agreement on Israel's withdrawal from Gaza and Jericho, fax exchanges were successfully employed in order to confirm the understanding reached.[7]

Radio, television, and internet broadcasting

Radio and television broadcasts, together with official websites, can also be used for direct communication between states.[8] Messages may be sent through channels controlled by government, like the Voice of Russia, Voice of America (VOA), and Radio and TV Marti,[9] or influenced by government, like the BBC World Service; or they may be sent by means of statements issued to the independent mass media.[10] In a crisis such channels are valuable if, for example, an urgent 'no change in policy' message needs to be sent to a large number of allied states simultaneously (Wriston, p. 2). The fact that the commitment has been made publicly also gives added reassurance. If all other channels of communication with the rival state or alliance have collapsed, broadcast communications may be indispensable. With its capacity to present visual images of political leaders, ministerial spokesmen, and ambassadors, television is particularly useful because it can send non-verbal as well as verbal messages (Cohen, 1987; May, pp. 686–8).

Official monitoring services pick up foreign broadcasts and then translate and summarize them with an eye to the special interests of their 'customers' in government. They are particularly adept at identifying significant messages, though only a handful of states enjoy such services. The most proficient appear to be the Foreign Broadcast Information Service (FBIS) of the United States and the BBC Monitoring Service (Rawnsley, 1999).[11]

Of course, governments do not always require sophisticated monitoring services in order to pick up publicly broadcast messages, especially if they are repeated in other prominent media. Such was the case in connection with Haiti in 1986. With 'Baby Doc' Duvalier's dictatorship tottering, US Secretary of State George Shultz announced on ABC-TV's 'Good Morning America' programme that the United States wanted to see a government in Haiti 'that is put there by the democratic process'. Very soon Duvalier was gone. 'Shultz's Word Heeded; Duvalier Saw Omen in Televised Remark', ran a *Washington Post* headline (Shultz, 1993, pp. 622–3). There are many other instances in which governments have sent messages to each other during a crisis via this sort of telecommunication, for example in the Cuban missile crisis in 1962 and the Gulf War in 1991 (Wriston, p. 2).

Routine diplomacy

Of course, radio and television broadcasts, and website messages, are not used for direct communication between governments – especially hostile governments – only during a major crisis. During normal times, leaders are always making speeches and governments are always issuing statements that are intended as much for the consumption of foreign leaders as for the public (May, pp. 665, 667, 685; Kornienko, pp. 3–4). Nor is direct telephone communication, even by heads of government and senior ministers, confined to crises, though it is true that their secure lines do tend to be called 'hot lines'. These connections are now a common device used to maintain regular contact between friendly states with strong common interests, though communication with states that are more peripheral to their concerns will generally go through more traditional channels.[12] A hot line was established between Washington and Beijing in 1998,[13] though this was not employed during the EP-3 spy plane incident in April 2001, as already mentioned above. As for the Washington–London hot line, it did not always require a crisis for President Reagan to use this to talk to Margaret Thatcher (Thatcher, 1995, pp. 435, 774). Nor did it require a crisis for him to talk on a secure telephone to King Hussein of Jordan, a frequent visitor to Washington whose English was impeccable (Shultz, 1993, pp. 435, 451).

The existence of a 'hot line' between heads of government is now as suggestive of an intimate link as it is of a dangerous relationship that might require instantaneous, top-level stabilization. A hot line, in other words, is a status symbol and one that is especially useful to advertise if there has been any indication that relationships are under strain. It is clear that this sort of motive was already a prominent one in the competition for hot lines to Moscow between France and the United Kingdom in the mid-1960s. A more recent example was observed in February 1994. The US administration, which had recently been at odds with Britain over Bosnia and Northern Ireland and now wished to make amends, was very keen to draw press attention to the hot line between the White House and 10 Downing Street. The monthly telephone calls that had previously been the norm between British prime minister, John Major, and Bill Clinton had also been stepped up sharply, British journalists in Washington were informed.[14]

The limitations of telecommunications

The drawbacks of *telephone* diplomacy, especially in the relations between hostile states, have already been noted. It remains to look at its disadvantages in normal relationships and to consider the limitations of telecommunication more generally as a medium of direct communication between foreign governments. These limitations are considerable, even though they are likely to diminish with further technological advance.

In the first place, there are logistical difficulties involved in using the telephone, especially at head of state or government level. In fact, one former senior minister and ambassador of Saudi Arabia has written recently that 'there are few diplomatic tasks more difficult than setting up a phone call between two heads of state ... preparing a phone call', he adds, 'can sometimes take days'. Apart from possible language problems, there are time differences and differences in congested daily schedules with which to cope (Algosaibi, p. 238). These problems are not, of course, entirely overcome by the installation of hot lines.

In his *Guide to Diplomatic Practice*, Sir Ernest Satow remarked upon a further problem of telephone diplomacy. 'The moral qualities ... of statesmen and nations', he noted, 'have not kept pace with the development of the means of action at their disposal: ... more than all, that of rapidity of communication by telegraph and telephone. These latter', he concluded, 'leave no time for reflection or consultation, and demand an immediate and often a hasty decision on matters of vital importance' (Satow, vol. I, p. 157). Satow's observation was perhaps exaggerated in regard to the telegraph, but remains apposite where the telephone is concerned. It is, as already noted, part of its attraction that it can be used to 'bounce' the party at the other end of the line into an agreement that further reflection might have cautioned against. Thus an advantage for the former is a disadvantage for the latter. It may turn out, however, to be a disadvantage for both if the latter recants and wriggles out of what was, after all, merely an 'oral' undertaking: the temperature of the relationship is bound to drop. The same effect can be produced if a leader is caught off balance by a telephone call and, rather than being 'bounced' into agreement, reacts too negatively. A case in point is provided by the late-evening call (London time) that President Reagan made to Mrs Thatcher in order, she believed, to try to persuade her to snatch diplomatic defeat from the jaws of military victory in the Falklands in 1982. 'It was not very satisfactory for either of us', she has since recorded, 'that I should not have had advance warning of what he was likely to say and as a result I was perhaps more forceful than friendly' (Thatcher 1995, p. 230). She had had an equally difficult telephone conversation with President Reagan earlier in the crisis (Thatcher, 1995, pp. 220–1).

Of course, there is greater familiarity with the telephone today than in Satow's time, and conventions and technology (and training in them) exist to help cope with this sort of problem. For example, advisers can listen in to telephone conversations conducted by ministers and heads of government. The bureaucracies of many modern states are also so vast and fractured that the need for internal consultation on 'matters of vital importance' raised in a telephone call is widely understood. Nevertheless, it is clear that for certain kinds of regime, especially those that are externally weak, internally dictatorial, and diplomatically unsophisticated, telephone diplomacy may still carry the risk of provoking a rash response, and it would be surprising if the risk was entirely confined to such states.

Unless exceptional precautions are taken, telecommunication in general is also vulnerable to eavesdropping. It is for this reason in particular that foreign ministries, not least the US State Department, have proceeded only with the greatest circumspection in the introduction of electronic mail (Stimson Center Project, pp. 20–4). And it is also chiefly for this reason that the internal regulations of many MFAs also expressly forbid the treatment of classified issues on the telephone at the sub-political level. Anxiety about the security of telecommunications helps to explain, too, why states still employ special envoys (Berridge, 1994, ch. 6) and sometimes diplomatic couriers, who enjoy significant protection in international law, to deliver orally or hand-carry messages of a particularly sensitive nature. If governments are forced, as for example during a crisis, to rely on radio or television broadcasts to communicate with each other (see above), the whole world is in principle able to 'eavesdrop' since the messages are immediately in the public domain. Knowing this, those responsible for sending such messages are unlikely to frame them in a manner suggestive of an accommodating attitude. In any case, public messages of this sort, however couched, are likely to fall victim to misrepresentation. Official websites can be faked (Baldi), and other organs of the mass media can distort messages and make it difficult for the intended recipient to distil them objectively. The 'peace offer' broadcast during the Gulf War by Baghdad Radio on 15 February 1991 is a perfect illustration in both of these regards. After careful translation of the broadcast had been made it was apparent that the conditions attached to the 'peace offer' were so fantastic that the US-led coalition could not take it seriously. However, prior to proper translation, the Western media had rushed to present it as virtually the end of the war, thereby exaggerating further the animosity towards Baghdad when the hopeful expectations unwisely raised came crashing down (Taylor, pp. 228–30; Rawnsley, 1999, pp. 143–4).

To the extent that it is confined to transmission of the spoken or written word, telecommunication also has the disadvantage that it is, by definition, insensitive to all forms of 'non-verbal communication' (Cohen, 1987). Unless one follows the absurd argument of Harold Nicolson that precision in diplomacy is so important that it is essentially a written art, this is a particularly significant limitation (Simpson, 1980, p. 74). When the representatives of states, whether leaders or junior officials, communicate by telephone and radio, and especially by e-mail and fax, they cannot – should they wish to do so – provide nuance or emphasis to their messages to the degree available in communication via personal encounters. The use of body language, dress, venue, and setting, by means of which a diplomat can also *say* one thing but *mean* another, are all forgone in telecommunication of this sort (Cohen, 1987, chs 3–6).

Video-conferencing

It is true, however, as already noted, that the visual images of television enable body language to be conveyed more readily. Furthermore, video-conferencing is becoming increasingly sophisticated and more secure, and is even better able to overcome the insensitivity of telecommunication to non-verbal communication. The UN is already using it on occasions in order to create 'virtual meetings' between discussants in New York, Geneva, and Vienna.[15] And the former deputy foreign minister of Canada, Gordon Smith, wrote in 1999 that '[t]he military in many countries has been doing this [holding virtual meetings via secure video links] for some time' (Smith, G. S. 1999, p. 21)

However, even the smartest video conference, in which the parties are in dedicated visual as well as oral contact, obviously cannot replicate entirely the personal encounter. The participants in such a 'virtual meeting' remain physically remote and thus quite incapable of exploiting the physical dimension of body language or, for that matter, the social rituals that help to create the atmosphere in which messages are most likely to be sympathetically received. In the brilliant chapter on body language in Raymond Cohen's *Theatre of Power*, it is significant that only two of its forms noted can be employed on television or in a video conference: facial expression and tone of voice. All of the others – the handshake, embrace, and displays of inconvenience[16] and triumph – require a personal encounter.[17] In some cultures, physical 'touch and proximity' are unusually important (Cohen, 1987, p. 103). Moreover, it is these forms of body language that are most useful in establishing the desired tone at 'threshold moments' in a relationship (Cohen, 1987, pp. 90–1). When it is further considered that it is especially in hostile relationships that it is so necessary to relieve the inevitable tension of a diplomatic exchange by gracious social ritual and acts of hospitality, the limitations of telecommunication become all too obvious. Even Smith, one of the best known apostles of 'virtual diplomacy', believes that '[n]egotiations are best done face to face, and even video does not work very well unless the parties know each other and the stakes are relatively minor' (Smith, G. S., 1999, p. 21). On the other hand, it should not be forgotten that in quite a lot of routine diplomacy the parties do indeed know each other well and are looking for a compromise on questions where the stakes are indeed relatively minor.

Summary

Direct telecommunication between governments is now a very important channel for the conduct of diplomacy, both in crises and in more
normal times. In crises, the telephone is especially valued as a means of
communication between allied and friendly states, not least at head of
state or government level. Here it seems to be used chiefly as a vehicle
for providing reassurance and intelligence, urging support, explaining
attitudes, and agreeing joint responses. Adversaries in a crisis are more
likely to use written telecommunication, whether over a hot line or via a
broadcast statement, though telephone exchanges are certainly not
unknown. Here, clarification of intention seems to be the main function
fulfilled. In routine diplomacy, direct telecommunication of all kinds is
even more common.

Nevertheless, even some of the most enthusiastic supporters of the
use of telecommunications in diplomacy acknowledge that its limitations remain considerable. These are particularly obvious in the field of
negotiation, especially between hostile states, though it also seems to be
true that most of the other functions of diplomacy can at best be
supplemented by direct telecommunication. Before turning to the conduct of diplomacy on a face-to-face basis, however, two cautionary
observations should be stressed. First, there is a variety of different
forms of 'telecommunication' and it is important to try to weigh up
the implications for diplomacy of each of these separately. Secondly, this
is not easy because the existing research on this subject is still very much
in its infancy.[18]

Notes

1   Albeit chiefly from foreign ministries to their own missions abroad rather
than to foreign governments. On the British corps of Queen's Messengers,
see Berridge and James, pp. 198–9. Of course, couriers also carry items that do
not lend themselves to delivery by means of telecommunication. At
the beginning of 2000, the U.S. Diplomatic Courier Service still had almost
a hundred couriers and carried on average ten tons of 'classified and sensitive material for State and other U.S. government agencies every day'
(Miles).

2   The report of the Washington-based Centre for Strategic and International
Studies, *Reinventing Diplomacy in the Information Age* (December 1998), was
critical of the State Department for its over-cautious telecommunications
strategy (p. 65).

3 Of course, it is not foolproof in this regard. The recipient of a call may fail to act on a promise to pass on a message, or may successfully impersonate the intended recipient.

4 On the available evidence, this seems to occur only in connection with calls at the highest levels.

5 Though apparently there was fierce debate over this question in the White House situation room (*The Guardian*, 4 April 2001). The official line was that he had taken the decision not to use the telephone in order to avoid suggesting that the White House was treating the situation as a crisis.

6 Similar connections were installed between Paris and Moscow in 1966 (the 'white telephone') and London and Moscow in 1967. The British desire for their own hot line to Moscow came from Downing Street rather than the FO. It was inspired by the refusal of the United States to allow them to be 'tied in' to the Washington–Moscow hot line and fear that the French would beat them to having their own line to the Kremlin. The British prime minister, Harold Wilson, first raised the issue with the Soviet government in February 1966. In the event, the French, who at this time had more pull in Moscow, beat them anyway (PRO, FO371/188931 and FCO28/387).

7 'Fax diplomacy breaks the impasse', *Financial Times*, 7 January 1994.

8 'Public diplomacy', of which this is an aspect, is also discussed in Chapters 1 and 7 (in the latter under the sub-heading 'Propaganda'). I have discussed the background to the subject, and described many of the radio and TV stations involved, in more detail in my textbook on international politics (Berridge, 1997, ch. 8).

9 American surrogate voices for Cuba.

10 These can easily be explored via their websites. See 'Philip M. Taylor's links', section headed 'Public and Cultural Diplomacy', http://www.leeds.ac.uk/ics/phillink.htm

11 Rawnsley notes that 'at least eleven other countries are known to have developed systems for monitoring foreign broadcasts, including France, Germany, Japan, Russia and most recently Australia ... ' (Rawnsley 1999, p. 135).

12 As long ago as the early 1960s, the American president, John F. Kennedy, pointed out that in Africa 'a chief of mission was on his own, in contrast to Bonn, Paris, and London, where the main business was done by telephone from Washington and through regular visits from the secretary of state and other top officials' (Kaiser, p. 182). Kennedy probably exaggerated this contrast in order to flatter the men he wanted to send as ambassadors to Africa, though not by that much. He had, after all, made Africa an unusually high priority for an American administration and, according to Kaiser (sent to Senegal), there was 'a certain cachet about being one of Kennedy's African ambassadors' (p. 184).

13 Henry Kissinger had offered one to Beijing in 1973, at the time of the US–PRC rapprochement. His idea was that it would be used to flash intelligence to Communist China of Soviet military movements. However, the offer was turned down (*The Kissinger Transcripts*, p. 2).

14 In *The Guardian*, this story was reported under the heading: 'US hotline to No 10 warms relationship', 25 February 1994.

15 I am grateful to Stefano Baldi for supplying this information.

16   That is, putting oneself out for visitors, for example by going to the airport to meet them.
17   It is true that a 'triumph display' can be executed by a single individual, as when the founder of the French Fifth Republic, General De Gaulle, held his arms aloft to create a 'V' for victory. However, it can only signify unity as well 'when it involves more than a single figure'. This typically involves one leader grabbing the arm of another and thrusting it into the air for the benefit of the television cameras (Cohen, 1987, pp. 100–1).
18   It is extraordinary that, as far as I am aware, there is not even a history of the US–Soviet hot line. It is treated merely as a footnote in the history of arms control agreements.

Further reading

Callaghan, James, *Time and Chance* (Collins: London, 1987), pp. 344–6.

Cohen, Raymond, *Theatre of Power: The Art of Diplomatic Signalling* (Longman: London and New York, 1987), ch. 5.

Cohen, Y., *Media Diplomacy: The Foreign Office in the Communication Age* (1986).

Davison, W. P., 'Mass communication and diplomacy', in J. N. Rosenau, Kenneth W. Thompson, and Gavin Boyd (eds), *World Politics* (1976).

Jones, R. A., *The British Diplomatic Service 1815–1914* (Smythe: London, 1983), ch. 7.

Kennedy, P. M., 'Imperial cable communications and strategy, 1870–1914', *English Historical Review*, vol. 86, October 1971, pp. 728–52.

May, Ernest R., 'The news media and diplomacy', in Gordon A. Craig and Francis L. Loewenheim (eds), *The Diplomats 1939–1979* (Princeton University Press: Princeton, New Jersey, 1994).

Rawnsley, Gary D., *Radio Diplomacy and Propaganda: The BBC and VOA in International Politics, 1956–64* (Macmillan – now Palgrave: Basingstoke, 1996).

Rawnsley, Gary D., 'Monitored broadcasts and diplomacy', in J. Melissen (ed.), *Innovation in Diplomatic Practice* (Macmillan (now Palgrave): Basingstoke, 1999).

Smith, Gordon S., *Reinventing diplomacy: a virtual necessity* (http://www.usip.org/oc/vd/vdr/gsmithISA99.html)

Solomon, Richard H., 'The Information Revolution and International Conflict Management', Keynote Address at the Virtual Diplomacy Conference, April 1997, http://www.usip.org/pubs/pworks/virtual18/inforev_18.html

United States Institute of Peace, *Virtual Diplomacy: Fact Sheet* (http://www.usip.org/oc/virtual_dipl.html)

7
Bilateral Diplomacy: Conventional

The term 'bilateral diplomacy' now usually means nothing more than communication limited to two parties at any one time; it signifies nothing about the method by or context in which they communicate. Thus bilateral diplomacy occurs when, say, a question is pursued with the Russian government by the British ambassador in Moscow or directly by a telephone call from London. However, it also takes place when British and Russian representatives confer at the United Nations on matters outside the formal agenda and of interest to themselves exclusively. Nevertheless, while bearing this in mind, for the purpose of this chapter 'bilateral diplomacy' will mean the conduct of relations on a state-to-state basis via formally accredited resident missions, which is the conventional method for conducting bilateral diplomacy. It will deal, in other words, with what the British scholar-diplomat Harold Nicolson called the 'French system of diplomacy' because of the dominant influence of France on its evolution and the gradual replacement of Latin by French as its working language (Nicolson, 1954). This chapter will commence with a discussion of the main features, including the drawbacks, of the French system as it evolved from the early modern period to the twentieth century. It will then proceed to a detailed examination of the working of bilateral diplomacy today.

The French system of diplomacy

In the Middle Ages, responsibility for diplomacy was placed chiefly in the hands of a *nuncius* and a plenipotentiary. The former was no more than a 'living letter', whereas the latter had 'full powers' – *plena potestas* – to negotiate on behalf of and bind his principal. Nevertheless, they were alike in that they were temporary envoys with narrowly focused tasks

(Queller, chs 1 and 2).[1] It was the mark of the system that began to emerge in the second half of the fifteenth century that these *ad hoc* envoys were replaced or, more accurately, supplemented by permanent or 'resident' embassies with broad responsibilities. Why did this occur?

Temporary embassies were expensive to dispatch, vulnerable on the road, and – because of the high status required of their leaders – always likely to cause varying degrees of trouble over precedence and ceremonial. As a result, when diplomatic activity in Europe intensified in the late fifteenth century,[2] it is not surprising that 'it was discovered to be more practical and more economical to appoint an ambassador to remain at a much frequented court' (Queller, p. 82; and Satow, vol. I, pp. 240–1). Furthermore, continuous representation produced greater familiarity with conditions and personalities in the country concerned and was thus likely to generate a more authoritative flow of information home. It also made easier the preparation of an important negotiation (even if this was not undertaken by the resident diplomat himself),[3] as well as launching it without attracting the attention that would usually accompany the arrival of a special envoy (Queller, p. 83).[4] The spread of resident missions was also facilitated by the growing strength of the doctrine of *raison d'état*, that is, the doctrine that standards of personal morality were irrelevant in statecraft, where the only test was what furthered the interest of the state. This sanctioned what in the seventeenth century Louis XIII's first minister, Cardinal Richelieu, called 'continuous negotiation', in other words, permanent diplomacy 'in all places', irrespective of friendship or religious hue (Berridge, Keens-Soper, and Otte, ch. 4). As early as 1535, the Most Christian King of France, François I, had established a resident embassy in Constantinople at the court of the Ottoman Sultan, Shadow of God on Earth and spearhead of the Muslim holy war against Christendom.

Resident missions were initially greeted in some quarters with intense suspicion. Nevertheless, their value was such that they were steadily strengthened by the customary 'law of nations', which evolved quite rapidly in this area after the late sixteenth century. Reflecting the change in practice, the premises rented by the envoy – as well as his person and entourage – were soon attracting special immunities from local criminal and civil jurisdiction (Adair; Young, E. 1966). As might have been expected, however, the more powerful and thus relatively more relaxed states – including France itself – were slower to dispatch than to receive resident embassies (Anderson, pp. 8–10; Hale, pp. 267–8). The Ottoman Empire did not experiment with residents of its own until 1793 (Naff). As for Manchu China, this first had to be encouraged to view foreign states as sovereign equals rather than as barbarous vassals whose representatives must acknowledge this status by the delivery of tribute and performance of the kow-tow at the feet of the Emperor (Peyrefitte). As a result, it did not entertain foreign relations on this basis until 1861 (Moser and Moser, p. 2ff).

Continuity in diplomacy via the resident mission was not the only characteristic feature of the French system. Another was secrecy. In current usage 'secret diplomacy' can mean keeping secret all or any of the following: either the contents of a negotiation; knowledge that negotiations are going on at all; the content of any agreement issuing from negotiations; or the fact that any agreement at all has been reached. Nevertheless, in the French system secret diplomacy normally meant keeping either the fact or the content of negotiations secret. This was considered important chiefly because a successful negotiation means, by definition, that each side will have to settle for less than its ideal requirements. This means that certain parties – radical supporters of the governments concerned, some other domestic constituency, or a foreign friend – will have to be in some measure 'sold out'. If such parties are aware of what is afoot at the time, they might well be able, and will certainly try, to sabotage the talks.

Protocol is the term given to the procedural rules of diplomacy, some but not all of which concern elaborate ceremonial. Ceremonial procedures, not least religious ones, were an important feature of diplomatic relations before the Renaissance and were developed even more fully in the following centuries to become another important feature of the French system. Ceremonial was used to burnish a prince's prestige, flatter his allies, and solemnize agreements (Anderson, p. 15). Ratification of agreements concluded by plenipotentiaries, which was juridically unnecessary, was also often accompanied by high ceremony in order to reinforce the compact (Queller, pp. 219–20). Ambassadors, in contrast to 'public ministers' of lower rank, were of special value in ceremonial because they were held to have the full 'representative character', in other words, to represent their sovereigns 'even in their dignity' (Vattel, p. 367).

Protocol in general has always had the task of making it unnecessary for diplomats to have to argue afresh about procedure each time they meet, thereby enabling them to concentrate on the substantive issues that divide their governments (Cohen, 1987, p. 142). In this regard, the regulation of diplomatic precedence, that is, the order in which diplomats are received and seated at official functions, or append their signatures to treaties, for example, has always been particularly important.

This is because of the sensitivities of princes to their prestige, which is such a valuable currency in international relations (Morgenthau, ch. 6). It was a major achievement of the French system to overturn, at the Congress of Vienna in 1815, the controversial scheme of precedence laid down by the Pope in 1504 (Box 7.1). Henceforward, diplomats would take rank according to the date of the official notification of their arrival in the capital concerned, the longest serving being accorded the highest seniority. It also became customary that plenipotentiaries at a conference would sign treaties in alphabetical order (Nicolson, 1963, p. 100).

Box 7.1   The papal class list

'The Pope, not unnaturally, placed himself first among the monarchs of the earth. The Emperor came second and after him his heir-apparent, 'The King of the Romans'. Then followed the Kings of France, Spain, Aragon and Portugal. Great Britain came sixth on the list and the King of Denmark last. This papal class-list was not accepted without demur by the sovereigns concerned' (Nicolson, 1963, pp. 98–9).

According to Nicolson, however, what really distinguished the French system was its adoption of the critical principle that deceit had no place in diplomacy. It is likely that Nicolson exaggerated the depravity of the diplomatic methods popularized by Machiavelli (Hale, pp. 272–5; Mattingly, p. 109; Queller, p. 109). Nevertheless, it does seem that as the resident ambassador became more accepted, achieved a higher social standing, and gradually became part of a profession (see below), he – and his prince – attached more importance to honesty in diplomacy. Callières emphasized, indeed, that the purpose of negotiation was not to trick the other side but to reconcile states on the basis of a true estimate of their enduring interests (Callières, pp. 33, 110). This was right; it was also prudent. For only if agreements are made on this basis are they likely to endure, and if they are unlikely to endure they are unlikely to be worth concluding in the first place. By contrast, if a state secures an agreement by deceit or subsequently throws over an agreement immediately it becomes inconvenient, it is likely to breed a desire for revenge in the breast of its victim (Callières, p. 83). It is also likely to find other states disinclined to enter negotiations with it in the future. Greater honesty in diplomacy was a sign of the maturing of the diplomatic system.

An additional feature of the French system was the professionalization of diplomacy, with controlled entry, proper training, clear ranks, and regular payment. For Callières in particular diplomacy was too important and too much in need of extensive knowledge and technical expertise to be treated otherwise (Callières, pp. 99–100). The transformation of diplomacy into a profession was a slow and fitful process and was not seriously under way, even in France itself, until well into the nineteenth century (Anderson, pp. 80–96, 119–28). Nevertheless, movement in this direction had been signalled well before this by the emergence of the *corps diplomatique* or diplomatic body.

The 'diplomatic corps', as it was corrupted in English, was the community of diplomats representing different states who were resident in the same capital.[5] The evolution of this institution, with its own rules of procedure, such as the rule that the longest-serving ambassador should be the spokesman or *doyen* (dean) of the *corps* on matters of common interest, was clear evidence of an emerging sense of professional identity among diplomats. Diplomats under the French system, in other words, had come to recognize that they had professional interests that united them as diplomats, as well as political and commercial interests that divided them as, say, Englishmen, Frenchmen, or Austro-Hungarians. Foremost among these professional interests was defence of their immunities under the 'law of nations'. The diplomatic corps perhaps reached its apogee – or at any rate its most glorious moment – in the successful defence of the Legation Quarter in Peking during the Boxer uprising in 1900 (Fleming; Moser and Moser, chs 6–8).

In his elegant lectures, Harold Nicolson remarked that the French method was 'that best adapted to the conduct of relations between civilised States' (Nicolson, 1954, p. 72). Nevertheless, he was aware of weaknesses and drawbacks, and others were less charitable still. Indeed, though Nicolson vigorously disputed this, some held the old diplomacy to have been one of the causes of the First World War. One of these, of course, and one already touched upon, was 'the habit of secretiveness' (Nicolson, 1954, p. 77). Others were the tendency of the resident diplomat to 'go native', the stranglehold on the profession of the traditional aristocracy, and the inclination of its members to conduct their business at an excessively leisurely pace.

'Localitis', as 'going native' is now sometimes known, is an occupational hazard experienced by the professional diplomat who has been posted for a long time in the same part of the world. It has been recognized since the birth of resident missions during the Italian Renaissance. At best the diplomat loses touch with sentiments at home; at worst he becomes a mouthpiece for the government to which he is accredited rather than the one that he nominally represents.

It is not difficult to understand the tendency of diplomats who had served at one post for a long time to 'go native'. In order to be effective in his foreign posting a diplomat had to learn at least something of the local culture, perhaps even – despite the widespread use of French in court and diplomatic circles – the language. This would not in itself lead to sympathy for the local point of view but it would present the opportunity to acquire it, especially if the culture in question prized values and personal attributes that were also important to the nation and social class from which the diplomat was drawn. This was certainly a part of the explanation of the fascination exerted over British diplomats by the desert tribes of Arabia (Monroe, pp. 116–17; Seale and McConville, p. 22). Diplomats could also, of course, be won over by gifts and decorations. This was why Queen Elizabeth I of England is said to have remarked, with her ambassadors in mind: 'I would not have my sheep branded with any other mark than my own' (Satow, 1922, vol. I, p. 369).

Without doubt generally a more important explanation of localitis, however, was the fact that the resident diplomat was in the front line of diplomacy, ideally in constant touch with local officials and other influential persons. In order to gain such access, it was difficult to avoid showing a certain sympathy for their point of view, though this usually varied with the discrepancy in power between the states concerned and the kinds of state involved.[6] Localitis also tends to grow in direct proportion to the resistance of the foreign ministry at home to the explanations of local behaviour offered by the embassy (Gilbert, p. 547). As Valentine Lawford, a junior member of the British Embassy in Paris in the 1930s, says in his memoirs: 'Naturally, being on the spot and having to put the British case, we were inclined to treat the opposing side's point of view rather less cavalierly than our colleagues in Whitehall. But perhaps, too,' he adds, 'the thought of them safely scoffing from the far side of the Channel did sometimes tend to prejudice one a little perversely in favour of a French thesis' (Lawford, p. 360). It was substantially because of recognition of the possibility that the resident diplomat might 'go native' that it became normal to rotate diplomats between postings, typically after three or four years, despite the costly sacrifice of hard-won area expertise that this involved.

What of the stranglehold on the profession of the traditional aristocracy? Though the earliest resident diplomats were not generally of the highest social standing, special envoys normally had considerable status. This was necessary to maintain the prestige of the prince and flatter the party with whom he was dealing, as well as to make it easy for the diplomat to move in circles of influence. As the French system matured with the institutionalization of resident diplomacy, permanent ambassadorships – at least in the important capitals – attracted leading notables and the emerging foreign services of the various European states became the province of the traditional aristocracy (Anderson, pp. 119–21).

Aristocratic dominance of diplomacy was significant because of the considerable uniformity of outlook that it fostered across the diplomatic services of different states. As Anderson says, 'The aristocracies which ruled so much of Europe could still see themselves even in 1914 as in some sense parts of a social order which transcended national boundaries ... A diplomat who spent most of his working life in foreign capitals could easily feel himself part of an aristocratic international to which national feeling was hardly more than a vulgar plebeian preju-dice.' For one thing, they often had foreign wives (Anderson, p. 121; Nicolson, 1954, pp. 78–9). Similarly, it made them uncomfortable with the growing trend towards more democratic control of foreign policy in Europe in the early twentieth century, and attracted hostility – generally unwarranted – towards their methods, such as secret negotiation. Since the traditional aristocracy was also contemptuous of 'trade', its domin-ance of diplomacy made this a poor instrument for promoting the commercial and financial interests of the state abroad (Platt, 1968). This, along with other menial tasks, was left to consuls, who were generally of a lower social standing and were treated correspondingly badly (Platt, 1971). This was unfortunate, since the consuls did import-ant commercial and other work and were often in a position to provide vital political information from outlying regions.

Finally, it has to be said that as the number of states increased, the complexity of the problems confronting them multiplied, and the ur-gency attending them grew, the French system of bilateral diplomacy became too slow. 'Ordinary diplomatic channels', namely communica-tion between individual governments via resident missions and even special envoys, were no longer sufficient alone. This was realized during the First World War and was demonstrated by the huge rash of confer-ences, many of them achieving permanent status, which were hurriedly organized to cope with the crisis (Nicolson, 1963, pp. 84–5). After the First World War, 'multilateral diplomacy' was properly inaugurated with the creation of the League of Nations, and it was widely believed that the old diplomacy had been replaced by a 'new diplomacy'. This was an exaggeration but some things clearly had changed, and these changes will be discussed more fully later in this chapter as well as in Chapter 9. Nevertheless, the French system remained at the core of the world

diplomatic system after the First World War, and remains – albeit sometimes disguised – at its core today. It is necessary, therefore, to turn to an
examination of its modern manifestation, which is legally anchored in
the Vienna Convention on Diplomatic Relations, 1961 (VCDR).

The Vienna Convention on Diplomatic Relations, 1961

Until 1961, diplomatic law, which provides diplomatic agents with
immunities under local criminal and civil law, was located chiefly in
customary international law, that is, in the accumulated practice of
states that had come to be accepted as binding upon them. What the
VCDR did was to codify the customary law on diplomacy, that is, clarify
and tighten it, refine its content, and relaunch it in the form of a
multilateral treaty. It did this under the impetus of concerns felt most
strongly by the established states of the West. First, there was a growing
anxiety that looseness in the existing rules was enabling some states to
use their embassies for illegitimate purposes; or alternatively, to submit
missions to improper harassment. Secondly, there was a fear that traditional diplomatic institutions would be dismissed as part of the machinery of neo-colonialism if the new states of Asia and Africa were not
allowed to give them official sanction. And thirdly, there was an appre-
hension that the existing rules were inadequate to cope with the great
increase in the 'armies of privileged persons' in the major capital cities
attendant upon the arrival of representatives from these states (Denza,
1976, p. 5).[7] The move towards codification had actually begun in the
late nineteenth century but the real breakthrough came in 1949, when
the UN International Law Commission (ILC) decided to inscribe the
subject on its agenda (Langhorne, 1992). This was treated with more
urgency after 1952 as a result of strong complaints from the Yugoslav
government about the activities of the Soviet embassy in Belgrade.

The hallmark of the VCDR, which issued from the Conference on
Diplomatic Intercourse and Immunities held in Vienna from 2 March
until 14 April 1961, was the unambiguously 'functional' approach to
diplomatic privileges and immunities adopted by its framers. This
meant simply that a resident mission's privileges were justified only by
the need to ensure its most efficient functioning, a point made by
Grotius at the beginning of the seventeenth century (Berridge, Keens-
Soper, and Otte, pp. 58–9). They were not justified, in other words, on
the two grounds formerly popular. These were either that the embassy
enjoyed 'exterritoriality', or that the head of mission, if of ambassadorial
rank, was a representative of a head of state, though there is an echo of

the latter theory in the VCDR's preamble. A League of Nations expert committee had itself thrown out exterritoriality as a suitable explanation of diplomatic privileges and immunity and, as Hardy suggests, its similar rejection by the Vienna Convention 'may be taken as conclusive' (Hardy, p. 10). Exterritoriality is not a justification of diplomatic immunity but merely, as Vattel had noted two centuries earlier, 'a figurative way' of expressing it (Vattel, p. 397).

Consistently with the functional approach of the VCDR, early attention was given in the document to listing the proper functions of a diplomatic mission (Box 7.2). It was the first time that this had ever been done in a formal legal instrument (Denza, 1998, p. 30). As might have been expected, too, privileges clearly important to the functioning of diplomatic missions were generally strengthened by the Vienna Convention, while those that are less so were reduced – as were the categories of those by whom they could be invoked. As Denza points out, 'the reduction of privileges and immunities to what is essential makes that minimum easier to defend to public opinion' (Denza, 1976, p. 6).

The most important functional privilege required by a resident mission has always been the inviolability of its premises. This refers to its right to operate without constraint, whether this should originate from the receiving state's own government, in the shape of forced police entry, for example, or from other elements. Indeed, the receiving state is obliged to provide all diplomatic missions with 'special protection' (Cahier, p. 20). In this area the Vienna Convention made very strong statements indeed. It noted starkly that 'The premises of the mission

---

Box 7.2   Article 3 of the Vienna Convention on Diplomatic Relations, 1961

1. The functions of a diplomatic mission consist *inter alia* in:
   (a) representing the sending State in the receiving State;
   (b) protecting in the receiving State the interests of the sending State and of its nationals, within the limits permitted by international law;
   (c) negotiating with the Government of the receiving State;
   (d) ascertaining by all lawful means conditions and developments in the receiving State, and reporting thereon to the Government of the sending State;
   (e) promoting friendly relations between the sending State and the receiving State, and developing their economic, cultural and scientific relations.
2. Nothing in the present Convention shall be construed as preventing the performance of consular functions by a diplomatic mission.

shall be inviolable' (Article 22,1) and ruled out any exceptions.[8] This also applied, of course, in the event of a breach in diplomatic relations or of armed conflict. The VCDR also elaborated on the importance of inviolability by singling out for particular emphasis certain of the facilities of a mission that are essential to its efficient functioning.

Thus it was stressed that inviolability of the mission extended to its contents, to bank accounts, and also to movable property. In the last regard, means of transport and 'archives and documents' were emphasized. The inviolability of the mission's communications was the subject of a long article, though the controversial qualification was added that 'the mission may install and use a wireless transmitter only with the consent of the receiving State'. This was a concession to the developing states, which feared that unrestricted diplomatic wireless would, among other things, permit inadmissible forms of intervention in their internal affairs (Kerley, pp. 111–16; Denza, 1998, pp. 175–9).

As for the inviolability of the person of the diplomat himself, the VCDR also made a particularly strong statement of the customary position. Diplomatic agents would remain immune from the criminal jurisdiction of the receiving state, and from its civil and administrative jurisdiction as well – except in some matters where they are involved in an entirely private capacity (Denza, 1976, p. 4). Of course, the Convention reiterated the right of receiving states to expel, rather than subject to court proceedings, diplomats whose actions were regarded as pernicious. Inviolability also implies the duty of the receiving state to provide special protection for the person of the diplomat as well as for the premises of his mission, and this, too, was made clear in the VCDR. Finally, it is worth noting here that it also underwrote the freedom of movement of the diplomatic agent, so vital to a number of his functions, not least that of information-gathering. Affirmation of this right had been made necessary by the Soviet bloc policy, introduced following the Second World War, of limiting the travel of foreign diplomats to 50 kilometres from the capital unless they obtained special permission to make longer trips. This had provoked a number of Western states, notably the United States, to retaliate in kind (Denza, 1998, p. 169). However, freedom of movement was also qualified by permitting receiving states to bar a diplomat from certain zones on grounds of national security, and the result was that state practice did not change a great deal (Denza, 1998, pp. 168–72).

In these and other ways, informed by the doctrine of functional necessity, the VCDR elaborated on the privileges of the diplomat and mission premises. It is worth noting, though, that in doctrine and practice the inviolability of the diplomatic agent is now somewhat less sacrosanct than the inviolability of the mission premises (Cahier, pp. 25–6). This is chiefly because constraints on a diplomat endanger the performance of a mission less than constraints on its premises, movable property and communications.

The Vienna Convention also detailed the duties towards the receiving state which missions must observe in carrying out their tasks. This was hardly surprising, since resident missions had always run the risk of being suspected of espionage and subversion, and this had been heightened by the Cold War activities of the super powers in the non-aligned world (Berridge, 1997, pp. 157–61). (This suspicion had, of course, been behind the Yugoslav case that had raised the profile of this whole question earlier in the 1950s.) Thus the VCDR contained 'an outright condemnation of all forms of espionage' (Cahier, p. 10), and stated that diplomats must 'respect the laws and regulations of the receiving State' and 'have a duty not to interfere in the internal affairs of that State'.

However, in order to reduce further the risk of domestic interference, the VCDR made five practical stipulations. Diplomatic missions were required to confine their conduct of official business to 'the Ministry for Foreign Affairs of the receiving State or such other ministry as may be agreed'. It also insisted that 'offices forming part of the mission' could not be established 'in localities other than those in which the mission itself is established', unless prior permission was obtained. *Agrément* might also be required for service attachés. Receiving states were given a right to insist on the slimming down of missions that they believed to be too large. And finally, as noted earlier, radio facilities could only be installed in missions with the consent of the receiving state.

The Vienna Convention on Diplomatic Relations was signed in Vienna on 18 April 1961 and came into force three years later when, on 24 April 1964, it had been ratified by 22 states. By the end of the 1960s 90 states had either ratified or acceded to the Convention. When Communist China acceded to the Convention in November 1975 it enjoyed the support of the entire Permanent Five (P5) on the UN Security Council. By the time that Eileen Denza was completing the second edition of her *Commentary* on it in the middle of the 1990s, she was able to note that 177 states were parties to the Convention – 'close to the entire number of independent States in the world' (Denza, 1998, p. 1). Practice, it is true, revealed certain gaps and ambiguities in this seminal instrument. Nevertheless, it remains 'without doubt one of the surest and most widely based multilateral regimes in the field of international relations' (Brown, p. 54).

The VCDR dealt only with traditional bilateral diplomacy, and thus excluded both relations with international organizations and special missions. This was one of the reasons for its success.[9] Among the other reasons was the fact that 'all states are both sending and receiving states'; furthermore, where there were serious disagreements, as for example over diplomatic wireless, the major powers – whether East or West – had tended to be on the same side (Kerley, p. 128).

The resident mission and the case for euthanasia

It is one of the ironies of the history of diplomacy that not long after the Vienna Convention had reinforced the resident mission, voices began to be heard – at least in the West – claiming that it had become an anachronism. Prominent among these were those of Zbigniew Brzezinski and Henry Kissinger (Kaiser, p. 262; Watson, p. 145).

The arguments for quietly putting the resident ambassador out of his misery are well known. First, the technology of travel and communications has advanced to such a degree that it is easy for the political leaders and home-based officials of different countries, especially friendly ones, to establish direct contact, so bypassing their ambassadors (see Chapters 6 and 10). Secondly, there are diplomatic as well as economic advantages to this since functions such as representation and negotiation (especially where experts are needed to deal with technical business) are actually better executed via direct contact (Eban, 1983, pp. 361–2, 367; Watson, p. 133). Thirdly, the opportunities for direct international dealing have multiplied with the growth of international organizations and regional integration, notably in the European Union. Fourthly, information gathering and political reporting by missions are at a discount as a result of the huge growth in the international mass media, an argument reinforced by the dramatic broadcasting from Baghdad of CNN (Cable News Network) reports during the Gulf War at the beginning of the 1990s. And fifthly, serious ideological tensions and deepening cultural divisions across the world mean that the exchange of resident missions by hostile states provides – quite literally – dangerous hostages to fortune.

The Iranian crisis at the end of the 1970s, during which the Shah's regime was replaced by a revolutionary theocratic government under Ayatollah Khomeini, seemed to provide spectacular confirmation that the resident embassy was both an anachronism and a liability. The US Ambassador in Tehran, William Sullivan (at the time the most senior member of the US Foreign Service on active duty), was repeatedly bypassed by direct communication between the White House and the Shah, and subsequently took early retirement (Sullivan, pp. 199–287). As for the embassy that he had left on 6 April 1979, nine months later this was seized by militant supporters of the new Islamic government and its staff held hostage for 444 days.[10] This humiliated the administration of Jimmy Carter and provoked a crisis that dominated his last year in office.

Against such a background, it is hardly surprising that supporters of the resident mission should have been on the defensive throughout most of the post-war period. This was particularly true in Britain, where traditional diplomacy came under increasingly hostile official scrutiny after the mid-1960s and suffered remorseless attacks on its budget. The same trend was observable in the United States. Nevertheless, the resident mission has enjoyed a reprieve. Why has the case for euthanasia been resisted? The best way to answer this question is to show how the functions of the resident mission cannot be performed as well, if in some cases at all, in its absence.

Generalizing about the significance of the work done by resident missions is perilous. For one thing, it varies with the diplomatic services of which they are part. The Saudi diplomat, Ghazi Algosaibi, for example, has conceded that Arab ambassadors generally compare unfavourably with their Western counterparts in this respect (Algosaibi, pp. 239–40) Their significance also varies with country of location within the same service. Thus Kaiser has noted that US embassies in Africa perform more of the real business of bilateral relations than US embassies in Europe (Kaiser, pp. 182–4). Nevertheless, many important tasks are performed in at least some degree by almost all well-run embassies of at least medium size. It is to these that we must now turn.

Representation

Representation, that often overlooked or naively minimized function of diplomacy, is chiefly concerned with prestige and is in certain instances impossible to distinguish from propaganda (see below). Devolving chiefly on the head of mission, it embraces entertaining, giving public lectures, appearing on television and radio shows, and attendance at state ceremonial occasions. Now, this sort of work certainly can be conducted by ministers and officials in direct contact with their foreign counterparts: indeed, they can perhaps conduct it best of all. When General de Gaulle, president of the 5th French Republic, towered over other mourners at the funeral of John F. Kennedy in 1963, he was representing France in the United States in a way that could have been done by no French Ambassador. The trouble is, first, that while he was in the United States he could hardly be representing France in the many other countries that were important to his government at that time; and secondly, he could not remain in Washington for very long. Permanent embassies are a permanent reminder of the importance and traditions of a state (Jackson, pp. 165–8). Besides, when government leaders or important officials go abroad on representative duties, it is generally indispensable for the security of their communications (and sometimes for their health) that they should enjoy the support of a local embassy. It is worth adding, too, that the existence of a permanent embassy broadens a state's representative options and thus its repertoire of non-verbal signals. For example, at the funeral of Soviet leader Leonid Brezhnev in Moscow in 1982, most foreign delegations were headed by dignitaries flown in for the occasion. Nevertheless, a few countries found it expedient to be represented merely by their resident ambassadors (Berridge, 1994, p. 142). In their absence, it may have been difficult to avoid showing either too much or too little respect. There are also, of course, many other ceremonial occasions when for either practical or political reasons it is simply much more convenient to be represented by a resident ambassador than by a special envoy. Resident missions are generally of special importance to the prestige of new states and of established ones in declining circumstances.

Promoting friendly relations

The first duty of an embassy is to promote its country's policy, and this may actually require a diplomat to behave in an unfriendly manner (James, 1980, pp. 937–8). Nevertheless, it remains an important task of the embassy to promote friendly relations with local elites *insofar as this is compatible with policy*. The Berrill Report into British diplomacy called this the 'cultivation of contacts' and commended it (Central Policy Review Staff, p. 259). This is not surprising since a well 'networked' embassy will obviously find it easier to gain influence and gather information; it will also be better placed to handle a crisis in relations should one subsequently develop. It is for this reason, as well as others, that a good embassy will honour local customs (provided they are not flagrantly objectionable), mark important local events, and engage in extensive social contact.

It is also an important job of the embassy to ensure that gratuitous offence is not given to the host government in the event that some unpleasant message has to be delivered. An ambassador who is liked, familiar with the understatement of his profession (Edwards, p. 81), fluent in the local language, fully acquainted with protocol, and sensitive to local prejudice – in short, a professional – is more likely to achieve this than anyone else. In sum, pursuing friendly relations means pursuing these as far as this is possible. Of course, friendly relations can be cultivated by other means, for example by summitry (see Chapter 10), though this can have the opposite effect when there are personality clashes between leaders. For this task, then, the resident embassy has the greatest opportunities and is likely to have the most appropriate knowledge and skills.

Negotiation

In negotiation, the most important function of diplomacy broadly conceived, the resident ambassador also continues to have more than a walk-on part, even when political and geographical proximity encourages political leaders and senior officials to take the lead. The ambassador may play an important supporting role, not least in following up negotiations when an envoy has departed (Henderson, 1994, pp. 214–16, 225–6). As Trevelyan observes, 'argument breeds argument and negotiation is a continuous process' (Trevelyan, 1973, p. 72). When the leaders of friendly states involved in a negotiation are not on 'easy telephoning terms', perhaps because of language or personality differences, the role of the ambassador will be further enhanced (Henderson, 1994, p. 214). In addition, employment of a resident ambassador in a negotiation still avoids the disadvantages of using special envoys, such as unwanted publicity, ignorance of local sentiment, and the existence of a temptation either to break off prematurely or make rash concessions in order to return home on schedule. Not surprisingly, in some negotiations the ambassador is still to be found taking the lead.

The embassy role is perhaps biggest in important negotiations that are difficult and long-drawn-out (Central Policy Review Staff, p. 117). A good example is provided by the part played by Leonard Woodcock, head of the United States liaison office to Communist China, in the talks during 1978–79 that led to the normalization of relations between Washington and Beijing (Vance, p. 117). An even more salutary example comes from Iran in the late 1970s, where it is well known that the British and American ambassadors were in constant touch with the Shah and his advisers on subjects of the greatest delicacy, not the least of which concerned the fate of his regime. Though able to speak directly to the Shah by telephone and fly in special envoys, the American administration was handicapped in its ability to dispense with the negotiating services of its own ambassador, even though its political differences with him mounted as the crisis deepened. This was a result of the daily preoccupation of the White House 'with other major issues', as has been more or less admitted by Zbigniew Brzezinski, the same man who had earlier tolled the bell for the resident ambassador (Brzezinski, pp. 361–2, 396, 526–7). Like it or not, therefore, ambassadors sometimes have to be permitted to play a leading role in important negotiations if only because their political masters cannot be everywhere, or in sustained and informed telephone conversation with everyone, at the same time. Sometimes in a negotiation, too, they are brought back to reinforce the home team. US ambassadors to Egypt, Herman Eilts, and Israel, Samuel Lewis, were so respected for their knowledge of their respective countries (see below) that they were brought back to be members of the 11-man US negotiating team at the Camp David summit in September 1978 (Carter, p. 327).

If embassies are thus still to be found playing either a supporting or a leading role in important negotiations, it should hardly be surprising that their role in negotiating on more humdrum matters is very great indeed (Henderson, 1994, p. 335; Jackson, pp. 149–51). Ministers and senior officials do not want to be bothered with these. Furthermore, the very advances in communication that have enabled home ministries to make direct contact with foreign governments similarly make the embassy itself a more responsive instrument in negotiations of all kinds.

Lobbying

Embassies are also often heavily involved in lobbying, that is, encouraging a favourable attitude to their countries' interests on the part of those with influence, to whom access is thus vital. Lobbying may have the object of preparing the ground for a new negotiation, supplementing a current one, or, among other things, trying to influence a vote at the United Nations.

In many states, lobbying is the most important work of the embassy. However, the targets of its attention, the extent to which lobbying is prudent, and the style judged most efficacious will obviously vary with the constitution and political culture of the state in which the embassy is established. The same activities employed for representation and fostering 'friendly relations', such as entertaining, are also commonly employed in lobbying, and typical targets are government departments and opinion leaders in business and the media. However, only where elected assemblies have real influence, as in the United States, do legislators (especially the chairmen of key committees) attract the embassy's attention. All former ambassadors to the United States report their heavy involvement in lobbying during their periods in Washington (Henderson, 1994, pp. 287–8; Eban, 1977, chs 7–9). Allan Gotlieb, who was Canadian ambassador in the US capital from 1981 until 1989, gives the impression that the head of mission in Washington has time for little else. This is not only because power is so widely diffused here but also because, compared to domestic pressure groups, the foreign embassy in Washington can deliver no votes. It is for this reason, he concludes, that an embassy 'often lives or dies by its capacity to find domestic allies' (Gotlieb, pp. 44, 56, 76), thereby, incidentally, overturning the traditional prohibition, inscribed in the VCDR, against intervention in the affairs of a receiving state.

Clarifying intentions

States often need to make sure that others know enough in order to behave conveniently. Depending on the situation, another government may, for example, need to be reassured ('relax – we're only invading your neighbour'), alarmed ('these sanctions are just the first step'), encouraged ('we like what you're doing'), or deterred ('do that and you'll regret it'). Once more, the resident ambassador is not the only option. For example, if a message needs special emphasis or flattery is important, telephone diplomacy might be employed (see Chapter 6) or a special envoy might be sent (Berridge, 1994, ch. 6). Nevertheless, there remain situations in which the resident embassy is either at least equally appropriate or distinctly preferable as the vehicle of clarification.

An ambassador can supplement a written message with an oral explanation and be more appropriate than a special envoy if it is thought advisable to keep the exchange in a low key. The manner of his presentation may also reinforce the message, as may his local reputation. If in fact reassurance is the import of a message, a statement by a trusted ambassador will be as good a medium as many and better than most. The embassy might also be employed for the clarification of intentions in order to avoid erosion of its local standing, which needs preserving for other aspects of its work.

Information gathering/political reporting

Gathering information on political, military and economic developments and reporting it home has long been recognized as one of the
most important functions of the resident embassy. Immersed in the
local scene and swapping information with other members of the diplomatic corps, embassy personnel are ideally situated to provide informa-
tive reports,[11] and it is difficult to see this function ever being
adequately performed in any other way.

A mission at the UN could obtain some information on, say, conditions in Iceland from the Icelandic mission in New York, but it would be
very limited. Special envoys can also obtain information but the brevity
of their visits and their slender resources make it likely that their reports
will be impressionistic. Spies, unless highly placed agents in place, do
not get regular high-level access. Nor do journalists, who in any case do
not always ask the questions in which governments are interested
(James, 1980, p. 939; Edwards, pp. 54–8) or attach the same priority to
the *accuracy* of their information (Hurd, p. 169). And while a journalist's
dispatch may be censored, a diplomat's may not. In 'closed societies' the
information provided by a diplomatic mission is especially important
(Central Policy Review Staff, p. 258).

What is particularly impressive is the extent of reliance on embassies
for knowledge of the mind of the local leadership. For example, during
the American-mediated negotiations between Israel and Egypt in the
1977–79 period, in which accurately sensing the mood of the Egyptian
president, Anwar Sadat, was of vital importance to the Carter administration, great reliance was placed on the reports of the US ambassador in
Cairo, Herman Eilts, who by 28 November 1978 had had more than 250
meetings with the Egyptian leader (Quandt, pp. 166, 284; Carter, pp.
320–1). Carter also paid close attention to the 'on-the-spot reports' of
the US ambassador in Tel Aviv, Samuel Lewis (Carter, p. 321).

It is true that during the last days of the Shah, President Carter
ultimately lost faith in the reports of his ambassador in Tehran, William
Sullivan, despite his regular meetings with the Iranian leader. However,
Carter continued to rely on some of Sullivan's reports for some time
after the two men found themselves at odds over policy. Moreover,
when the president lost faith in him he did not dispense with a resident
envoy but sent another (Carter, pp. 443–9). This case shows, too, that
intelligence on a foreign government can also be sought by gentle
interrogation of its own ambassadors abroad. Both Carter and Brzezinski
testify to the usefulness in this regard of the Iranian ambassador in

Washington, Ardeshir Zahedi, who was known to be close to the Shah (Carter, p. 441; Brzezinski, pp. 359–60).

Policy advice

It follows naturally from the respect still generally accorded to the local knowledge of the competent embassy that its advice on policy, sometimes subsumed under 'political reporting', is usually welcomed as well. The Duncan Report in Britain picked this out for special emphasis in 1969 (Review Committee on Overseas Representation, pp. 18, 91), as did the Murphy Commission Report in the United States six years later. Advice on policy is particularly valued if the ambassador has acquired a high professional reputation. Moreover, advances in telecommunications, widely believed to have weakened his office, also enable the head of mission to communicate his views to his own government with great rapidity (Kaiser, p. 263; Faber, p. 207). The advice of an ambassador may be obtained by recalling him for consultation as well as by direct telecommunication. In the United States there is also a tradition of discussing policy at periodic and ad hoc conferences at which chiefs of diplomatic and consular missions from an individual region meet senior State Department officials. However, it appears that these have now been replaced by the expedient of collecting regional views from Washington (Vance, p. 126).

Consular services

Citizens of one state who find themselves in another, whether for purposes of holiday, education, business or permanent residence, have interests that may usefully be supported by a resident mission. For example, a tourist charged with a criminal offence will need moral support and legal advice. Such concerns are the responsibility either of diplomats in the consular sections of embassies or consular officers (who have similar immunities to diplomats) at consular posts[12] in the provinces. As foreign travel has become easier and cheaper, consular work has generally become much more important. Of course, whether citizens abroad – distressed or otherwise – should be 'nannied' by diplomats is another matter, and the Berrill Report certainly took a severe view of the matter (Central Policy Review Staff, ch. 9). Nevertheless, as the Report admitted, the issue is politically sensitive in a democracy with a welfare state tradition and a free press. Rightly or wrongly, citizens of such states tend to expect this support (Edwards, ch. 11) and can make life difficult for a foreign minister whose missions are found wanting in this regard. In short, resident missions with efficient and compassionate consular branches are likely to be vote-winners.

As well as protecting the interests of individual citizens abroad, the consular function also includes the processing of categories of potential travellers to the home country who are legally subject to entry control, notably those seeking permanent settlement. In light of the spread of poverty, chaos and disease in most areas of the world beyond North America, Western Europe, certain parts of the Far East and Australasia, this is work of enormous and increasing significance (Herz, pp. 5–8; Edwards, ch. 11). Once more, however, there is great variation in the emphasis given to this work not only between embassies of the same diplomatic service located in different countries but also between diplomatic services themselves. In Britain, for example, a great deal of the burden of processing potential immigrants is placed on overseas missions, whereas in others, such as France, most of this is done at home. The British view, which is similar to the American one (Herz, p. vii), is that, although expensive, this reduces delays at ports of entry, facilitates investigation of the applicant's circumstances, and minimizes his inconvenience – especially if he is refused (Central Policy Review Staff, p. 163). Another probable reason is the avoidance of heartrending scenes at ports and airports and fear of what the media would do with them.

Commercial diplomacy

Until well into the twentieth century, the diplomatic services of most states regarded commercial work either as the responsibility of the socially inferior consul or of an autonomous or semi-autonomous foreign trade service. However, a major change was foreshadowed in the 1960s when trading states such as Britain began to grow increasingly concerned at their diminishing share of total world exports and took off against the background of the profound global economic turbulence of the 1970s. As a result, since that time commercial work has generally been regarded as a top priority within a unified diplomatic service (Rana, pp. 96–7).[13] This is true even in Germany, where the powerful chambers of commerce were formerly left to get on with it themselves. In Britain, the first major post-war push to commercial diplomacy came from the Duncan Report in 1969, which concluded that export promotion 'should absorb more of the [Diplomatic] Service's resources than any other function' (Review Committee on Overseas Representation, p. 68).

Not to be confused with economic diplomacy (Berridge and James), commercial diplomacy includes use of the resident mission's resources to promote not only exports but also inward investment. Important features of the work of the embassy's commercial section are the supplying of market intelligence and helping to smooth the way for trade missions from home. If the state in question is also an arms exporter, service attachés are expected to devote as much time to promoting weapons sales as to gathering military intelligence. When the foreign government is itself the customer, and in 'closed, remote, or unfamiliar places', the embassy's political expertise is especially valuable to businessmen (Rana, p. 111).

Whether or not the benefits of commercial diplomacy to the balance of payments are achieved at the expense of the political work of embassies is a controversial question (Donelan, pp. 612–15). Its defenders tend to argue that political work does not suffer since it is precisely political analysis and advice on local conditions and personalities that most businessmen and financiers now require from resident heads of mission. Nevertheless, the frank account by the highly respected British ambassador in Tehran, Sir Anthony Parsons, of his belated grasp of what was happening in Iran during the last years of the Shah's regime does not support this. '[T]he Embassy', he notes, 'was primarily organised as an agency for the promotion of British exports and for the general commercial, financial and economic interests of Britain. This was true both of the civilian and the military staff while even the political officers had a brief to be on the lookout for fresh export opportunities' (Parsons, p. 40). There were, of course, other reasons for this failure in political reporting but Parsons clearly implies that the overwhelmingly commercial outlook of the embassy did not help.

Propaganda

Propaganda designed to influence a foreign government is not diplomacy. It is a form of political advertising. The aim of this is usually to persuade a foreign government to accept a particular view by winning over to this view those with influence upon it: its own general public, the media, pressure groups, and foreign allies. Nevertheless, propaganda directed towards a foreign state's external policy is generally considered acceptable, and the resident ambassador is now heavily involved in it. This is known as 'public diplomacy'. The embassies of some countries also attempt to influence the foreign policy of the receiving state by helping to export their own cultures to them. This is known as 'cultural diplomacy'.

Of course, the ease with which the resident mission can conduct propaganda – even restricted to foreign policy questions – varies with the local political culture and the sensitivities of the regime. It would, for example, have been inconceivable for any ambassador in Tehran whose political masters valued their relationship with the Iranian government – either before or after the fall of the Shah – to make public appeals over the latter's head on questions of any kind (Parsons, pp. 72–3). Even in France 'it would be thought odd and might prove counter-productive with the French government for a foreign diplomat in Paris to appear to be advancing his country's cause in public' (Henderson, 1994, p. 287). Nevertheless, there remain many countries where the ambassador is able to undertake a propaganda role with relative freedom. In the main, these are the liberal democracies, and the United States is the best and most important example.

Again it is convenient to call on the testimony of Sir Nicholas Henderson, who was moved from Paris to the American capital in 1979: 'In Washington it is quite different … It would be regarded there as a sign of lack of conviction in his country's case if an Ambassador did not go out of his way to promote it publicly' (Henderson, 1994, p. 288). Henderson put the British point of view directly to the American people on a number of issues of considerable sensitivity in Washington, notably Northern Ireland and the Falklands crisis (Henderson, 1994, pp. 397–9, 421–5, 450ff.). But Washington is hardly unique. Foreign ambassadors can be heard regularly on the radio and seen on the television. During the Gulf War in early 1991, Iraq's ambassadors in Europe and the United States were at the forefront of Baghdad's propaganda campaign. This is perhaps one reason why Saddam Hussein did not sever diplomatic relations with the Coalition powers until three weeks after the outbreak of the war (Taylor, pp. 97–8, 106, 181).

The resident ambassador is well placed, at least in the liberal democracies, to make propaganda for the obvious reason that he is attractive to the local media as an interviewee and to a variety of local bodies as a speaker. In the absence of a high-ranking visitor from home, he is the most accessible spokesman for his government. He is also likely to have mastered the sound-bite and the after-dinner address. It is improbable that he will make any great fuss about having to appear at an inconvenient time. And he will expect neither a fee nor even payment of his expenses. Cultural diplomacy is conducted by the embassy's cultural attachés and agencies such as the British Council that have a more or less arm's-length relationship to it.

The versatility of the embassy

It has already been mentioned that the core work of resident embassies varies in range and emphasis between different national diplomatic services and, within the same service, between countries of location. It is now necessary to elaborate the point that embassies also vary in the range of subsidiary or optional functions that they fulfil. While not all of these can be defined as 'diplomatic', reference to them is another way of stressing that the resident embassy is an extremely versatile institution. This is a further reason for its reprieve.

The administration of foreign aid is an important function of the embassies of donor states in the developing world. One reason for this is that the bigger powers commonly have a variety of agencies involved in aid work and the embassy is the natural vehicle for the coordination of their efforts.[14] Another is that the political relationship between givers and receivers is notoriously delicate (Trevelyan, 1973, p. 106).

A second non-core function is political intervention, that is, intervention by the embassy in the domestic affairs of the receiving state. If we ask why the resident mission has survived the communications revolution, part of the answer must lie here. For the incontrovertible fact is that the major powers – during the Cold War notably the Soviet Union and the United States – found their embassies to be excellent forward bases from which to conduct political operations in unstable but nevertheless important countries. Such operations might be aimed at propping up a friendly regime or undermining a hostile one, and involve anything from the secret channelling of funds, arms and medical supplies to the friendly faction to organizing a military coup against the opposition. Zbigniew Brzezinski, who, as we know, saw no use for embassies before he joined Jimmy Carter's administration, wanted the US ambassador in Tehran to persuade the Iranian military to seize power. The ambassador had no objection to this in principle, opposing it only on the grounds that it would not work.

Thirdly, and in even more flagrant violation of the Vienna Convention on Diplomatic Relations, resident missions have also proved useful to some states in providing cover for the prosecution of their wars. These include wars against domestic enemies exiled abroad and wars against other states. The embassies of Middle East states throughout the world have notoriously been involved in this sort of activity, an example being the implication of the Iranian embassy in Buenos Aires in the savage bombing of Jewish targets in the Argentinian capital in 1994.

Finally, the work of some embassies in conducting relations between hostile states on the territory of a third might be mentioned. If the United States and Communist China had not both had resident missions in such places as Geneva, Warsaw, and Paris, a channel of communication which played an important role in limiting their conflict and ultimately in facilitating their rapprochement would have been unavailable (Berridge, 1994, ch. 5). Similarly, communication between the United States and the Socialist Republic of Vietnam and between the United States and North Korea would have been hindered by the absence of missions in third places – in fact, Bangkok and Beijing respectively. Indeed, this point is an appropriate one on which to conclude, since it underlines the value of the resident mission by illustrating the lengths to which states go to make contact via other resident missions following a breach in relations. These also include 'disguised embassies', which will be the subject of the next chapter.

Summary

The resident embassy, concerning which obituaries were so confidently drafted in the 1970s and early 1980s, is still alive. It has survived the communications revolution chiefly because it remains an excellent means by which to support if not lead in the execution of key diplomatic functions. However, it is also exceptionally versatile, and enjoys a strong legal regime in the Vienna Convention on Diplomatic Relations. Furthermore, the communications revolution has made it both more responsive and more able to make inputs into policy-making at home. It is not surprising that the death of the resident ambassador has been indefinitely postponed.

Notes

1 Plenipotentiaries with general responsibilities did exist but were rare (Queller, pp. 35–6).
2 The process started among the city-states of the Italian peninsula, where the balance of power was wobbling even before the catastrophic invasion by the French in 1494.
3 It remained customary for long to continue sending higher-ranking special envoys to conduct important negotiations.
4 However, this point should not be exaggerated since a diplomatic initiative by a resident was often quite literally heralded by the arrival of a special messenger.

5 The 'diplomatic corps' is commonly confused with the 'diplomatic service', which is an error since the whole point of the former is that it is multi-national while the latter is definitely not: the London diplomatic corps but the British diplomatic service.

6 Gilbert maintains that the risk of adopting the standpoint of the host government is particularly great for diplomats from democracies who find themselves in totalitarian states. In the first place, this is because the propaganda to which they are subjected is so relentless. In the second, it is because the sheer oddity of the regime to which they are accredited requires unusual explanatory exertions – 'The person who explains glides easily into the role of the person who justifies and advocates' (Gilbert, p. 547).

7 According to the Yugoslav jurist, Milan Bartos, 'Whereas in the past the diplomatic corps in an average capital had numbered only 200, there might now be 4,000 on the diplomatic list and four or five times as many subordinate mission staff' (*Yearbook of the ILC, 1957, vol. I*, p. 124).

8 Cahier regrets this, and draws attention to the fact that the draft text submitted to the ILC by its Special Rapporteur in 1955 included provision for exceptions to the inviolability rule in 'extreme emergencies' (Cahier, pp. 20–1). However, it is reasonable to assume that if an emergency is extreme and therefore as self-evident as all that, then the local authorities would probably have little difficulty in securing the permission of the head of the mission to enter his premises (Kerley, pp. 102–3).

9 Among the reasons for avoiding consideration of representation at international organizations was the relative absence of customary law in this area and the danger of producing conflicts of law by attempting to codify the conventions which dominated. (On the unhappy attempt to grapple with this in 1975, see Fennessy.) By contrast, the ILC had from the beginning thought it important to consider special missions (*Yearbook of the ILC 1957, vol. I*, pp. 2–6, 46–8) and, indeed, submitted a short draft on them. However, this was postponed by the conference for later consideration.

10 The US embassy was actually occupied twice following the departure of the Shah, in February 1979 as well as in November. On the first occasion the government acted properly to extricate the militants. It was only when Ayatollah Khomeini publicly endorsed the occupation of 4 November two days afterwards that it was clear that this was an entirely different situation.

11 There are, of course, exceptions. The position of many embassies in Peking during the Cultural Revolution provides a good example. Virtually besieged by Red Guards, they often had little idea of what was going on (Cradock, chs 2–7).

12 In descending order of importance, these are consulates-general, consulates, vice-consulates, and consular agencies.

13 Though the Department of Commerce still supplies most of the commercial officers in American embassies.

14 The necessity for this was one of the reasons for the introduction into the US Foreign Service in the early 1950s of the idea that the ambassador should be the leader of a 'country team' (Blancké, pp. 137–44).

Further reading

Bassiouni, M. Cherif, 'Protection of diplomats under Islamic law', *American Journal of International Law*, vol. 74, 1980, pp. 609–33.

Berridge, G. R., *Talking to the Enemy: How States without 'Diplomatic Relations' Communicate* (Macmillan – now Palgrave: Basingstoke, 1994).

Berridge, G. R. and Alan James, *A Dictionary of Diplomacy* (Palgrave: Basingstoke, 2001), for the full text of the Vienna Convention on Diplomatic Relations, 1961, with 'A Guide to the Key Articles'.

Boyle, F. A., *World Politics and International Law* (Duke University Press: Durham, North Carolina, 1985), ch. 13 ('The definitional context of the Iranian hostages crisis').

Brown, J., 'Diplomatic immunity – state practice under the Vienna Convention', *International and Comparative Law Quarterly*, vol. 37, 1988.

Cahier, P., 'Vienna Convention on Diplomatic Relations', *International Conciliation*, no. 571, 1969.

Central Policy Review Staff, *Review of Overseas Representation* ['The Berrill Report'] (HMSO: London, 1977).

Cradock, P., *Experiences of China* (Murray: London, 1994).

Dembinski, L., *The Modern Law of Diplomacy: External Missions of States and International Organisations* (Nijhoff: Dordrecht, 1988, for UNITAR).

Denza, E., *Diplomatic Law: A Commentary on the Vienna Convention on Diplomatic Relations*, 2nd edn (Clarendon Press: Oxford, 1998).

Donelan, M., 'The trade of diplomacy', *International Affairs*, vol. 45, no. 4, 1969.

Eban, A., *The New Diplomacy: International Affairs in the Modern Age* (Weidenfeld & Nicolson: London, 1983).

Edwards, R. D., *True Brits: Inside the Foreign Office* (BBC Books: London, 1994).

Faber, R., *A Chain of Cities: Diplomacy at the End of Empire* (Radcliffe Press: London and New York, 2000), esp. ch. 10.

Fennessy, J. G., 'The 1975 Convention on the Representation of States in their Relations with International Organizations of a Universal Character', *American Journal of International Law*, vol. 70, no. 1, 1976.

Gotlieb, A., *I'll be with you in a minute, Mr. Ambassador: The Education of a Canadian Diplomat in Washington* (University of Toronto Press: Toronto, 1991).

Henderson, N., *Mandarin: The Diaries of an Ambassador, 1969–1982* (Weidenfeld & Nicolson: London, 1994).

Hurd, D., *The Search for Peace* (Warner Books: London, 1997), ch. 6.

James, A. M., 'Diplomacy and International Society', *International Relations*, vol. 6, no. 6, 1980.

Jennings, Sir Robert and Sir Arthur Watts (eds), *Oppenheim's International Law*, 9th edn (Longman: London, 1992), vol. I, ch. 10: 'Diplomatic envoys'.

Kaiser, P. M., *Journeying Far and Wide: A Political and Diplomatic Memoir* (Scribner's: New York, 1992), esp. pp. 262–99.

Kerley, E. L., 'Some aspects of the Vienna Conference on Diplomatic Intercourse and Immunities', *American Journal of International Law*, vol. 56, 1962.

Langhorne, R., 'The regulation of diplomatic practice: the beginnings to the Vienna Convention on Diplomatic Relations, 1961', *Review of International Studies*, vol. 18, no. 1, 1992.

Lee, L. T., *Consular Law and Practice*, 2nd edn (Clarendon Press: Oxford, 1991).

Loeffler, J. C., *The Architecture of Diplomacy: Building America's Embassies* (Princeton Architectural Press: New York, 1998).

Mayers, D., *The Ambassadors and America's Soviet Policy* (Oxford University Press: Oxford and New York, 1995).

Morgenthau, H. J., *Politics Among Nations: The Struggle for Power and Peace*, 5th edn (Knopf: New York, 1978), ch. 31.

Office of Inspector General [US Department of State], *Report of Inspection. Embassy Bucharest, Romania, ISP/I-99-29, Sept. 1999.* http://oig.state.gov/pdf/buchar est.pdf

Parsons, A., *The Pride and the Fall: Iran 1974–1979* (Cape: London, 1984).

Rana, K. S., *Inside Diplomacy* (Manas: New Delhi, 2000).

Review Committee on Overseas Representation, *Report of the Review Committee on Overseas Representation 1968–1969* ['The Duncan Report'] (HMSO: London, 1969).

Seitz, R., *Over Here* (Weidenfeld & Nicolson: London, 1998).

Shaw, M. N., *International Law*, 4th edn (Grotius: Cambridge, 1998).

Stearns, M., *Talking to Strangers: Improving American Diplomacy at Home and Abroad* (Princeton University Press: Princeton, New Jersey, 1996), esp. chs 5, 7 and 8.

Sullivan, W. H., *Mission to Iran* (Norton: New York, 1981).

Trevelyan, H. , *Diplomatic Channels* (Macmillan (now Palgrave): London, 1973).

Vienna Convention on Diplomatic Relations, 1961 [full text] (http://www.un.org/ law/ilc/texts/diplomat.htm); see also Berridge and James.

Wolfe, R. (ed.), *Diplomatic Missions: The Ambassador in Candian foreign policy* (School of Policy Studies, Canadian Centre for Foreign Policy Development: Queen's University, Kingston, Ontario, 1998).

8
Bilateral Diplomacy: Unconventional

In some bilateral relationships resident embassies of the conventional kind cannot be maintained because of a formal decision of at least one of the states in question. This decision, which is usually the product of a history of marked political hostility, may be a refusal to recognize the other as a state[1] or, more commonly, a refusal to recognize its government as the legitimate government of that state.[2] The result is the same when, in the event of war or as a protest against its policies, a state cuts 'diplomatic relations' with another even while continuing to recognize its government (Peterson, 1997, p. 102). However, even if states start to fight, they usually understand, either from the beginning or before too long, that they have a mutual interest in communicating with each other. This may be dictated by a need to minimize the consequences of the breakdown in their relations, or edge towards a restoration of normality. This chapter deals with the attempt to achieve communication in such circumstances by means of resident missions other than the normal embassy, that is, by bilateral diplomacy of an unconventional kind.[3] It is because such diplomacy is now so widespread and because so much turns on its success that this subject warrants extended discussion (Berridge, 1994).

Where normal embassies are politically embarrassing, diplomatic functions may be performed on a more or less restricted scale by four main kinds of alternative resident mission. These are interests sections, consulates, representative offices, and front missions.[4] For obvious reasons, missions of all four kinds are sometimes referred to as 'disguised embassies'. This chapter will consider the advantages and disadvantages of each and why one is thus preferred to another in different relationships. It will also be necessary to consider whether the differences between at least some of these missions (especially interests sections and representative offices) and formally accredited embassies are indeed merely nominal.

Interests sections

Though there are exceptions to this, an interests section is generally understood to consist of a group of diplomats of one state working under the flag of a second on the territory of a third. For example, since shortly after the outbreak of the Gulf War in early 1991 there has been an Interests Section of Iraq attached to the Embassy of Jordan in London, the capital of the United Kingdom. Until the mid-1960s, however, this practice was more or less unknown,[5] the usual custom being for a state that lacked a resident mission in a second to entrust the protection of any interests it might have there exclusively to the diplomats of a third state. This state was known as the 'protecting power', and protection was arranged by trilateral agreement, that is, agreement between this power, the protected power, and the local power. To understand the interests section, however, it is necessary to understand the protecting power, since the former is an elaboration of the latter.

The institution of the protecting power appears to have originated in the sixteenth century with the assertion by Christian powers such as France of the right to protect co-religionists in 'heathen' lands such as those ruled by the Ottoman Empire. It was then strengthened by two developments in the nineteenth century. The first was the great expansion in trade and travel, 'which far outstripped the increase in diplomatic and consular posts throughout the world' (Franklin, p. 23). The second was the growing tendency to expel enemy consuls upon the outbreak of war (Franklin, pp. 27–9). A variety of motives also ensured that a protecting power would come forward to meet the increased need for protection. Apart from considerations of religious and racial solidarity, chief among these was the prestige that accrued to a power able to demonstrate its influence by playing this role. States with neutralist traditions such as Switzerland and Sweden became especially popular as protecting powers, though Austria (a permanent neutral after 1955), Belgium, Spain and the United States have also been important (Blake, pp. 6–7). The practice was duly codified in the Vienna Convention on Diplomatic Relations, 1961 (see Box 8.1).

Useful though the institution of the protecting power proved to be, it had obvious drawbacks. For one thing, the embassy of the protecting power could not be expected to have any special familiarity with the

---

Box 8.1   Protecting powers and the Vienna Convention on Diplomatic Relations, 1961

Article 45
If diplomatic relations are broken off between two States, or if a mission is permanently or temporarily recalled:

(a) the receiving State must, even in case of armed conflict, respect and protect the premises of the mission, together with its property and archives;

(b) the sending State may entrust the custody of the premises of the mission, together with its property and archives, to a third State acceptable to the receiving State;

(c) the sending State may entrust the protection of its interests and those of its nationals to a third State acceptable to the receiving State.

Article 46
A sending State may with the prior consent of a receiving State, and at the request of a third State not represented in the receiving State, undertake the temporary protection of the interests of the third State and of its nationals.

---

interests of the protected power, especially if they were complicated. For another, the protecting power could not be expected to look upon the interests of the protected power as equivalent to its own, for the very good reason that these would not necessarily be in harmony (Franklin, pp. 110–11, 146). Finally, employing a protecting power also tended to bring with it the general drawbacks of using intermediaries of any description (see Chapter 11). These could include having to pay a price of some sort to persuade a third state to take on what could well prove to be a delicate, even dangerous, job.[6]

In view of the drawbacks of protecting powers, therefore, it is not really surprising that when diplomatic relations began to be severed for largely symbolic reasons, which was a feature of the 1960s (Berridge, 1994, pp. 7–10), this very old diplomatic institution was widely and significantly modified. What happened was that certain states, after withdrawing their head of mission and formally closing their embassies, arranged for some of their diplomats to be left behind and attached to the embassy of a protecting power. An echo of the nineteenth-century practice of leaving consuls in place despite the outbreak of war, the 'interests section' was the result. Its beauty was that it permitted resident diplomacy to continue while simultaneously making it possible to claim that relations with an unsavoury government, or a government currently pursuing an unsavoury policy, had been 'severed'.[7] The burden placed on the protecting power was also reduced, and any hostility redirected to its own embassy perhaps diluted – especially if the interests section was established in the embassy building of the nominally departed state.

An interests section, then, consists of diplomats of the protected power operating under the legal auspices of the protecting power, whether physically within the embassy of the latter or in their own 'embassy', nominally closed following a breach in diplomatic relations. The arrangement still requires trilateral agreement, though the pattern of the accord varies. Thus the protected power normally negotiates a formal agreement, but this may be concluded either with the protecting power or the local power, the consent of the one left out being granted informally or tacitly.[8]

The first interests sections were established in Cairo and Bonn in May 1965 following the decision of Egypt to break diplomatic relations with West Germany in retaliation for the decision of the latter to open them with Israel. Shortly afterwards, Britain introduced them in order to maintain contact with the more important of the nine states that broke off relations with London in protest at the refusal of the Wilson government to put down by force the rebellion in Southern Rhodesia. Some of these states also reduced their high commissions or embassies in London to interests sections. Following this the interests section spread rapidly as its advantages became apparent (Berridge, 1994, pp. 36–7). It was first used by the United States in the aftermath of the Six Day War in the Middle East in 1967, when a number of Arab states severed relations with Washington, alleging that the United States had supported Israel's attack on Egypt. Not surprisingly the new device also proved particularly useful to Israel itself, especially in Africa, where over twenty states severed relations with it at the time of the Yom Kippur War in 1973 (Klieman, pp. 63–4).

Since their invention in the mid-1960s interests sections have also been used increasingly as a tentative first step towards the restoration of diplomatic relations following a long period in which there was no sustained direct contact. Two examples of this can be seen in US–Cuban and Soviet–South African relations. Interests sections were opened in Washington and Havana in September 1977, though in fact no further improvement in US–Cuban relations occurred and at the time of writing (May 2001) these missions are still being employed. The Soviet and South African governments had severed relations, on the latter's initiative, in 1955 and had thereafter been implacable enemies. However both had strong common interests in the economic sphere (especially in controlled gold and diamond marketing) and domestic changes in both countries at the end of the 1980s began to make normal diplomatic contact once more conceivable. The Soviet government, moreover, had decided to encourage the African National Congress (ANC) to negotiate with, rather than fight, the South African government. As a result, by virtue of an agreement of February 1991, interests sections were opened under the protection of the Austrian embassies in both Moscow and Pretoria.

Interests sections may have become popular since the mid-1960s, and on the 'upside' as well as the 'downside' of diplomatic relations. But are they really, as American diplomats with experience of work in them sometimes claim, embassies in all but name?[9] It is true that they frequently operate from former embassy premises and are sometimes permitted confidential, *direct* communication with their home governments, and independent access to their own local funds (Bergus, p. 71). However this is what one would expect of US interests sections. Since the United States is a superpower, it is hardly surprising that Third World states should often want the symbolic gratification of breaking relations with it while wishing the substance of diplomatic contact to remain, including reciprocal rights in Washington. But where other states are concerned the situation may well be different.

It must be admitted to begin with that, while there are exceptions, even non-US interests sections tend to be permitted to operate from former embassy premises (Berridge, 1994, pp. 37–40). Further, the members of all interests sections enjoy the privileges and immunities provided to diplomatic agents under the VCDR. This, of course, is because they possess the legal status of diplomatic agents of the embassy of their protecting power. Nevertheless there is evidence that even American interests sections work under significant handicaps compared with embassies. This applies especially in the first days of their establishment and if they represent an adjustment to a recent severance rather than a first step towards a rapprochement. These handicaps may derive either from the new circumstances in which the diplomats find themselves operating or from formal restrictions placed upon them.

One handicap concerns the need for *agrément*, that is, the need for the approval of the receiving state to be given to the appointment of a named diplomatic agent prior to any public announcement. Under the terms of the VCDR, only heads of mission certainly, and service attachés possibly, require *agrément*. However, on the available evidence, a sending state needs *agrément* for every member of an interests section (Bergus, p. 70; Lowe, p. 473). Now this might be thought a relatively insignificant handicap for the interests section to labour under compared with the embassy, since in any case the VCDR states that receiving countries have the absolute right to declare any diplomat in a conventional embassy *persona non grata*. In principle, therefore, embassies might be as weakly supplied as interests sections with staff considered offensive or dangerous, or simply too effective. Nevertheless discreetly preventing the arrival of such persons in the first place is less provocative than having to expel them after they have been installed, and therefore a tactic more readily employed. Under what appears to be an emerging norm concerning comprehensive *agrément*, therefore, interests sections may well be rather more limp and passive than embassies as instruments of the policy of the sending state.

A second handicap under which the interests section generally labours, in contrast to the embassies of all but the smallest states, is the diminutive size of its staff.[10] Interests sections are normally only a fraction of the size of the former embassy. For example the 19-strong British embassy in Argentina was replaced at the time of the Falklands War by an interests section containing only two British diplomats, while two years later the 18-strong embassy in Libya was replaced by an interests section enfeebled to exactly the same extent. Even the United States suffered. Its embassy in Cairo was the biggest US mission in the Middle East at the time of the Six Day War in 1967, occupying premises and grounds that gave it an atmosphere 'something like a university campus' (Bergus, p. 70). However the interests section that replaced it was initially limited to a mere four diplomats, and by 1970 it had been allowed to grow to an establishment of no more than 16 (Bergus, p. 71).

What this drastic scaling-down in personnel means, of course, is a huge reduction in the numbers of specialist personnel and the elimination altogether of many specialist categories, even if such categories of staff are not explicitly excluded under the local agreement. This obviously produces considerable difficulties for these interests sections, difficulties compounded by the atmosphere of political crisis in which they are born. This will normally generate not only a huge increase in workload in some areas (especially consular if there is a large expatriate community over which to watch) but a severe reduction in the local cooperation that they can expect. In such circumstances, and even if not specifically prohibited, it is likely that many traditional embassy functions, such as commercial and information work, will go by the board. Remaining resources will have to be concentrated on the core functions of message transmission, political reporting, policy advice, and consular work. In this connection it is interesting to note the State Department announcement of 7 May 1991 on the agreement to permit an Iraqi interests section to operate from the former chancery building under the protection of Algeria. It was emphasized that this was designed to 'facilitate maintenance of *minimal* communications between the United States and Iraq and provide *basic* consular services'. The Iraqi interests section was to be staffed by only three Iraqi nationals (two diplomats and one of administrative and technical rank) and none was to be allowed to travel, without special permission, beyond a 25-mile 'zone of free movement' (*US Department of State Dispatch*, p. 347).

A third handicap of the interests section compared with the embassy relates to the question of direct access to the government of the local power. While this is normally permitted, restrictions are sometimes experienced. For example the tiny British interests section in the Swiss embassy in Buenos Aires was 'boycotted' by the Argentine foreign ministry for at least the first eighteen months after the Falklands War (*The Times*, 4 November 1983). And even the US interests sections in Algiers (1969–74) and Iraq (1980–4) were only able to secure 'mid-level' contacts with the host governments (Eagleton, pp. 92–6).

It is thus clear that many – probably most – interests sections for the greater part of their lives are *not* 'embassies in all but name'. They tend to be extremely small, unable to employ staff to whom objection might be taken by the receiving state, and have no guarantee of regular, high-level access. Nevertheless, they remain a most useful means of preserving, or initiating, resident bilateral diplomacy in the absence of diplomatic relations.

Consular posts and sections

As noted in the previous chapter, consular functions are performed at consular posts established in major cities and ports removed from the capital as well as in the consular sections of embassies. There is also a long tradition of employing these posts as the usual device for conducting resident diplomacy in the absence of diplomatic relations, though for a long time this was the subject of some legal uncertainty (James, 1992, p. 383; Peterson, 1997, pp. 114–17). It is of particular interest, therefore, that when consular law was codified in the Vienna Convention on Consular Relations, 1963, it was made formally clear that consular relations do not depend upon the existence of diplomatic relations (see Box 8.2). There is thus now no legal argument that consular posts may survive a breach in diplomatic relations, as well as the temporary closure of an embassy. Like interests sections, they may also be created as a first step towards the restoration of diplomatic relations. It is also now

Box 8.2   **Diplomatic acts and the Vienna Convention on Consular Relations, 1963**

Article 2
Establishment of consular relations
1. The establishment of consular relations between States takes place by mutual consent.
2. The consent given to the establishment of diplomatic relations between two States implies, unless otherwise stated, consent to the establishment of consular relations.
3. The severance of diplomatic relations shall not ipso facto [by virtue of that fact] involve the severance of consular relations. ...

Article 17
1. In a State where the sending State has no diplomatic mission and is not represented by a diplomatic mission of a third State, a consular officer may, with the consent of the receiving State, and without affecting his consular status, be authorized to perform diplomatic acts. The performance of such acts by a consular officer shall not confer upon him any right to claim diplomatic privileges and immunities.

unambiguous that, with the agreement of the receiving state, consular posts may also be empowered to engage in explicitly 'diplomatic' acts (see Box 8.2; James, 1992, p. 355). But why should states still occasionally prefer to talk to their enemies via consulates, as they certainly do,[11] now that interests sections are available? For, as the first part of this chapter has been at pains to stress, this new institution has made it possible to leave existing *diplomatic* officers securely in place following a breach in diplomatic relations.

One obvious advantage of using the older device of a consular post rather than an interests section sheltered by a protecting power is the avoidance of the general drawbacks of relying on a third party: indebtedness, possible misunderstandings, the necessity to share secrets, and so on. The unostentatious and outwardly mundane consular post is also unlikely to carry overtones of any political dealings between sending and receiving state. By contrast, interests sections are known to be more political – their denizens may have boasted too much about how little difference there is between them and the embassies they replaced.[12] Consular posts may also be larger and come in multiples; spread around the country, they are better placed than the interests section to gather intelligence. Finally, with the general integration of the consular and diplomatic services in the course of the twentieth century, consular officers are now much more likely to have had previous diplomatic experience and thus to be able to cope with any diplomatic tasks thrust upon them.

Consular representation may also be a convenient method of conducting limited relations with unrecognized states when these states were created out of provinces of larger ones in which external powers happened already to have consulates. Here a very important case in the post-war period is provided by North Vietnam, which was effectively cut off from the rest of Vietnam following the Geneva Conference in 1954. A similar case is provided by Taiwan,[13] which became the redoubt of the Kuomintang forces following the success of the Communists on the Chinese mainland in 1949. The British government (among others) had well-established consular offices in Hanoi and Haiphong in North Vietnam, and Tamsui in Taiwan, and attached even more importance to them in the new circumstances. The consulate-general in Hanoi was retained by Britain throughout the Vietnam War and was regarded as an important source of intelligence to pass on to the United States (Kear).

Representative offices

In some circumstances, typically when businesslike relations between two governments are desired but one continues to grant recognition to a rival of the other, neither interests sections nor consular posts are attractive. For example when the governments of the United States and the (Communist) 'People's Republic of China' wanted to consolidate their rapprochement in 1973, interests sections could not be contemplated because their employment would have amounted to a denial of a firmly held American position. This was that 'Chinese interests' in the United States were already protected by the Washington embassy of the government of the 'Republic of China' (temporarily confined to the island of Taiwan), which the United States recognized as the legitimate government of the Chinese state. As for consular posts, Chou En-lai, the Chinese Communist prime minister, regarded these as insufficiently political to advertise the new Sino-American relationship and thus inadequate for the purpose of deterring any Soviet attack (Kissinger, 1982, p. 61). In such circumstances, an increasingly common expedient is now the 'representative office', sometimes also known as a 'liaison office'. This is a mission that looks like and operates much like an embassy, the only difference being its *informality*.

According to Henry Kissinger, the liaison offices exchanged between the United States and Communist China were indeed embassies in all but name. 'Their personnel would have diplomatic immunity; they would have their own secure communications; their chiefs would be treated as ambassadors and they would conduct all exchanges between the two governments. They would not become part of the official diplomatic corps,' adds Kissinger, 'but this had its advantages since it permitted special treatment without offending the established protocol orders' (Kissinger, 1982, p. 62). Both countries sent senior and trusted diplomats to head these offices. According to Kissinger the establishment of full diplomatic relations with the PRC on 1 January 1979 thus produced nothing more than an entirely nominal change to the resident missions in Beijing and Washington (Kissinger 1982, p. 63).

Representative offices have also proved useful to the government of the 'Turkish Republic of Northern Cyprus' (TRNC), which is recognized only by Turkey, and – in the past – to the Republic of South Africa. It might be added that unlike interests sections, representative offices do not have the disadvantages of reliance on a third party; and unlike consular posts their staff and premises have the somewhat stronger measure of inviolability enjoyed by diplomatic missions.

Front missions

It is finally necessary to note those missions which, as defined in the introduction to this chapter, are on the surface altogether innocent of diplomatic purpose but in fact pursue it with zeal. Distinct from the representative office by virtue of their genuine 'cover' function, though sometimes confused with them, front missions come in all shapes and sizes. Trade missions or commercial offices,[14] information or tourist offices, travel agencies, scientific missions, and cultural affairs offices, are all favourite covers for diplomatic activity (Berridge, 1994, pp. 53–8; Peterson, 1997, pp. 117–18). Some front missions, notably those of Taiwan and states represented in Taipei, cover most of these functions – and more – and are accordingly little different from representative offices.[15] Foreign newspaper correspondents are also sometimes employed in this role, as in the case of the two North Vietnamese journalists resident in London in the 1960s with whom the Wilson government dealt as representatives of Hanoi (Wilson, p. 167). The Holy See's apostolic delegate, whose mission in a foreign country is formally 'religious', has also served as a diplomatic conduit in states where the Vatican was unable to accredit a 'political' nuncio or (in non-Catholic states) pronuncio.[16]

Front missions are obviously of most value where visible relations between unfriendly powers could lead to great embarrassment on one or both sides of a bilateral relationship. Their drawbacks are, however, equally obvious. Precisely because they have to preserve their 'cover' by pursuing work which in any case is normally important in its own right, their remaining diplomatic resources may be comparatively slender.[17] Furthermore, while the staff of some trade missions gained partial immunities after 1945 (Peterson, 1997, p. 117), it seems unlikely that – with some important exceptions – many front missions enjoy anything like full diplomatic or even consular immunities. This means that their staff must be unusually circumspect in their activities. Their access to local officials is also likely to be restricted and may have to be conducted through intermediaries (Cross, pp. 257–8).

Summary

A state may refuse to recognize another as a state or refuse to recognize its government as the legitimate government of that state. While maintaining recognition in both senses, it might also simply refuse to have anything to do with it, that is, 'sever diplomatic relations'. In any of these eventualities, resident diplomatic missions of the conventional kind cannot be maintained. If the parties wish to preserve some degree of communication by resident means, therefore, alternatives have to be found. These are interests sections, consular posts and sections, representative offices, and front missions – with the exception of consular posts and sections, all allegedly 'disguised embassies'.

All of these means of keeping personnel on the spot have their advantages in different situations but their similarities to conventional diplomatic missions should not be exaggerated. All labour under handicaps that embassies do not experience, except for the representative office. If one of these modes of unconventional diplomacy is indeed an 'embassy in all but name', it is the representative office rather than the interests section.

Notes

1   For example, almost universal adoption of this attitude towards the Turkish Republic of Northern Cyprus (TRNC) has meant the absence from the Turkish sector of Nicosia of all but a Turkish embassy.
2   A well-known and particularly significant example of this was the refusal of the United States to recognize the Communist government of the People's Republic of China (PRC) as the government of the Chinese state. This was

responsible for the absence of an American embassy on the Chinese mainland from 1949 until 1979.

3   There is a long tradition that limited bilateral relations might continue to be conducted by an embassy resident in a state, at least for a short period, where a new government is not recognized by the sending state (Peterson 1997, ch. 7). Such 'informal diplomacy' is not the subject of this chapter.

4   In an earlier book (Berridge, 1994) I used the term 'diplomatic front'. However, I have concluded that this is unsatisfactory since it might be taken to imply that the mission in question pursues a non-diplomatic purpose behind a diplomatic façade, which is exactly the opposite of the idea I wish to convey. I have derived 'front mission' from the term 'front organization'. Historically associated with the operations of the Communist Party of the Soviet Union and the CIA, a front organization concealed unacceptable aims behind acceptable ones.

5   There had, however, been much earlier harbingers of this development. For example, when Stratford Canning, the British ambassador in Constantinople, closed his embassy following the destruction of the Turkish fleet at Navarino in 1827, he entrusted the protection of British interests to the Dutch ambassador. However, since some of his dragomans (interpreters) wished to remain behind, he arranged for one of them to be attached to the Dutch embassy 'with the duty of assisting those British subjects who had also determined on staying after the departure of the Ambassador', PRO, Canning to Dudley, 31 March 1828, FO78/165. Referring to the complicated circumstances of British merchants at Smyrna, Canning later suggested to the Foreign Office that 'the Netherlands Authorities might perhaps be willing to allow one of the clerks or interpreters of the British Consular office to transact in their cancellaria and agreeably to their forms, the whole of the British business, under the title of assistant cancellari to the Dutch Embassy. This is the only expedient which has occurred to my mind', Canning to Dudley, 14 April 1828, FO78/165.

6   This point is illustrated by a case that post-dates the invention of the interests section. Thus when the US embassy in Kampala was forced to close for security reasons in 1973, the West German ambassador in Uganda was not at all keen to fall in with the request from Washington to assume the protection of American interests. His humour was not improved by the unwillingness of the Americans – for the same reasons that were prompting them to close their embassy – to leave behind any of their own personnel to open an interests section in his embassy. As a result, German protection was only agreed after protracted and clearly difficult negotiations (Keeley, 1995).

7   However it is important to note that, because of the depth of animosity in some relationships, the rise of the interests section by no means eliminated all trace of the traditional practice whereby the protecting power's own diplomats were required to carry out this work. For example Switzerland operated in this mode on behalf of the United States in Iran after 1979, as did Poland in Iraq after the outbreak of the Gulf War in 1991. Confusingly, though, the Polish-staffed office operating from the former US Embassy in Baghdad is known as the 'US Interests Section'.

8   For example, the British Interests Section that was established in the Swedish Embassy in Tehran in 1989 was created by virtue of a formal bilateral agreement between Sweden and Britain; Iran's consent was informal (Lowe,

pp. 471–4). By way of contrast, the agreement of May 1977 that created an American interests section in Havana and a Cuban interests section in Washington was formally concluded between the principals themselves. The protecting powers, Switzerland and Czechoslovakia respectively, were on this occasion the informal participants (Smith, p. 103).

9   This is the thrust of the US contributions in Newsom.

10   The enormous US interests section in Havana is a famous exception to this rule.

11   As for example in Soviet–South Korean and Soviet–Israeli relations in 1990 (Peterson, 1997, p. 116; James, 1992, pp. 356, 384). This was also a common ploy in the conduct of South Africa's foreign relations (notably with Japan, Israel, Norway, Denmark, New Zealand and Rhodesia) during the period of its greatest diplomatic isolation (Geldenhuys, pp. 14–15, 132–3; Barber and Barratt, pp. 113, 230; Hunter, pp. 23–5).

12   In this context it is interesting that in 1988 the Bush administration resisted Congressional pressure to open an interests section in Hanoi on the grounds that this 'would in fact represent the establishment of a US diplomatic presence in Vietnam. This would be seen,' the spokesman added, 'as a major political victory by Hanoi (*The implications of establishing reciprocal interests sections with Vietnam*, p. 41).

13   Similar but not identical because the Republic of China (Taiwan) has always maintained that it was the legitimate government of the whole of China.

14   A natural ploy for a trading state, this was the device employed at the end of the 1950s by Britain as a half-way house to the restoration of 'full relations' with Egypt following the Suez crisis (Parsons, pp. 41–2). Taiwan and Israel have also made widespread use of commercial offices for diplomatic purposes, as did South Africa during the apartheid era.

15   The government in Taipei actually places all its own unconventional missions abroad (other than three consular posts) in the general category of 'representative office', in 2001 registering a total of 61 of them. However, the great majority of these are actually called the 'Taipei Economic and Cultural Office' (http://www.mofa.gov.tw/emofa/erelate/Bilateralism.htm). Clearly, though, these are borderline cases. The American front mission in Taipei, headed by a 'Director' rather than an 'Ambassador', is known as the 'American Institute in Taiwan' (Cross, ch. 19; http://ait.org.tw/ait).

16   This device was used in Britain until 1979 and in the United States until as late as 1984 (Berridge, 1994, pp. 54–6).

17   There are, of course, exceptions to this, notably the large, quasi-representative offices involved in Taiwan's bilateral relations. The American Institute in Taiwan (Taipei), for example, in 2001 had a staff of over 300.

Further reading

Berridge, G. R., *Talking to the Enemy* (Macmillan – now Palgrave: Basingstoke, 1994), chs 1, 3.

Cross, Charles T., *Born a Foreigner: A Memoir of the American Presence in Asia* (Rowman & Littlefield: Lanham, Maryland, 1999), ch. 19 [Taiwan].

Franklin, W. M., *Protection of Foreign Interests: a study in diplomatic and consular practice* (US Government Printing Office: Washington DC, 1947).

Hertz, Martin F. (ed.), *The Consular Dimension of Diplomacy* (University Press of America: Lanham, Maryland, 1983).

James, Alan, 'Diplomatic relations and contacts', *The British Yearbook of International Law 1991*, vol. 62 (Clarendon Press: Oxford, 1992), pp. 347–87.

Kear, Simon, 'The British Consulate-General in Hanoi, 1954–73', *Diplomacy and Statecraft*, vol. 10(1), March 1999, pp. 215–39.

Kissinger, Henry A., *Years of Upheaval* (Weidenfeld & Nicolson: London, 1982), pp. 60–3.

Lee, Luke T., *Consular Law and Practice*, 2nd edn (Clarendon Press: Oxford, 1991).

Lowe, V., 'Diplomatic law: protecting powers', *International and Comparative Law Quarterly*, 39(2), Apr. 1990.

Melissen, Jan (ed.), *Innovation in Diplomatic Practice* (Macmillan – now Palgrave: Basingstoke, 1999), ch. 13.

Newsom, David E. (ed.), *Diplomacy under a Foreign Flag: the protecting power and the interests section* (Hurst: London, 1990; St. Martin's Press – now Palgrave: New York, 1990, for the Institute for the Study of Diplomacy).

Peterson, M. J., *Recognition of Governments: Legal Doctrine and State Practice, 1815–1995* (Macmillan – now Palgrave: Basingstoke, 1997), ch. 7.

Rawnsley, Gary D., *Taiwan's Informal Diplomacy and Propaganda* (Palgrave: Basingstoke, 2000).

Sullivan, Joseph G. (ed.), *Embassies Under Siege* (Brassey's for the Institute for the Study of Diplomacy: Washington DC, 1995).

Vienna Convention on Consular Relations, 1963 [full text] (http://www.un.org/law/ilc/texts/consul.htm).

Whiteman, M. M., 'Diplomatic missions and embassy, protection of interests by third states', *Digest of International Law* (1970), pp. 450–1.

9
Multilateral Diplomacy

If the role of the resident ambassador was substantially modified in the course of the twentieth century, this is at least in part because of the explosion in the number of conferences attended by three or more states, an explosion, that is to say, in multilateral diplomacy.[1] These conferences, where communication is conducted principally by means of verbal, face-to-face exchanges rather than in the predominantly written style of bilateral diplomacy (Webster, p. 152), vary hugely in subject, scope, size, level of attendance, longevity, and extent of bureaucratization. At one extreme is a relatively insignificant ad hoc conference, say a six-nation conference on air-traffic control, lasting perhaps for a week and attended at the level of officials and experts; at the other a major permanent conference, or intergovernmental organization (IGO), such as the United Nations. In 1909 there were already 37 intergovernmental organizations and by 1962 the number had risen to 163 (see Table 9.1). In 1985 a peak was reached when the existence of 378 was recorded (*Yearbook of International Organizations*, p. 2357). This chapter will consider why this enormous expansion has occurred, and look at the characteristic procedures associated with what in the earlier decades of the twentieth century was called, inevitably, the 'new diplomacy'.

The origins of multilateral diplomacy

Though it is common to assume that multilateral diplomacy is essentially a twentieth-century phenomenon, its origins in fact lie much earlier. It was important in diplomacy between allies in ancient India (Watson, p. 91) and even in diplomacy beyond alliances in the Greco-Persian world of the fourth century BC (Watson, pp. 85–8). Within the European system of states, somewhat chaotic multilateral conferences

Table 9.1 Intergovernmental organizations (IGOs) and non-governmental organizations (NGOs), 1909–2000: number in selected years by main categories*

	1909	1954	1962	1970	1981	1988	1996	2000
Universal membership organizations								
IGO	...	...	...	...	31	33	36	35
NGO	...	...	...	...	370	422	493	474
Intercontinental membership organizations								
IGO	...	...	...	...	50	45	37	33
NGO	...	...	...	...	859	796	1007	1041
Regionally oriented membership organizations								
IGO	...	...	...	...	255	230	186	172
NGO	...	...	...	...	2991	3259	3933	4384
Federations								
IGO	...	...	...	...	1	1	1	1
NGO	...	...	...	...	43	41	39	37
Total IGO	37	118	163	242	337	309	260	241
Total NGO	176	997	1324	1993	4263	4518	5472	5936

... indicates number not available.

* excludes the many borderline cases of 'international organizations' listed in the source from which this table was compiled, e.g. 'internationally oriented national organizations' and 'religious orders and secular institutes'.

Source: adapted from Appendix 3: Table 2 [types A–D] of the *Yearbook of International Organizations: Guide to Global Civil Society Networks*, Edition 37, 2000/2001, vol. 1B, edited by the Union of International Associations (K. G. Saur, Munich)

devoted to peace settlements (referred to as 'congresses' when of special importance) were a feature of the seventeenth century. Nevertheless, multilateral diplomacy did not begin to take on modern form until the early nineteenth century, following the end of the Napoleonic Wars (Satow, vol. II, pp. 3–4; Webster, ch. 4; Langhorne 1981). Since the global states-system of today emerged most directly from the European states-system, the immediate origins of modern multilateral diplomacy are to be found here. Why, then, did it emerge most emphatically in the nineteenth century and blossom in the twentieth?

In order to provide a comprehensive explanation of the development of multilateral diplomacy at this historical juncture, it is insufficient to note the great improvements in transport that made it possible and the advantages that made it attractive; for this leaves out of account accidents of personality and circumstance. With this caveat, it is clear nevertheless that the coincidence of motive and opportunity during these years provides a substantial part of the story, and the emphasis in the following account is placed on the motives that prompted states to embrace multilateral diplomacy with such unprecedented enthusiasm.

Emergence of the view that in certain circumstances multilateral diplomacy actually provides the best chance for a successful negotiation was of obvious importance. A conference is subject-focused and thus concentrates minds on one issue or series of related issues. It brings together all the parties whose agreement is necessary. It encourages informality (Hankey, pp. 35–7). Its members may even develop a certain *esprit de corps*. It has a president with a vested interest in its success. And – at least if it is an ad hoc conference – it will embody a deadline that will also help to concentrate minds, because the conference cannot go on for ever (see Chapter 4). When issues are complex, when many parties are involved, and when speed of decision is of the essence, there is a particularly high premium on proceeding by means of the conference. Sir Maurice Hankey, who played such an important role in the development of multilateral diplomacy himself, laid great stress on the impetus given to this device by 'the perils and the overwhelming press of war business' during the great conflict of 1914–18 (Hankey, p. 14). Whether multilateral diplomacy *always* has a beneficial effect on negotiation is another matter. Other things being equal, this depends very much on the adequacy with which it is prepared and the procedures that are adopted for its conduct (see below). In the event, there has, of course, been a sufficient number of highly successful multilateral conferences to sustain the view that this is an effective diplomatic device. Among recent ones are the Arab–Israeli 'multilaterals' (Peters) and the Uruguay Round of the General Agreement on Tariffs and Trade (GATT).[2]

It seems reasonable to suggest that multilateral diplomacy was also encouraged because a conference of the great powers – and conferences in the European states-system were essentially conferences of the great powers[3] – was a magnificent device for both identifying and advertising membership of the great power club. Those who managed to secure an invitation to such a conference were, by definition, and irrespective of any thoughts the Pope might retain on the matter to the contrary,[4] great powers. This was obviously of enormous value to a state's prestige. For the one that could secure a home venue for the conference, and thus by custom secure the presidency as well, so much the better; this counted in terms of prestige and also in influence over the subjects of immediate concern (Webster, p. 59 and ch. 9). Because it inevitably raised the question of the authority by which the great powers presumed to dispose of the fate of the world, the great power conference was also an unrivalled opportunity to affirm and justify their special rights (Webster, pp. 65–6; Bull, ch. 9). Finally, such a conference was a subtle device whereby a great power could express respect for, and a bond of solidarity with, its most dangerous rivals. With such a calculus of great power interest behind it, it is hardly surprising that multilateral diplomacy should have developed with such impetus once the idea got off the ground. It reached its twentieth-century apogee in the Security Council of the United Nations.

The great power conferences of the nineteenth century that gave birth to the multilateralism of the twentieth might have been important because they advertised the great powers. However, they were also important because they advertised other things, and such conferences remain important today for the alignments or priorities – climate change at the Kyoto and Buenos Aires conferences in the late 1990s, for example – that they highlight. Indeed, the vastly improved opportunities for propaganda provided by the revolution in mass communications made this an increasingly important consideration. It is much easier to demonstrate a commitment to the resolution of an urgent international problem by 'staging' a conference on it than it is by discussing the issue through normal diplomatic channels. And even if an invitee thinks that a conference on a subject is untimely, it may find it difficult to resist participation. Apart from the possibility that it may wish to avoid giving offence to the conference sponsors and the fear that any decisions taken in its absence may threaten its interests, it will not wish to risk being thought hostile to its aims (Webster, p. 66). For example, the British were secretly opposed to a conference on West African Defence Facilities that the French were so anxious to promote in the early 1950s. They agreed to support it nevertheless. They did this because Paris had been cooperative over an earlier one that they had held themselves in Nairobi. They were also suitably flattered by the French suggestion that Britain as well as France should be an inviting power. And they took consolation from the fact that at least the conference would provide 'a welcome opportunity to show Anglo-French solidarity' in colonial Africa at a time when the relationship between the two metropolitan powers was under some strain (Berridge, 1992a, pp. 72–7).

If conference diplomacy has prospered because it has been felt to be a valuable device for advancing negotiations between numerous parties simultaneously, it has also gained support because of the impetus that it can give to bilateral diplomacy. This point has two aspects. First, a multilateral conference can provide opportunities for participants to discuss matters outside the formal agenda and that are only of immediate concern to themselves. This is particularly true of major standing conferences such as the United Nations, and is of special value to states that do not enjoy diplomatic relations (Berridge, 1994). Secondly, powerful mediators can hold a multilateral conference in order to kick-start a series of essentially bilateral negotiations that subsequently develop elsewhere. This was the extremely valuable function performed for the Arab–Israeli bilateral talks by the Geneva Conference of December 1973 (Kissinger, 1982, ch. 17) and then by the Madrid Conference in October 1991.

Multilateral diplomacy was also encouraged in the early years of the twentieth century by that strain in liberal thought which emphasizes the importance of popular consent in sustaining governmental authority. If governments were to be democratically accountable in the domestic sphere, it followed that they should be similarly accountable in the international sphere. An important means for achieving this was 'open diplomacy': the conduct of negotiations under the glare of a public scrutiny which (this was axiomatic) was 'creative and pacific' (Keens-Soper, pp. 76–7). In an extension of the same thinking, the procedures of 'open diplomacy' also permitted some formal influence, however limited, to the smaller states. Of course, conference diplomacy was not necessarily 'open diplomacy'. This was certainly not what Hankey, for example, had in mind when he sang the praises of conference diplomacy in his lecture to the Royal Institute of International Affairs in 1920. Nevertheless, conference diplomacy was a necessary if not a sufficient condition for 'open diplomacy'; hence the one tended to encourage the other. The League of Nations Assembly was the first great example of open diplomacy (Armstrong, chs 1 and 2), and was followed after the Second World War by the United Nations (Berridge and Jennings, 1985; Luard).

Finally, multilateral conferences hold out the prospect of making agreements stick. They do this partly by solemnizing them through signing ceremonies that display the consensus achieved in the most visible manner conceivable; and partly by their reflexive disposition to provide monitoring or follow-up machinery of one sort or another (Aurisch, p. 288).

International organizations

The advantages of multilateral diplomacy noted so far do not altogether explain why some conferences have become permanent: standing diplomatic conferences or, as they are more commonly known, 'international organizations' or 'intergovernmental organizations'.[5] No doubt this is partly because, in the case of politically important ones such as the United Nations or the International Monetary Fund (IMF), it suits the powers with the greatest influence in them to have the world permanently reminded of their claims to high status. After all, a constant process of creating, dissolving, and then re-creating ad hoc conferences on these subjects would cause much justified anxiety to those over whom a question mark had appeared concerning their real international weight. Indeed, had a series of ad hoc great power conferences been employed for the purposes of preserving 'international peace and security' instead of the UN, Britain and France would probably have lost their seats at the top table many years ago. It is also fair to note that some multilateral conferences have become permanent under the impact of the enduring 'functionalist' notion that it is out of such structures that regional and perhaps even ultimately global integration will grow. Nevertheless, it seems clear that the multilateral conferences that achieve permanent status do so principally because the problem with which they were established to grapple is itself seen as a permanent problem. The paradigm case is the unceasing problem for the UN of preserving international peace without jeopardizing the security of its member states.[6]

An international organization, properly so-called, has a constitution or 'charter' in which, among other things, its aims, structure, and rules of procedure are laid out. Most important is provision for a governing body and a permanent secretariat housed in permanent headquarters.[7] In important cases such as the UN, the governing body – in this instance the 'Security Council' – is in virtually continuous session. The organization will have meetings of the full membership but at less frequent if nevertheless regular intervals. In normal circumstances these meetings do not have great influence but this may be greater in emergencies, when special meetings can normally be held. It is also important that substantial contributions to the budget of the international organization should come from at least three countries (*Yearbook of International*

Organizations, p. 2404). A good example, and a very important one, is the International Atomic Energy Agency (Box 9.1).

Apart from their permanent secretariats, none of the assemblies, councils, committees or working groups of international organizations would find it possible to operate in the absence of temporary delegations and diplomatic missions permanently accredited to them by the member states. As a result, in 1975 an attempt was made to extend to them the same sort of privileges and immunities in which permanent missions accredited to states had been confirmed by the Vienna Convention on Diplomatic Relations, 1961 (see Chapter 7). In the event, this attempt, made at a conference also held in Vienna, foundered because most international organizations are hosted by a small number of wealthy Western states, while the vast majority of states are only sending states. Clearly, the host states were appalled at the extent to which the armies of specially privileged diplomats in their capitals would be swollen were this proposal to go through, and in effect they killed it (Fennessy).[8] Nevertheless, these diplomats have some protection, their positions being regulated by specific agreements between individual host states and the organization concerned.

A multilateral conference that settles down to permanent status has obvious advantages. It permits the initial breakthrough to be consolidated. It keeps the problem under constant surveillance. It encourages the accumulation of specialized knowledge. It signals serious commitment. It creates a lobby for the cause in question. It often provides

---

Box 9.1   The International Atomic Energy Agency

The IAEA, which was established in 1957, is an autonomous organ linked to the UN General Assembly. At the end of 1999 it had 130 states members. Its chief aims are to promote the peaceful uses of atomic energy and ensure that any assistance with which it is associated is not diverted to military ends. Thus its 'safeguards system' is of great importance, and by the end of 1998 it had carried out inspections at 897 installations in 68 states. It is this activity that has brought it into conflict with Iraq and North Korea. The Agency has a 'General Conference' that meets annually, a 35-strong 'Board of Governors' that generally meets five times a year, a 'Secretariat' of over 2000, and a plethora of scientific committees, advisory groups, and working groups. In addition to its headquarters in Vienna, it has offices in the USA, Switzerland, Canada, and Japan.

Source: *Yearbook of International Organizations*, pp. 1231–2. The IAEA's website can be found at www.iaea.org/worldatom/

technical assistance to states requiring it. And it does all this without raising the excessive expectations often generated by ad hoc conferences. That rudimentary international organization, the joint commission, is an expression of exactly the same set of reflexes (Berridge, 1994, ch. 7). There is a price to be paid for this, it is true: permanently constituted conferences tend to freeze the power structure in existence at the time of their creation, together with the culture convenient to it. In this connection it is perhaps significant that the real negotiations seeking to restrain the nuclear ambitions of North Korea in the late 1980s and early 1990s did not take place within the ambit of the IAEA, from which indeed it resigned in June 1994. Nor did they take place within the UN, of which it had never been a member. Instead, they took place in an altogether bilateral context with the United States (Berridge and Gallo).

Questions of procedure

Whether multilateral conferences are ad hoc or permanent, they tend to share similar procedural problems – though the solutions with which they come up are by no means identical. Among others, these problems include questions of venue, participation, agenda, style of proceedings, and decision-making.

Venue

This is sometimes a question of symbolic and always one of practical significance in prenegotiations, and this has already been discussed at some length in Chapter 2. Nevertheless, it must also be mentioned here since, for obvious reasons, venue is of special importance when the creation of a *permanent* conference, or international organization, is contemplated; and the more important the organization the greater the excitement that this issue tends to generate. An outstanding case in point is, of course, the controversy surrounding the site for a permanent home for the United Nations, a question which fell into the lap of the UN's Preparatory Commission in late 1945. Though many different sites were suggested, the argument – inspired in the main by concerns over prestige but rationalized in a different language – basically resolved into one over whether it should be located in Europe or America. The argument for Europe was that this had always been the major cockpit of international conflict and hence where the UN was likely to have most of its work to do. Besides, the pro-Europe camp maintained, the old buildings of the League of Nations remained available in Geneva, itself in a neutral country and 'easy to reach from Europe and the Middle East and from the East coast of the Americas' (Gore-Booth, 1974, p. 151). For America 'it was contended that an American headquarters was necessary to retain American interest and avoid a return to isolationism' (Nicholas, p. 44), while many Latin Americans preferred this solution for practical and political reasons of their own (Gore-Booth, 1974, p. 152). In the end, a decision was made for the United States but the question of precisely where in the United States the UN's permanent home would be located then had to be addressed. New York was finally chosen over the opposition of the Arabs, who 'stood out for San Francisco against the strongly Jewish environment of New York' (Gore-Booth, 1974, p. 152). For sound political reasons, however, the UN's other major agencies were distributed among other important cities, notably Paris, Vienna, Geneva, Washington, and Rome.

Venue may be of special importance for permanent conferences but it is also significant for ad hoc conferences. Today this is principally because only a limited number of cities have the communications systems, hotel space, and pools of qualified interpreters to cope with the huge size of many of these conferences. Venues are also sometimes chosen, however, because it is believed that they will assist the publicity of the conference, which is no doubt why Botswana was chosen as the site for the 1983 meeting of the signatories of the Convention on Endangered Species (Aurisch, pp. 283–4). Finally, an old and enduring reason why the venue of ad hoc conferences is important is that it is customary for the presidents of such conferences to be the foreign minister or principal delegate of the host country (Thompson, p. 395; Gore-Booth, 1979, p. 232). Conference presidents have important duties: stating the background and purposes of the conference, and setting its tone in an opening speech; directing administrative arrangements; orchestrating any 'diversions' (which might include showing off local achievements); and, above all, chairing plenary sessions and perhaps drawing up any final report. It is true that the host country will generally have a special interest in the success of the conference and that this may put it under pressure to make concessions of its own to ensure that this is achieved (Putnam, p. 61). Nevertheless, its possession of the conference presidency is a position of influence, as it was in the 'Council of Europe' in the nineteenth century. 'The question of president never raised any difficulty,' noted Sir Charles Webster. 'It belonged to the state in whose territory the meeting took place, an advantage', he added, 'of which both Palmerston and Metternich were very conscious' (Webster, p. 63).[9]

Participation

The sponsors of conferences dealing with matters of peace and security are traditionally great powers or regional 'great powers'. In other matters, they are those – great powers or not – who have a major interest in the subject and are anxious to get something done about it, prepared to shoulder the administrative and financial burden (often considerable), and prepared to risk the possible political complications of staging the conference.

Who should be invited? This is a question that has a parallel in bilateral diplomacy: who should be consulted among the friends and allies of the two parties? However, the question is more sensitive in multilateral diplomacy since the invitation list is usually public knowledge. As a result, prestige – possibly even de facto recognition of a government or a state – is at stake, since an invitation is regarded as acknowledgement of the importance of the invitee to the outcome of the conference, and lack of one the opposite. An invitation also publicly confers legitimacy of interest, which may have far-reaching consequences, especially for a state or other entity hitherto somewhat marginal to the question in hand.

Before the twentieth century, the rule of thumb was that invitees should be limited to important states with a direct interest in the subject matter of the conference. Those with an important indirect interest or whom it was hoped might be encouraged to take a future interest, could be accorded observer status. This remained substantially the case in the twentieth century with the great majority of ad hoc conferences other than those of the 'open-to-all' type spawned by the UN system. For example, the Geneva Conference on Indo-China in 1954 was limited to the USA, the Soviet Union, France, Britain, Communist China, Vietnam, Cambodia, Laos, and the Vietminh (Touval, 1989, pp. 160–1). To cite another case, the Arab–Israeli multilaterals, inaugurated in January 1992, have been limited to the main regional parties together with those external parties who have in effect assumed a mediating role of some kind (Peters, p. 6).

However, employment of the criterion of interest in determining the membership of a conference is often insufficient to remove all problems. For one thing, the concept of 'interest' itself is so slippery that there is ample room for disagreement on whether or not a state or other agency has a 'legitimate' interest in a subject. In this connection, it is interesting that the century just ended witnessed some broadening of the basis of ad hoc multilateral diplomacy to include small states – broadening to the point of universality, of course, in the case of UN conferences.

Nevertheless, there was resistance to including representatives of bodies other than states. This was particularly noticeable in conferences dealing with the termination of military hostilities and territorial settlements. For example, the Vietminh were not admitted to the Indo-Chinese phase of the Geneva Conference in 1954 until the last minute (Randle, pp. 159–60). As for the Afghan *mujahedin*, they were not present at any stage of the Geneva talks on Afghanistan in the 1980s. And neither SWAPO, UNITA nor the ANC was a participant in any round of the decisive Angola/Namibia talks in 1988. In each of these cases there is little doubt that the excluded, or nearly excluded, parties had an extremely strong interest in the outcome, and not a little power to shape future developments.

Apart from the slipperiness of the concept of interest, conference participation is also problematical since in practice the sponsors are often influenced by considerations of political rivalry. When this happens, they sometimes find themselves in a classic dilemma. On the one hand, they are inclined to refuse an invitation to interested rivals for fear of adding to their prestige and making the deliberations of the conference more difficult. On the other, they will be tempted to extend them an invitation in order to 'carry' them along and forestall the subsequent sabotage of any agreement reached. This was the uncomfortable position occupied by US Secretary of State, John Foster Dulles, apropos the British agitation to invite the Chinese Communists to the Geneva Conference on Indo-China in 1954. It was also that in which US President Jimmy Carter found himself in 1977 in relation to the issue of whether or not to keep the Soviet Union involved in the multilateral diplomacy over the Arab–Israeli conflict. In view of their quite different reputations, it is ironical that it was Dulles who agreed to open the door to his rival and Carter who decided to keep it closed.

A special case of problematical conference participation which in some measure reflects the dilemma described in the last paragraph is the question of the permanent, veto-wielding membership of the UN Security Council. Fixed at five in the Charter in 1945 and presently consisting of the USA, Russia, the People's Republic of China, France and Britain (the Permanent 5 or P5), there is a growing belief that this membership is no longer appropriate. The UN General Assembly has had an 'Open-ended Working Group' considering this and related questions since January 1994, and in 2000 the need for reform was endorsed even by the major powers at their G8 summit (Global Policy Forum).

Supporters of reform claim that Britain and France are no longer great powers, and that Russia is but a pale reflection of the former Soviet

Union; besides, they point out, the third world has no representation at all. According to one view, the Security Council would carry more authority if, at a minimum, Germany and Japan (the second largest contributor to the UN's general budget) were to be added to the permanent membership. Among other variations on this theme is the neat but still politically unrealistic suggestion that Britain and France should step down in favour of one seat for the European Union. Being influential members of the EU, this would ensure a significant degree of continuing representation for them. Germany, also an EU member, would be similarly represented, and Japan could then join without increasing the permanent membership beyond its existing limit of five (Wilenski, p. 442). More radical proposals, for example those contained in the Razali Paper (Box 9.2), argue for a net increase in the number of both permanent and non-permanent members of the Council, though the veto would be withheld from the new permanent members.

Against the reformers it is argued that it is a mistake to tamper with the Security Council when it has at long last started to work – 'if it ain't broke, don't mend it' sums up their position. In any case, steps have been taken to ensure greater 'transparency'. It is also said that powerful members such as Japan are virtually permanent members in any case

---

Box 9.2   The Razali Paper on Security Council reform

This paper was presented by the Chairman of the General Assembly's 'Open-ended Working Group' on Security Council reform on 20 March 1997. It took the form of a draft resolution of the General Assembly. Its main points were as follows:

- The 'effectiveness, credibility and legitimacy' of the work of the Security Council depend, among other things, on its 'representative character'.
- Membership of the Security Council should be increased from 15 to 24 by adding five permanent members and four non-permanent members.
- The five new permanent members should be elected on the following pattern: one each from the developing states of Africa, Asia, and Latin America and the Caribbean; and two from 'industrialized States', understood to mean Germany and Japan.
- The four new non-permanent members should be elected on the following pattern: one each from Africa, Asia, Eastern Europe, and Latin America and the Caribbean.
- The 'original permanent members' should restrict use of the veto to actions taken under Chapter VII of the Charter (use of force).
- The new permanent members should not acquire veto power.

For the full text, see http://www.globalpolicy.org/security/reform/raz-497.htm

since they are re-elected so often to a non-permanent seat, and are carefully consulted by the P5 even when they are not. Defenders of the status quo add that reform that entails enlargement would make the Security Council 'unwieldy', and conclude their case by underlining the undeniable fact that there is no consensus on how the membership should be altered anyway.

Of course, the defence of the status quo on the Security Council glosses over the issue of prestige. It also begs the question as to whether the Council is working because of or in spite of its present composition – if it is in fact working that well anyway. And it stumbles, even if it does not fall, on a tension between the claim that consulting powerful outsiders informally is effective while bringing them formally into the decision-making by enlargement of the Security Council would not be.[10] Nevertheless, this is a sophisticated rearguard. It generally takes a cataclysmic upheaval to alter the composition of the councils of the major powers.

Finally, it is important to note that states or other agencies that are widely acknowledged to have a legitimate interest in a particular subject, and that may be prepared to engage in confidential bilateral discussions, may be reluctant to be observed on the same conference platform. This was a constant problem for the multilateral diplomacy in Africa sponsored by the South African government in the 1950s, and – until the early 1990s – for all attempts to involve the Israeli government in multilateral talks in which the PLO was a participant.

In many international organizations the problem of participation is in principle solved, as already noted, by admitting all states. These are the so-called 'universal membership organizations', which have the added advantage of permitting discreet contact between states lacking diplomatic relations. Of these the United Nations is now probably the paradigm case. However, it was certainly not such at the start of its life or for many years after, when membership was confined to the founding members and 'all other peace-loving states which accept the obligations' of the Charter and 'are able and willing to carry out these obligations'. This permitted the blackballing of many important states for long periods (Nicholas, pp. 86–7), most signally in the case of the People's Republic of China, which was not admitted to membership until October 1971. Unpopular countries such as South Africa were also forced out of some international organizations, despite being founder members (Luard, pp. 164–7).

However, universal or near universal membership brings problems of its own. The most important of these returns us to the concept of interest. This is because throwing the doors of a conference wide open permits, and may even encourage, each participant to have a say in the affairs of all of the others, whether they have a direct interest or not. Such problems will be exacerbated if discussion is conducted in public and decision-making proceeds, as it does in the UN General Assembly, by majority-voting on the basis of 'one state, one vote' (see below). In short, universal membership may well be anti-diplomatic, gratuitously worsening relations between states that in an earlier era would either have had little contact at all or would have had contact only on issues where both had a direct interest. It is, for example, unlikely that relations between Britain and Ireland would have suffered as a result of the Falklands crisis in 1982 had they not both been members (the one permanent and the other temporary) of the Security Council of the United Nations.

Agenda

Problems concerning the agenda of a multilateral conference, that is to say, the list of items that are to be discussed, vary in some degree between ad hoc and permanent conferences. If a state is invited to an ad hoc conference, whether it will attend or not is likely to be significantly influenced by the draft agenda circulated in advance by the prospective host. This can present thorny issues. For example, the draft might contain embarrassing items. Alternatively, it might contain items that in themselves are innocuous though prejudgement is obvious from the manner in which they have been worded – for instance, 'Chinese aggression against Vietnam', rather than 'the situation concerning China and Vietnam' (Nicol, p. 41; Bailey and Daws, pp. 83–4). As in any kind of negotiation, the proposed agenda might even contain a particular juxtaposition of items that amounts to the proposition of a thinly disguised deal (see Chapter 2).

There is, however, an agenda problem peculiar to *permanent* multilateral conferences, and that is that they are provided with a general agenda by their founding charters or statutes, usually under the heading of 'functions' or 'purposes'.[11] This is translated into a working agenda by the most influential members before each session (Peterson, 1986, ch. 2), and those who do not like it can only refuse to attend with difficulty since they have already accepted permanent membership. Even one of the P5 on the Security Council cannot veto the inscription of an item on the agenda or veto its inclusion at a particular point on the agenda. This is because the customary law of the Council states that these are procedural rather than substantive matters (Nicol, p. 102; Bailey and Daws, pp. 84–5).

It is true, of course, that devices exist to ensure that the sessional agendas of the permanent multilateral conference are broadly acceptable and that the discomfort that might be inflicted by them on minority states is thereby reduced. Even if vetos are not permitted, their approval by special majorities – two-thirds of the members present and voting being typical – is normally required. In any case broad consultation usually ensures that a vote on the agenda does not need to be taken. If some states remain hostile to the inclusion of a particular item on the agenda, they may be mollified by a vague, general or altogether obscure formulation of it. This is the practice that the UN Security Council has increasingly adopted (Bailey and Daws, pp. 83–4). And in the final analysis they can temporarily absent themselves from meetings or maintain only a token presence, as South Africa did at the General Assembly for several years after November 1956. This was in protest at the Assembly's habit of discussing its racial policies.

In practice, therefore, the difference between ad hoc and permanent conference diplomacy in regard to the question of the agenda is not by any means as great as might at first sight appear. Nevertheless, it remains true that states in a minority may have to endure discussion of an embarrassing item on the agenda of a permanent conference and that, to this extent, multilateral 'diplomacy' is unlikely to serve the real purposes of diplomacy and may even exacerbate tensions. States in a minority tend to stay for the discussion of items on which they would prefer silence to prevail partly because they want their answer to any charges to be heard, and partly because they have other reasons for wishing to remain a part of the organization.

Public debate and private discussion

It is because of the style of practices under the heading of 'public debate' that multilateral diplomacy has, with justice, earned an extremely bad name. When debate takes place between a large number of delegations in a public setting without any serious attempt to achieve prior agreement in private, the political necessity of playing to the audience outside is inescapable and the give and take of genuine negotiation goes out of the window. The style of proceedings is self-consciously 'parliamentary', and the result is that propaganda is substituted for diplomacy (Keens-Soper, pp. 78–86). Until recent decades this was typically the case with both the UN General Assembly and the formal meetings of the UN Security Council. Even 'closed' plenary sessions of conferences are hardly likely to encourage real negotiation when, as is often the case, well over a hundred states are represented and the corridors outside are crawling with journalists and lobbyists from NGOs. At the International Conference on Population and Development, held in Cairo in September 1994, there were 182 participating countries.

Widespread recognition of the drawbacks of over-reliance on public debate in multilateral diplomacy has led to increased employment of subcommittees, private sessions, and informal consultations. Since the 1970s the UN Security Council itself has regularly met informally in private (Berridge, 1991, pp. 3–6) and the P5 have caucused in secret since the mid-1980s (Berridge, 1991, ch. 5). Conferences within the broader UN system are now preceded by preparatory committees and, once launched, now employ an elaborate mix of different kinds of session – private and public, plenary and small group (Aurisch, pp. 284–5). In the Arab–Israeli multilaterals, overseen by a largely ceremonial 'Steering Group', the real business is conducted in five functionally defined and informally conducted 'working groups'[12] and in their 'inter-sessional' activities (Peters, ch. 3). Where there is a constitutional tradition of public meetings, however, these are generally retained. In any case, while public sessions of conferences that effectively rubber-stamp agreements thrashed out in private might induce cynicism, they are valuable in demonstrating unity on important international problems.

The number of participants and the technicality of the issues in most multilateral conferences held today make them extremely complex. Despite the procedural advances just noted, therefore, it might be imagined that this alone would vitiate the advantages of conducting diplomacy by this method. Complexity is indeed a problem but it is not normally fatal. This is because in most large conferences the order of battle is simplified by the formation of coalitions. In the UN Conference on the Law of the Sea, for instance, 150 states participated but in reality this boiled down to the West Europeans, the East Europeans, and the 'Group of 77' (Touval, 1989, p. 164). Furthermore, there is invariably a small number of states that is prepared to make the running, while their need to carry the rest usually inclines them to make their demands with moderation. The opportunities for package deals are also far more numerous than in bilateral diplomacy (Touval, 1989, pp. 165–7).

Decision-making

The method by which decisions are finalized in bilateral talks has never been an issue since it is obvious that when there are only two parties there can be no agreement unless both concur, which is another way of saying that each has a veto. A vote involving two parties where there is disagreement can only result in stalemate. Of course, one might impose its will on the other but in that case it would hardly be a negotiation at all. In short, in bilateral diplomacy the unanimity method is the only method available. By contrast, multilateral conferences provide the opportunity to make decisions by majority voting. As a result, the strength of the democratic idea, together with the fear that the unanimity rule might induce paralysis when large numbers of states were involved, produced widespread support for voting after 1945. In the second half of the twentieth century, and despite important exceptions,[13] this has been at least a formal feature of decision-making in most major international organizations, notably the United Nations.

Where majority voting is employed there are typically differences in the treatment of procedural and substantive issues. Furthermore, some international organizations employ weighted voting while others do not, and some require special majorities (Jenks, pp. 53–5) while others require only simple majorities (over fifty per cent). In the UN Security Council, for example, an affirmative vote of only nine of the fifteen members is required for a decision on a procedural question. Decisions on 'all other matters', however, require 'an affirmative vote of nine members *including the concurring votes of the permanent members*' (emphasis added) – the great power veto.[14] For its part, the UN General Assembly was authorized to pass resolutions on a simple majority of members 'present and voting', except in the case of 'important questions', which require a two-thirds majority.

In practice, however, decision-making by voting has not been as significant across the whole spectrum of multilateral diplomacy as the picture painted so far might suggest. To begin with, ad hoc conferences, especially those involving relatively small numbers of participants and not constituted under the auspices of the UN system, have rarely if ever even claimed to employ voting. Secondly, those that have tended to do so, including the permanent ones with large memberships within the system, have generally found it necessary to their survival to introduce modifications to the way their voting arrangements work in practice. This has been observed at least since the mid-1960s (Buzan, p. 325).

The problem for the UN system, of course, is that its 'one state, one vote' rhetoric has collided head-on with political reality as a result of the admission, especially since the late 1950s, of a huge number of small, weak states, including 'micro-states' (Berridge, 1997, pp. 18–21). In these circumstances even the requirement for a two-thirds majority can fail to block the 'wrong' decision (Jenks, p. 55). As Buzan puts it, this has rendered 'majority voting increasingly useless for lawmaking decisions because of the danger of powerful alienated minorities' (Buzan, p. 326).

Having lost its own majority following in the United Nations in the 1960s, the United States emerged as the most powerful member of just such a minority. Increasingly being expected to provide the lion's share of the money for programmes that it found objectionable, in the 1980s it drastically scaled back its funding of the organization. The result was that the UN, together with particularly anathematized satellites such as UNESCO, were threatened with collapse (Berridge, 1991, ch. 4).

Could this dangerous position not have been prevented by giving more votes to the bigger battalions, that is to say, by using a system of weighted voting? Though perhaps attractive in principle, this idea has three main problems. In the first place, it is politically sensitive because it draws attention to real differences in standing between states when all are supposed to be equal. In the second, where unweighted voting runs the risk of alienating powerful minorities, weighted voting runs the opposite risk, namely, the alienation of weak majorities. In the third place, it raises complex practical questions concerning the criteria to be employed in computing the differences between states (Jenks, pp. 52–3). As a result weighted voting has only proved acceptable in specialized economic organizations such as the IMF and the World Bank, where the size of financial contributions provides a ready claim on the size of votes, and other organizations that subsequently modelled themselves on their procedures (Zamora, pp. 576–7). Rather than general adoption of weighted voting, then, what has happened is that multilateral diplomacy has witnessed a growing acceptance of decision-making by consensus, especially following its successful employment at the Third UN Conference on the Law of the Sea in the period from 1973 until 1982 (Buzan, pp. 325–7; Peters, pp. 7–8). It is this that has saved the United Nations.

Consensus decision-making is the attempt to achieve the agreement of all the participants in a multilateral conference without the need for a vote and its inevitable divisiveness. A consensus exists when all parties are in agreement, which on the face of it is another way of saying that they are unanimous. However, a consensus may include some members whose support has been given only grudgingly and have simply registered no *formal* objection, whereas unanimity implies broader enthusiasm; hence the view that in fact they are not the same. It might be more accurate to say that a weak consensus is not the same as unanimity but that a strong one is.

But is consensus decision-making, that is to say, the method by which consensus is obtained, simply negotiation by another name? After all, if the reluctant agreement of all participants is to be obtained, those most in favour of a proposal must either water it down, make concessions to the unenthusiastic in some other area, or alarm them with the prospect of isolation. In short, they must negotiate with them. Nevertheless, it is now common to find even a strong consensus fostered by novel procedural devices, notably in the area of chairman's powers, and under the charter of some international bodies voting is still required, even if it now does little more than ratify a consensus already negotiated. As a result, it seems reasonable to conclude that consensus decision-making is something more than ordinary negotiation; it is the 'unanimity system' adjusted to the prejudices of the twentieth century.

The return of a system of decision-making in which the more powerful states were able to exert the influence to which they thought they were entitled also marked a 'crisis of multilateralism' (Aurisch, p. 288). At least it marked a crisis of the kind of multilateral diplomacy from which the weaker states had hoped to shape a world much more congenial to their interests, notably in the kind of 'New International Economic Order' about which so much was heard in the 1970s. It is perhaps not surprising, therefore, that the number of intergovernmental organizations should have gone into sharp decline after the mid-1980s, dropping by over a third by the turn of the millennium, though the level of universal membership IGOs remained steady. The total number of NGOs, by contrast, rose by roughly the same proportion (Table 9.1).

Summary

Multilateral diplomacy took firm root in the early twentieth century under the impact of world war and democratic ideas. It blossomed after the Second World War with the great expansion in the number of states and the belief of the new states that conference diplomacy within the UN system – based on majority voting – was their best chance of securing influence. Ultimately they were disappointed. The major Western powers became tired of paying for programmes to which they took strong political objection, and gradually, under the name of 'consensus decision-making', began to make their weight felt. In the 1980s, with the UN system reeling under the impact of American budgetary withholdings and the poorer states increasingly disillusioned with the meagre results obtained by their big voting majorities, a 'crisis of multilateralism' set in. The fashion for creating intergovernmental organizations had passed and existing numbers dropped. Of course, even multilateral spectaculars are still staged, and as an important mode of diplomacy multilateralism is here to stay. It has weathered its crisis, and it has emerged a little leaner. It has also emerged a little more diplomatic.

Notes

1 Technically, 'conference diplomacy' and 'multilateral diplomacy' are not synonyms since, of course, conferences may be held between only two states and thus be a device of bilateral diplomacy. In this connection it is interesting that Hankey's classic lecture on 'conference diplomacy' should have revolved substantially around the Anglo-French dialogue during the First World War, though he naturally goes on to show how the bilateral conference grew into a multilateral one (Hankey, ch. 1). In general, nevertheless, the two phrases are used interchangeably.

2 Now the World Trade Organization (WTO).

3 If their vital interests were closely touched, small states might be invited to attend. However, they invariably found themselves in the wings rather than centre stage – '*at* but not *in* the conference' (Webster, p. 60).

4 See Box 7.1.

5 It is important to note that, contrary to the practice followed here, the *Yearbook of International Organizations* does not regard 'international organization' and 'intergovernmental organization' as synonymous terms. Its usage instead is that IGOs are merely one of the two main kinds of international organization, the other being international NGOs.

6 Of course, the UN is a collective security organization as well as a standing diplomatic conference.

7 The *Yearbook of International Organizations* acknowledges that the officers in the secretariat may be of the same nationality in order to facilitate management operations but adds that in this event 'there should be rotation at designated intervals of headquarters and officers among the various member countries' (p. 2404).

8 As of 1999 there were still insufficient ratifications for this to enter into force.

9 While certainly not merely ceremonial figures, the presidents of plenary sessions of *permanent* conferences tend to be less influential than the presidents of ad hoc conferences. This is substantially for political rather than procedural reasons. They are commonly chosen from smaller states and also lack the ability to determine the ambience of a conference that is available to a senior politician operating on his home territory. UN Security Council presidents in any case rotate every month in the English alphabetical order of the names of the Council's members (Bailey and Daws, pp. 124–5). However, this also means, of course, that at least for a third of the time in this case the president comes from the ranks of the Permanent Five.

10 It is true that formal membership for a larger number will provide more procedural devices for blocking or delaying decisions.

11 For example, the Statute of the IAEA (1956) has a brief statement of 'objectives'. Following this, it lists functions (seven in all) such as encouraging 'the exchange and training of scientists and experts in the field of peaceful uses of atomic energy'.

12 On arms control and regional security, environmental questions, refugees, regional economic development, and water.

13 Notably the North Atlantic Council (the governing body of NATO, which is in permanent session at ambassadorial level but also meets twice-yearly at ministerial level) and the Organization of Economic Cooperation and

Development (OECD). The unanimity rule is retained in both of these organizations (Zamora, p. 574).

14 It was subsequently accepted that an abstention did not amount to a veto (Luard, p. 13).

Further reading

Armstrong, D., *The Rise of the International Organisation: A Short History* (Macmillan – now Palgrave: Basingstoke, 1982).

Aurisch, K. L., 'The art of preparing a multilateral conference', *Negotiation Journal*, vol. 5, no. 3, 1989.

Bailey, S. D. and S. Daws, *The Procedure of the UN Security Council*, 3rd edn (Clarendon Press: Oxford, 1998).

Berridge, G. R., *Return to the UN: UN diplomacy in regional conflicts* (Macmillan – now Palgrave: Basingstoke, 1991).

Berridge, G. R. and A. Jennings (eds), *Diplomacy at the UN* (Macmillan – now Palgrave: Basingstoke, 1985).

Bourantonis, Dimitris and Marios Evriviades (eds), *A United Nations for the Twenty-First Century* (Kluwer: The Hague, 1996), ch. 3 (by Henrikson).

Buzan, B., 'Negotiating by consensus: developments in technique at the United Nations Conference on the Law of the Sea', *American Journal of International Law*, vol. 72, no. 2, 1981.

Caron, D. D., 'The legitimacy of the collective authority of the Security Council', *American Journal of International Law*, vol. 87, 1993, pp. 552–88.

Daws, S., 'Seeking seats, votes and vetoes', *The World Today*, vol. 53, no. 10, October 1997, pp. 256–9.

Fennessy, J. G., 'The 1975 Convention on the Representation of States in their Relations with International Organizations of a Universal Character', *American Journal of International Law*, vol. 70, 1976.

Global Policy Forum, *Security Council Reform: Crucial Documents*, http://www.globalpolicy.org/security/reform/ (This is an excellent website for any student wishing to plunge into this debate.)

Hankey, Lord, *Diplomacy by Conference: Studies in Public Affairs 1920–1946* (Benn: London, 1946).

Jenks, C. W., 'Unanimity, the veto, weighted voting, special and simple majorities and consensus as modes of decision in international organisations', *Cambridge Essays in International Law: Essays in honour of Lord McNair* (Stevens: London. Oceana: Dobbs Ferry, New York, 1965).

Kahler, M., 'Multilateralism with small and large numbers', *International Organization*, vol. 46, no. 3, 1992.

Kaufmann, J., *Conference Diplomacy: An Introductory Analysis*, 3rd rev. edn (Macmillan – now Palgrave: Basingstoke, 1996).

Keens-Soper, M., 'The General Assembly reconsidered', in G. R. Berridge and A. Jennings (eds), *Diplomacy at the UN* (Macmillan – now Palgrave: Basingstoke, 1985).

Kissinger, H. A., *Years of Upheaval* (Weidenfeld & Nicolson and Michael Joseph: London, 1982), ch. 17.

Langhorne, R., 'The development of international conferences, 1648–1830', in *Studies in History and Politics*, vol. 11, part 2, 1981.

Leigh-Phippard, H., 'Remaking the Security Council: the options', *The World Today*, vol. 50, nos. 8–9, August–September 1994, pp. 167–71.

Luard, E., *The United Nations: How it works and what it does*, 2nd edn, revised by D. Heater (Macmillan – now Palgrave: Basingstoke, 1994).

Luck, E. C., *Mixed Messages: American Politics and International Organization, 1919–1999* (Brookings: Washington DC, 1999).

McDermott, A., 'Making reform an event', *The World Today*, vol. 53, no. 7, July 1997, pp. 172–4.

Parsons, A., 'The United Nations in the Post-Cold War era', *International Relations*, vol. 11, no. 3, December 1992, pp. 189–200.

Peters, J., *Building Bridges: The Arab–Israeli Multilateral Talks* (RIIA: London, 1994).

Peterson, M. J., *The General Assembly in World Politics* (Allen & Unwin: Boston, 1986).

Randle, R. F., *Geneva 1954: The Settlement of the Indochinese War* (Princeton University Press: Princeton, New Jersey, 1969).

Roberts, A. and B. Kingsbury (eds), *United Nations, Divided World*, 2nd edn (Clarendon Press: Oxford, 1993).

Ruggie, J. G., 'Multilateralism: anatomy of an institution', *International Organization*, vol. 46, no. 3, 1992.

Ruggie, J. G., *Multilateralism Matters: The Theory and Practice of an Institutional Form* (1993).

Sizoo, J. and R. T. Jurrjens, *CSCE Decision-Making: The Madrid Experience* (1984).

Thompson, K. W., 'The new diplomacy and the quest for peace', *International Organization*, vol. 19, 1965.

Touval, S., 'Multilateral negotiation: an analytic approach', *Negotiation Journal*, vol. 5, no. 2, 1989.

Webster, Sir C., *The Art and Practice of Diplomacy* (Chatto & Windus: London, 1961), ch. 4.

White, N. D., 'Accountability and democracy within the United Nations: a legal perspective', *International Relations*, 13(6), Dec. 1997, pp. 1–18.

Wood, M. C., 'Security Council working methods and procedure: recent developments', *The International and Comparative Law Quarterly*, vol. 45, January 1996, pp. 150–61.

Zamora, S., 'Voting in international economic organizations', *American Journal of International Law*, vol. 74, 1980.

10
Summitry

Today an astonishing degree of multilateral diplomacy takes place at the summit, at the level, that is to say, of heads of government or heads of state. But this is multilateral diplomacy of a very special kind; besides, bilateral diplomacy also takes place at the summit, as for example in the Franco-German summit that has occurred formally at regular intervals since 1963, and this is special too. For these reasons, then, it is necessary to treat summitry separately. This chapter will consider the origins of summitry, its advantages and disadvantages, and the bearing on summitry's contribution to diplomacy – as opposed to propaganda – of the different patterns that it assumes.

The origins of summitry

Since summitry[1] is often a special case of multilateral diplomacy, it is hardly surprising that the history of its development should have followed similar lines, and for similar reasons. It had ancient origins (Goldstein, p. 23; Plischke, p. 2) and at least by the middle ages was indeed a normal method of conducting diplomacy. At this time 'countries were little more than the private estates of their absolute rulers' (Ball, 1976, p. 29) and personal encounters were relatively easy to arrange since 'diplomatic relations were largely confined to neighbouring states' (Queller, p. 225). During the modern era, however, it fell into disuse as a result of the rise of the modern state and the introduction and spread of resident embassies. In the nineteenth century the Concert of Europe saw summit diplomacy flicker sporadically into life (Goldstein, pp. 27–9) but it did not become a significant technique again until the first half of the twentieth century. Growing out of the pall that had spread over professional diplomacy during the First World War and the belief that important decisions needed to be taken by men close to the people (Eubank, pp. 5–8), the return of summitry was announced by the Paris Peace Conference in 1919. Here Lloyd George, Clemenceau, and Woodrow Wilson held centre stage. In mid-century the wartime conferences of the Big Three – Roosevelt, Churchill, and Stalin – confirmed that it was unlikely to go away.

Encouraged at great power level especially by Churchill (Eubank, pp. 136–7), within about a decade after the Second World War summitry had really begun to take off. In addition to be being stimulated by the same political and technological trends promoting multilateral diplomacy (see Chapter 9), summitry increased as a result of concern over developments in the Cold War. These led politicians to believe that 'diplomacy in the nuclear age was too important to be left to the diplomatists' (Dunn, p. 5). Summitry also increased rapidly as a result of the decolonization of the European empires in the 1950s and 1960s, because the new states rarely possessed competent and extensive diplomatic services. And the regional organizations that were becoming fashionable gave summitry a natural focus (Dunn, pp. 4–13). Trends in international human rights law, which suggest that heads of state no longer enjoy immunity from charges of crimes against humanity, may well in future dampen the enthusiasm for summit travel.[2] However, there is as yet no evidence that this is having a significant impact.

Professional anathemas

Not surprisingly, however, the return on such a massive scale to this 'mediaeval dynastic practice' (Ball, 1976, p. 30) produced deep unease among professional diplomats. As a result, it caused many, recalling the objections to summitry of Philippe de Commynes (Box 10.1), to make it the target of biting criticisms. Since summitry is an insult to their competence and at least a limited threat to their careers, this might be put down to special pleading. Nevertheless, their arguments are persuasive and find loud echoes outside their ranks. Most eloquent among their number is George Ball, who was US Under Secretary of State during the Democratic administrations of the 1960s and on whose account this section draws heavily. What is the case against summitry?

The case against summitry turns on certain assumptions about heads of government[3] as a class, among which the following are prominent. First, they constitute the sovereign authority of their regimes, and thus the court of final appeal on all important policy questions. Secondly, they are ignorant of the details of policy. Thirdly, they are vain.

Box 10.1   Philippe de Commynes

Commynes (*c.* 1447–1511) was a French diplomat and historian and wrote the best-known political and diplomatic memoirs of the late fifteenth century. For these pages, his most apposite remark is that 'Two great princes who wish to establish good personal relations should never meet each other face to face but ought to communicate through good and wise ambassadors'. He took this view largely because he believed that great princes were in general spoiled, vain, and badly educated: in short, poorly equipped for diplomacy. However, he also noted at more than one point that the leaders of his time were unusually suspicious persons. A state of mind produced by the many false stories and groundless reports that were brought to their attention by court flatterers, this made them too ready to believe that the prince with whom they were negotiating was up to no good. Furthermore, summitry could place them in physical danger. Finally, Commyne's attitude may not have been entirely unconnected to the role that he was required to play when his master, Louis XI, met Edward IV on a bridge over the Somme at Picquigny in order to discuss the peaceful retreat of the English invasion force of 1475. Louis instructed Commynes to wear identical clothes to his own as a precaution against assassination.

Fourthly, they are oversensitive to the needs of their fellow heads of government, whom they tend to regard as members of the same trade union (Ball, 1982, p. 427). And fifthly, all of their activities are surrounded by massive publicity, by which, indeed, they live; this does not exclude their forays into diplomacy. Many disadvantages for diplomacy flow from these and other characteristics of the typical head of government.

In the first place, heads of government may conclude agreements that are inconsistent with or irrelevant to their national interests. They may also conclude no agreement at all. This could be a result of ignorance of the detail of the issue under discussion. It could also be a result of inadequate time because summits have to be brief and much of the time is usually taken up with protocol functions. If there is a cultural divide, it could quite easily be caused by a failure to understand nuances in the position of the other side. Diplomatic failures of one sort or another may also occur because heads of government develop personal likes or dislikes for their interlocutors or because they are fearful that enjoyment of generous hospitality may lead a tough bargaining position to be construed as bad manners (De Magalhães, p. 55). They may also occur because leaders get carried away by the atmosphere – the theatre – of the occasion, or because they fall ill (Eubank, p. 205). Illusory break-throughs captured by such slogans as the 'Spirit of Geneva' are a summit speciality (Ball, 1976, pp. 303). It is in any case far more difficult for heads of government than for ambassadors or even foreign ministers to contemplate bringing a negotiation to an end without something substantial to show for it. Under the glare of the television cameras, their personal prestige and the prestige of their country is on the line in a way that simply would not be the case were the negotiations being conducted even at foreign minister level. The result is that, even if none of the earlier problems are present, they always court two dangers. The first is the risk of making unwise concessions in order to achieve a 'success'. The second is making a 'tremendous row' (Watt) and breaking off the negotiations prematurely if it seems that they will be unable to get one. Worse still, since a president is the ultimate plenipotentiary, 'there is no recourse' in the event of a deadlock (Kissinger, 1979, p. 769), and there is no going back – except at the price of great humiliation – on a presidential promise, even if this turns out to have been a mistake:

> If he ignores subtleties of policy or some relevant fact, he may well commit his government to an action he would never favour had he had the chance to study the problem with care, follow the advice of better informed assistants, factor in all relevant information, and prepare a reply in precisely written language that took into account the context of total policy.
>
> (Ball, 1976, p. 39)

Dean Acheson made this point more succinctly: 'When a chief of state or head of government makes a fumble, the goal line is open behind him' (Acheson, p. 480). In short, diplomacy conducted at the summit is not only likely to lead to more mistakes but to irrevocable ones. Finally, and because this is so, relations between the states concerned may actually be exacerbated. There will be an unusually high incentive to argue over the interpretation of any agreement, and the scope for this will be greater since key points may have been vaguely formulated in the absence of aides and even in the absence of any written record (Ball, 1976, pp. 37–9). In any case, agreements or understandings achieved by means of summitry and thereby in some measure personalized tend to be weakened by the fall from office of one or other of the leaders concerned (De Magalhães, p. 56). In short, summitry 'obscures the concept of relations between governments as a continuing process' (Ball, 1976, p. 40).

Summing up the argument, David Watt wrote in 1981: 'Heads of government, with their massive egos, their ignorance of the essential details and their ingrained belief in the value of back-slapping ambiguity, simply mess everything up.' The examples, of course, are legion, and are quoted sometimes with sadness, sometimes with anger, by the professionals. The mistakes made in the Treaty of Versailles were in part ascribed by Harold Nicolson to the decision of the American president, Woodrow Wilson, to attend in person – a 'historical disaster of the first magnitude' (Nicolson, 1937, p. 71). In order to underline his own hostility to summitry, Acheson chooses the example of President Truman. '[I]n the privacy of his study', he remarks, the president unwittingly altered American policy in a most sensitive area by informing the British prime minister, Clement Attlee, that the United States would not use nuclear weapons without first consulting the British (Acheson, p. 484). William Sullivan's story is how the Shah of Iran, on a visit to the United States, told President Carter of his belief that the Organization of African Unity was an 'im*po*tent' body, and the president – a Southerner – agreed that it was indeed 'im*poh*tant' [important] (Sullivan, p. 129). And George Ball, in the course of his own savage polemic, gives us a list of summits that have been a 'source of grief'. First among these is Chamberlain's conference with Hitler at Munich in 1938, from which he returned with the conviction that he had secured 'peace for our time'. Second are the East–West summits of the 1950s and 1960s that did nothing but raise false expectations. Third are the personal encounters between President Johnson and Harold Wilson in the 1960s that impaired Anglo-American relations because the two men simply did not like each other. Fourth is the meeting in 1962 at which Kennedy gave Polaris to Macmillan because he had a soft spot for the avuncular older man, though this fitted ill with American policy on nuclear proliferation and gave de Gaulle an excuse to veto Britain's application to the EEC. Fifth, there are the discussions, dogged with misunderstandings, between Nixon and Prime Minister Sato of Japan which blighted US–Japanese relations in the early 1970s. And so on (Ball, 1976, ch. 3). After looking closely at seven great power summit conferences between 1919 and 1960, Keith Eubank echoed the professionals.[4] There was no evidence, he concluded, that the presence of heads of government at these meetings produced better agreements than would have been generated otherwise, while 'often the reverse was true' (Eubank, p. 196).

But this is not the end of the case against summitry. Leaders who employ the technique find that it mushrooms: despite the cost of these events, they have to attend even more summits for fear of causing offence. Heads of government who overindulge the habit may also find themselves giving insufficient time to domestic affairs, and may as a result even lose their jobs. This was the fate of General Smuts in the election of 1948 that gave South Africa the hateful racist doctrine of apartheid.

Case for the defence

Summitry has been so roundly anathematized by historians as well as professional diplomats, that it is at first glance not easy to understand why it remains such an important feature of the international scene. But only at first glance. In fact, of course, summitry is valued chiefly for its enormous symbolic or propaganda potential. For example, East–West summits were valued during the Cold War mainly because they enabled both sides to advertise their attachment to peace, while intra-alliance summitry was taken seriously because it advertised alliance solidarity. The end of the Cold War was also, of course, advertised by a summit, held in Paris in November 1990, which also bound the countries participating more tightly to their agreements by publicly solemnizing them at the highest level. In democracies, summits are of special value to political leaders because they demonstrate to their voters that they are personally 'doing something' about a current problem and are important actors on the world stage. Add to this pot the power of television and sprinkle the surface with exotic locations of great symbolic significance, and it is clear why summit diplomacy is an irresistible dish. President Nixon simply could not pass over the opportunity virtually to 'kow-tow' before Mao Zedong in Beijing in 1972 and pose for cameras on the Great Wall, even though Washington still did not recognize the Communist government (Ambrose, pp. 512–17). And President Bush obviously saw great political mileage in meeting the leaders of the South American drug-producing countries at a 'Cocaine Summit' in the Colombian seaside resort of Cartagena in February 1990.[5] At the Western Economic Summit which was held in Paris in 1989, during the Bicentennial of the French Revolution, 6000 journalists were in attendance on the assembled heads of state and government (Kirton, 1989, p. xxvii).

There is no doubt, however, that while summitry may well be irrelevant and even highly damaging to diplomacy, and may often serve principally foreign and domestic propaganda purposes, it can also be valuable for diplomacy – provided, of course, that it is employed judiciously. It is at this point that it is necessary to do something often overlooked when the case against summitry is being made, and that is to distinguish between different types within the same broad species; for while all summits share some of the same purposes and procedures some have different ones.

There are, then, three main kinds of summitry.[6] First, there is what might be called (at the risk of being accused of the subliminal suggestion that summits regularly murder diplomacy) the serial summit conference. This is a summit that is part of a regular series. Secondly, there is the ad hoc summit conference. This is generally a one-off meeting though it may turn out to be the first of a series. Such encounters usually have a fairly narrowly focused theme, and invariably have a high profile. Finally, there is the high-level 'exchange of views'. This may be part of a series but is more likely to be ad hoc. Rather than being concerned with a set-piece negotiation, it has the more modest purposes of clarifying intentions, gaining intelligence, and giving an extra push (perhaps a final push) to a continuing negotiation at lower level. The agenda of such an exchange of views may be focused but is often a miscellaneous collection. The meeting is also more likely to be bilateral than multilateral. While the 'exchange of views' is not necessarily conducted in low-key fashion, it often is, and sometimes it is even secret. What are the diplomatic purposes served by all these summits, those served more by some than others, and those served by some but by others not at all?

Bearing in mind the functions of bilateral diplomacy discussed in Chapter 7, there are five functions that might usefully be advanced by summitry. These are promoting friendly relations, clarifying intentions, information gathering, consular work (principally export promotion and interceding on behalf of detained nationals), and negotiation. Let us consider the degree to which the different types of summit are suited to carrying out these functions, broad though these categories are and treacherous though this makes the task of generalizing about them.

Serial summits

Important examples of the serial summit can be seen in Box 10.2. Of all three types of summit, this is probably the best suited to the key function of negotiation, though the extent to which this is true turns to some extent on its length and frequency. As a general rule, the greater each of these the greater will be the suitability of the summit to serious negotiation during the meeting itself. The reasons for this are clear. Longer meetings allow subjects to be treated in greater depth. Most importantly, too, they allow time for a return to the table following a deadlock rather than, as with brief summits, having the onset of deadlock coincide with the leaders' scheduled departure for the airport. The Commonwealth Heads of Government Meeting (CHOGM), which lasts between five and seven days, is one of the best in this regard. Frequent summits at predetermined intervals are also more conducive to serious

---

Box 10.2 Serial summits: some important examples

- US–EU summit. Presidents of USA, European Council, and European Commission. Inaugurated in 1990 by Transatlantic Declaration and met once a year until announcement of the New Transatlantic Agenda in 1995. Since then has met twice a year.
- US–Russian summits. US–Soviet summits had achieved serial summit status by the second half of the 1980s, by which time they were taking place once a year. Following the breakup of the Soviet Union at the end of 1991, US–Russian summits have taken place on average three times a year.
- Franco-German summit. Started following signing of Franco-German Treaty of Friendship and Cooperation in January 1963. Meets at least twice a year.
- ASEAN summit. Members of the Association of South-East Asian Nations, established in 1967. Meets formally every three years but, following a decision in 1995, informally in each intervening year. There is (technically at least) no formal agenda at the informal summits.
- SAARC summit. Members of the South Asian Association for Regional Cooperation, established in 1985. Meets annually.
- Western Economic summit. The G7 countries (France, USA, Britain, Germany, Japan, Italy, and Canada) plus the EU and, since 1991, Russia (hence now the G8). Inaugurated at Rambouillet in France in 1975. Meets annually.
- Commonwealth Heads of Government Meeting (CHOGM). Meets every two years.
- Arab League summit. There have been at least 20 'Arab summits' since the early 1960s but they have not been held on a regular basis and some have been convened by Egypt rather than the Arab League. In 2001 it was decided to hold Arab League summits annually.

---

negotiation because they are likely to arouse fewer public expectations and to have developed clear and comprehensive rules of procedure. In this regard, the Franco-German summit, which in practice often meets as many as five or six times a year, is one of the best. Unfortunately, but not surprisingly, frequent summits tend to be brief and long ones less frequent.

Whether serial summits are frequent or separated by a year or more, and whether they last for hours or days, they may contribute to a successful negotiation between the parties concerned for one or more of the following reasons. First, they educate heads of government in international realities. They are forced to do their homework in order to avoid embarrassment, and the personal encounters at the summit give them a first-hand feeling for the influences shaping the attitudes of their fellow leaders. '[I]f no significant domestic pressure for an internationally cooperative line of policy exists,' says Putnam, 'summitry cannot create it, but where such pressure exists, the summit process can amplify its effectiveness' (Putnam, pp. 73–5, 86). Secondly, and related to this, these summits make package deals ('linkage') easier. Sitting astride the apex of policy-making within their own administrations, heads of government are well placed to make trades involving bureaucratically separate issue areas. This is a capability to which a premium began to attach in the 1970s as matters such as financial markets, raw material and energy sources soared to the top of the foreign policy agenda (Bulmer and Wessels, p. 17). Thirdly, summits of this kind set deadlines for the completion of an existing negotiation, or a stage of an existing negotiation, between the parties. (Deadlines in general are discussed in Chapter 4.) Because heads of government may be publicly embarrassed by a failure to announce an agreement at a summit, their junior ministers and officials are put under intense pressure to have effectively concluded much the greater part of the negotiation with their opposite numbers before the summit is held. In short, serial summits sustain diplomatic momentum. Fourthly, if the negotiations have indeed been brought to this stage, the summit – even if brief – may serve to break any remaining deadlocks by virtue of the authority of the assembled negotiators and their greater breadth of vision (point two above). This is the 'final court of appeal' function of the summit.

As for the other functions, it is self-evident that the serial summit – or at least the series of which it is part – is also the best suited to information gathering, including the gathering of information on personalities. Summiteers themselves stress this point, in 1992 Chancellor Kohl of Germany noting in its support that he had met President Mitterrand of France in excess of 80 times (Bower, p. 37). The serial summit is probably the best for clarifying intentions as well, not least because these rarely appear more clearly than in the give and take of genuine – and therefore private – negotiations. The serial summit is probably not altogether useless for pressing the case of detained nationals, though its qualifications in this area are not self-evident. Precisely because it is the summit most suited to negotiation, it is also the summit that is perhaps least well suited to the promotion of friendly relations. Serious negotiation invariably generates tensions and these are almost bound to be greater at summits, as their critics have so frequently pointed out, since the protagonists can rarely pretend that their word is anything other than the last word of their governments.[7] Besides, politicians tend to find it harder to resist point-scoring than professional negotiators. Summits where serious negotiation occurs also allow little time for the elaborate courtesies, observance of which is so important to the pursuit of friendly relations by the resident ambassador. On the other hand, serial summits would not occur if there were not an appreciation of some significant overlap of interests or strong sense of cultural affinity among the participants. This will usually ensure that tensions are not permitted to become destructive, as the Franco-German summit and the CHOGMs demonstrate. Also worth mentioning here is the summit of the South Asian Association for Regional Cooperation that was held in Islamabad in 1988. This was the setting for a warm encounter between the Indian prime minister, Rajiv Gandhi, and Benazir Bhutto, whose election had been widely welcomed in India.

The paradigm case of the serial summit is the French-inspired European Council, the regular conference of heads of state and government of the European Union that was designed principally to ensure that supranationalism in Europe did not get out of hand. This had its origins in informal summits starting in 1957, formally came into being in Paris in December 1974, and was finally embodied in the treaty regime of the (then) EC in the Single European Act in 1986. Despite a deliberate attempt to maintain flexibility and informality, clear rules of procedure have developed, some of which are to be found in documentary sources (Werts, p. 77) and some in custom and practice. Among the more important are the requirement that the Council shall meet at least twice a year, though in practice it is normally summoned three times,[8] usually in March/April, June/July and November/December, with ministers and members of the Commission also in attendance. A first draft of the agenda is prepared by the Committee of Permanent Representatives in Brussels but the final draft is submitted by the country holding the presidency; the agenda is only finally agreed, however, at the start of the meeting (Werts, pp. 78–9; Bulmer and Wessels, pp. 51–3). The chairman is the head of government of the country holding the presidency. The Council normally lasts for no more than twenty-four hours, starting at noon and ending at noon on the following day. In order to encourage frank exchanges, and although it can subsequently lead to arguments, no official minutes of the plenary sessions are recorded (Bulmer and Wessels, pp. 57–8). These sessions are also intimate and restricted (ministers and officials are kept in a separate room), though 'not at all secret' since 'everybody goes out and tells great numbers of people exactly what they think has happened' (Jenkins, p. 75). After dinner on the first day there is a very informal 'fireside chat' on general political questions beyond the formal agenda (Callaghan, pp. 316–17; Werts, p. 80). Decision-making is, of course, by consensus (see Chapter 9).

What role has the European Council played? In theory, it was designed to promote frank exchanges of views, and to enable government heads to negotiate agreements on matters of high policy, especially those on which the Council of Ministers was deadlocked. In practice, the informal sessions have proved particularly useful, at least during some periods; they appear to have been vital, for example, in facilitating the establishment of the European Monetary System (Bulmer and Wessels, p. 84). And in general the European Council has proved valuable in signalling to the world European solidarity on some key foreign policy questions. It must be admitted, however, that as the scene of sometimes extremely tough negotiations in the plenary sessions, it has not been famous for its contribution to the promotion of friendly relations. Nor did this begin with the appearance of Margaret Thatcher in its ranks and the bitter and protracted arguments that she stimulated in the 1980s over Britain's budgetary contributions. Even in Paris in 1974, when Britain was represented by Harold Wilson, the exchanges on this subject were 'long, argumentative and tense at times' (Callaghan, p. 315). But this is simply the price of seriousness.

Ad hoc summits

Examples of this type of meeting are the Sino-American summit and the 'Cocaine Summit' mentioned above. As with the serial summit, the usefulness of this type of summit meeting in negotiation is to some extent a function of its length: the longer the better. The Camp David summit, for example, which took place in September 1978, lasted for a full thirteen days. Extremely tough negotiations took place between the American, Israeli, and Egyptian leaders and their senior advisers, and a dramatic breakthrough was eventually made with the announcement of the 'Camp David Accords'. The Camp David summit, in other words, did not merely ratify an agreement made earlier by the 'sherpas'[9] (Quandt, chs 9 and 10). As ad hoc summits go, however, Camp David was the exception rather than the rule. Most of them last no more than two or three days. Because of this, and because they also tend to generate more publicity than the serial summit, and lack its clear procedural rules,[10] ad hoc meetings are unlikely to be so useful for negotiations during the meetings themselves.

Nevertheless, precisely because the ad hoc summit is a more remarkable event, with the potential to produce more publicity, it is perhaps better suited than the serial summit to generating or regaining diplomatic momentum. Moreover, because there is no guarantee of a subsequent meeting to which consideration of an unresolved agenda item can be put back, the ad hoc summit represents a better deadline for an existing negotiation than the serial summit. The ad hoc EC summits of the early 1970s, including the Paris summit in 1974 that launched the European Council, are good examples of summits which (some more than others) had an 'energizing' effect on extant negotiations (Bulmer and Wessels, pp. 27–46). In the same period, in May 1972, the prospect of the Nixon–Brezhnev summit in Moscow put huge pressure on the arms control negotiators of both sides to wrap up the first Strategic Arms Limitation Treaty in time for a signing at the summit.[11] To give a final example, President Carter expressly conceived the Camp David summit in September 1978 as a 'dramatic' last throw of the dice. His aim was to use it to regain the momentum in the Middle East negotiations that had faltered when direct Egypt–Israel talks following Sadat's visit to Jerusalem in November 1977 had failed to make progress (Brzezinksi, p. 250; Carter, p. 305).

Since ad hoc summits are characteristically designed principally for symbolic purposes rather than negotiation, it seems reasonable to suggest that, whether they have an emphasis on ceremonial functions or not, they are better suited to the promotion of friendly relations than the serial summit. Indeed, many ad hoc summits are designed deliberately and openly for this purpose: the summit symbolizes this and fosters it by providing a format that encourages relaxed encounters between the leaders. Good bilateral examples of such summits are provided by the encounters between President Clinton of the United States and President Hafez al-Assad of Syria in Geneva in January 1994. A multilateral summit with heavy symbolic emphasis and the general aim of fostering increased economic and cultural ties between its participants was the two-day Ibero-American summit held in Mexico in July 1991.

As for clarifying intentions and gathering information, the qualifications of the ad hoc summit are a mixed blessing. On the one hand, the typically low emphasis on negotiation and high emphasis on ceremonial will reduce the opportunities for these purposes to be pursued. On the other, the more relaxed and less adversarial atmosphere may produce a frankness in the exchanges that suits these purposes very well. As for raising the cases of any detained nationals, it is highly unlikely that the ad hoc summit will be an appropriate occasion for such a sensitive exercise. This will be especially so if nurturing an old friendship or putting the seal on a new one is the main object of the event.

An important and interesting special case of the ad hoc summit is the funeral of a major political figure that is attended by high-level delegations from the region concerned or, as is now very common, from all over the world.[12] The 'working funeral' actually resembles the serial summit to the extent that at least by the 1960s it had established a predictable pattern of procedure. It is a special case, however, because it is more or less useless for the diplomatic purpose for which, it has been argued here, the typical ad hoc summit is principally conceived: generating significant diplomatic momentum on a major issue. This is partly because of its theme and partly because of the unavoidable shortness of notice that the countries sending delegations receive. Furthermore, funeral summits carry risks: existing diplomatic schedules are upset; and decisions on attendance and on level of attendance sometimes have to be made in the absence of perfect knowledge about what other states will be doing and of how the delegation will be received.

Nevertheless, funeral summits are of considerable value to the world diplomatic system. This is partly because the shortness of notice available to the 'mourners' has compensating advantages. First, it provides heads of government with an acceptable excuse to break an existing schedule in order to have urgent discussions on a current problem with other leaders in circumstances that will not arouse public expectations. Secondly, a decision to attend is unlikely to prove embarrassing as a result of changed circumstances by the date of the funeral. Thirdly, if attendance at the funeral is likely to cause controversy, there is little time for domestic opposition to be mobilized.

A working funeral is of special diplomatic significance if it is the funeral of an incumbent head of government. This is because the funeral is almost certain to be the first occasion both for foreign friends of the deceased to confirm that the new leadership remains wedded to their relationship and for foreign rivals to explore the possibility of a change of heart. The leaders of Warsaw Pact satellite states always attended the funerals of Soviet leaders for the former purpose, while Western leaders attended them for the latter, at least in the 1980s. The funeral summit also provides a perfect cover for discreet consultations between foreign rivals seeking to keep their conflict within peaceful bounds or striving for a way out of an impasse. Funerals of this kind are times of political truce.

Because there is so little time for preparation or for discussions during the event, funeral summits rarely serve for serious negotiation. Their functions are diplomatic signalling, promoting friendly relations (particularly between the mourners and the bereaved), clarifying intentions, and gathering intelligence.

The high-level 'exchange of views'

Heads of government who visit a number of countries on a foreign tour are usually engaged in this kind of activity, which is extremely common. For example, in September 1994 the British prime minister, John Major, accompanied by officials and businessmen, went on a week-long trip of this kind. It took in both the Gulf, where he had 'several hours of "very friendly" talks' with King Fahd of Saudi Arabia before proceeding to Abu Dhabi, and South Africa (*Financial Times*, 20 September 1994). Newly elected American presidents have a particular weakness for this least ambitious form of summitry, or perhaps are just able to gratify it more readily.

Where new leaders are concerned, the educational argument for this kind of summitry is a strong one, though perhaps more in friendly relationships than adversarial ones. In the latter there is hardly likely to be such frankness and, as illustrated by the famous Soviet–American summit encounter in Vienna in 1961, the pitfalls for the inexperienced are in any case more numerous. In the prior White House discussion on whether or not President Kennedy should seek a 'face-to-face talk' with Nikita Khrushchev, the American ambassador to Moscow, Llewellyn Thompson, strongly supported the idea. His argument was that 'it was impossible for the new President to get at second hand the full flavour of what he was up against' (Schlesinger, p. 277). However, while the subsequent encounter was clearly educational for both leaders, Kennedy came to the conclusion that Khrushchev's own education had been poor, the latter having wrongly formed the impression that the new American president lacked the necessary resolve to defend Western positions.

With its more modest ambitions and in general relatively low-key proceedings, the 'exchange of views' summit is probably the best suited of all summits to promote friendly relations. It also serves well in the promotion of trade and in taking up serious cases of maltreatment of nationals. It is not self-evident, however, despite its self-styling, that the 'exchange of views' summit is necessarily better at clarifying intentions and gathering information than the serial summit or even the average ad hoc summit. As for serious negotiations, this kind of summit can nudge forward continuing talks and even rescue those deadlocked on a particular point, though it will not generally be up to the standard of the serial summit in the last regard or the ad hoc summit in the first.

Secrets of success

It is a cliché of studies of summitry that is some consolation for professional diplomats and other officials, and no less true for being a cliché, that meticulous preparation is the key to success, whatever kind of summit is involved. Indeed, the conventional wisdom is that a successful summit is one that merely ratifies an agreement previously negotiated at lower level (Kissinger, 1979, p. 781; Weihmiller and Doder, pp. 103–5). Though sometimes disregarded without mishap,[13] this is obviously of greatest importance when the summit is the highly delicate kind designed to seal a new friendship between erstwhile enemies, as in the case of the Sino-American summit in February 1972.[14] However, it is also important when it is a friendly encounter but one that is only scheduled to last for hours rather than days, as in the case of the European Council or the Western Economic summits.[15] Ministers or senior officials close to the heads of state or government normally conduct the preparatory negotiations.

The 'sherpas' who prepare the ascent to the annual Western Economic summits 'typically meet three or four weekends a year, once in the winter to review the aftermath of the previous summit and to conduct an initial *tour d'horizon* for the next, and then roughly monthly from March until the summit itself in June or July' (Putnam, p. 59; also Kirton, 1989, p. xxxi). First they agree the agenda and then, assisted by contributions from appropriate subsidiary forums such as the OECD, the World Bank, the IMF, and the IAEA, they agree the chief lines of the final communiqué or 'declaration'. At a fairly late stage in the cycle of sherpa meetings,[16] foreign ministry officials join in. Their aim is to help prepare the 'political statements' that will be announced separately at the end of the summit in order to preserve the fiction that it is chiefly an economic affair (Kirton, 1989, pp. xxxii–xxxiii). Such, however, is the anxiety to ensure that the summit is a success that it is now usual for the host head of government to engage in a series of bilateral pre-summit summits. These take place not only with the other participants but also with important outsiders (Kirton, 1989, pp. xxv–xxvi). At the Houston Summit in 1989, the heads of government actually arrived two days early in order to conduct 'pre-Summit bilaterals' (Kirton, 1991, p. xii).

It is not only the communiqué that ideally should be prepared well in advance of the summit. Prior agreement or agreement at the outset on what might and might not be said to the media is another important requirement for successful summitry, as, of course, it is for any diplomatic encounter that entails private discussion. There must also be detailed planning of the choreography of the summit. This means the pattern of meetings and events such as visits, speeches, motorcades, 'walkabouts', joint press conferences, and so on, the mix depending on the character of the summit. Preplanned choreography is always important but is especially so if symbolism is expected to take precedence over substance, as at the Reagan–Gorbachev summit in Moscow in 1988. In preparation for this occasion, the White House planning group worked for three months to 'write a script that would resemble an American political campaign with strong emphasis on visual impressions'. Not surprisingly, the analogy that sprang to the mind of former B-movie film star Ronald Reagan was a Cecil B. De Mille epic (Whelan, p. 89). Among other requirements for successful summitry is not arousing excessive expectations. This might involve repeated prior statements that, say, a planned ad hoc summit will merely involve an 'exchange of views', which was the line taken by the Americans in the run-up to the Churchill–Eisenhower–Laniel summit at Bermuda in December 1953 (Young, J. W., 1986, p. 901).

These 'secrets of success' are, of course, necessary conditions of success; they are not sufficient ones. The best actors can fumble their lines when the curtain goes up, or simply fall ill. Churchill was unwell at the Bermuda summit, while the French prime minister, Laniel, took to his bed with a high temperature on the second day (Young, J. W., 1986, p. 906). Boris Yeltsin, President of the Russian Federation, apparently fast asleep, failed altogether to emerge from his Tupolev after it landed at Shannon airport in the Irish Republic in September 1994. What was going through the mind of the Irish prime minister, Albert Reynolds, who was waiting for his guest on the tarmac, complete with band, red carpet, and local dignitaries, is not difficult to imagine. Unforeseeable external events can also poison the atmosphere of a summit or cause acute embarrassment. The shooting down over the Soviet Union of an American U-2 spy-plane two weeks before the opening of the East–West summit in Paris in May 1960 reduced this event to a fiasco (Weihmiller and Doder, pp. 38–40). In another example, the occupation of Tiananmen Square in Beijing by pro-Democracy students prior to the Gorbachev–Deng summit in May 1989 turned this into a humiliation for the Chinese Communist leadership. The programme had to be hastily revised and the Soviet leader brought into the Great Hall of the People through the back door (Cradock, p. 221). In short, thorough preparation can minimize the risks of summitry but not eliminate them.

Summary

Summitry may sometimes be highly damaging to diplomacy and is always risky; and it may serve only foreign or domestic propaganda purposes. Nevertheless, judiciously employed and carefully prepared, it can – and does – serve diplomatic purposes as well. This is especially true of the serial summit, an institution to which resort seems to have become reflexive following the establishment of an important international relationship. But the ad hoc summit and the high-level 'exchange of views' are of some importance to diplomacy as well, if only as devices to inject momentum into a stagnant negotiation. The pattern of summitry has changed in the past and may change again. Nevertheless, there seems little reason to believe that it will go into a general decline as a mode of communication between states as it did with the rise of the resident ambassador at the end of the Middle Ages. Television and democracy have seen to that.

Notes

1 The term itself was not used until the 1950s, when it was developed in the press following Churchill's use of the word 'summit' during a speech in Edinburgh in February 1950. For an excellent discussion of its changing connotations, see 'What is summitry?' (Dunn, ch. 1).

2 I am grateful to David H. Dunn for drawing my attention to this possibility, which first arose when the former Chilean dictator, General Augusto Pinochet, was arrested and detained at the request of a Spanish judge during a visit to Britain in October 1998. The issue of a head of state's immunity was revived again in early 2001 with the arrest by Serbian authorities of the former Serb leader, Slobodan Milosevic, and reports that New Scotland Yard was investigating the possibility of bringing charges for war crimes against the Iraqi leader, Saddam Hussein, together with his deputy, Tariq Aziz (*The Guardian,* 26 April, 2001).

3 Some heads of government are also, of course, heads of state, as in the case of the President of the United States. In these circumstances the following arguments usually apply with even greater force.

4 Paris, 1919; Munich, 1938; Tehran, 1943; Yalta, 1945; Potsdam, 1945; Geneva, 1955; and Paris, 1960.

5 The follow-up was held at San Antonio (Texas) in 1992.

6 The following categories are sometimes subdivided according to their being bilateral or multilateral in composition.

7 Sometimes they can, though. Where there is a real separation of powers, as in the United States, the head of the executive branch could claim that any agreement to which he assented was subject to endorsement by the legislative and even judicial branches as well. And in a political system with a strong tradition of cabinet government, as in Israel and Britain, a head of government

can claim that in effect he is little more than an 'ambassador' answerable to the cabinet at home. This was invariably the tactic of Menachem Begin, the Israeli prime minister, during the Camp David negotiations.

8 The original agreement, in 1974, was that it should meet three times a year, which it did over the following decade. It was the Single European Act that changed the rule to 'at least twice a year'. The frequency of meetings thereafter was as follows: 1986 (2); 1987 (2); 1988 (3); 1989 (3); 1990 (4); 1991 (3); 1992 (2) (Werts, pp. xvii–xviii).

9 The term comes from the locally hired bearers who assist mountaineers in the Himalayas.

10 Except, of course, for the admittedly large number generated by the UN system.

11 By contrast, the knowledge that arms control would be on the agenda of another superpower summit before too long was no doubt one reason why the Moscow summit of May/June 1988 failed to generate adequate pressure for the conclusion of an agreement on long-range missiles (Whelan, pp. xi, 84–6).

12 I have written at length on this subject elsewhere (Berridge 1996).

13 In his account of the first two Reagan–Gorbachev summits, at Geneva in November 1985 and Reykjavik in October 1986, George Shultz records the impatience with the 'pre-cooking' of summit agreements that he shared with the president. This was in part because it provoked 'bickering' between the different departments and agencies of the administration. As a result, real negotiations involving both leaders occurred at the summits and both were a success. However, strict press blackouts were essential (Shultz, pp. 596–607).

14 The famous 'Shanghai Communiqué' released at the end of President Nixon's visit to Communist China in February 1972 was substantially negotiated by Henry Kissinger on his own visit to China in the previous October. However, it still took Kissinger a further 20 hours of negotiation in the wings of the summit itself to finalize it (Kissinger, 1979, pp. 781–4, 1074–87).

15 Though the original 36-hour encounters of the Western Economic summit had expanded to three days by the late 1980s (Kirton, 1989, p. xxiv).

16 Earlier if, as in 1990, political circumstances warrant it.

Further reading

Ball, G., *Diplomacy for a Crowded World* (Bodley Head: London, 1976), ch. 3.

Bulmer, S. and W. Wessels, *The European Council: Decision-Making in European Politics* (Macmillan – now Palgrave: Basingstoke, 1987).

Carter, J., *Keeping Faith: Memoirs of a President* (Bantam: New York and London, 1982).

Clift, A. D., *With Presidents to the Summit* (George Mason University Press: Fairfax, Virginia, 1993).

Cohen, R., *Theatre of Power: The Art of Diplomatic Signalling* (Longman: London and New York, 1987).

Commynes, Philippe de, *The Memoirs of Philippe de Commynes*, Vol. One, ed. Samuel Kinser, trsl. by Isabelle Cazeaux (University of South Carolina Press: Columbia, South Carolina, 1969).

Dunn, David H. (ed.), *Diplomacy at the Highest Level: The Evolution of International Summitry* (Macmillan – now Palgrave: Basingstoke, 1996).

Eubank, K., *The Summit Conferences 1919–1960* (University of Oklahoma Press: Norman, Oklahoma, 1966).

Fairbanks, C., *The Allure of Summits* (Foreign Policy Institute, Washington, DC, 1988).

Kirton, J. J., 'The significance of the Seven Power Summit', in Hajnal, P. I. (ed.), *The Seven Power Summit: Documents from the Summits of the Industrialized Countries 1975–1989* (Kraus: Millwood, New York, 1989).

Kirton, J. J., 'The significance of the Houston Summit', in Hajnal, P. I. (ed.) *The Seven Power Summit: Documents from the Summits of Industrialized Countries. Supplement: Documents from the 1990 Summit* (Kraus: Millwood, New York, 1991).

Kissinger, H. A., *The White House Years* (Weidenfeld & Nicolson and Michael Joseph: London, 1979), pp. 769, 781, 919–21.

Nicolson, H., *Peacemaking 1919*, rev. edn (Constable: London, 1943).

Plischke, E., *Summit Diplomacy: Personal Diplomacy of the United States Presidents* (Greenwood Press: New York, 1974).

Putnam, R., 'The Western Economic Summits: a political interpretation', in Merlini, C. (ed.) *Economic Summits and Western Decision-making* (Croom Helm: London; St. Martin's Press – now Palgrave: New York, 1984).

Putnam, R. and N. Bayne, *Hanging Together: Cooperation and Conflict in the Seven Power Summits*, 2nd edn (Sage: London, 1988).

Shultz, G. P., *Turmoil and Triumph: My Years as Secretary of State* (Scribner's: New York, 1993), chs 30, 36, 46 and 49.

Weihmiller, G. R. and D. Doder, *US–Soviet Summits* (University Press of America: Lanham, New York, and London, 1986).

Werts, J., *The European Council* (North-Holland: Amsterdam, 1992).

Whelan, J. G., *The Moscow Summit 1988* (Westview Press: Boulder, 1990).

11
Mediation

Mediation, which has a long and generally honourable record in the history of diplomacy, is by definition multilateral and may occur, as in the momentous talks on the Middle East at Camp David in September 1978, at the summit. It is particularly necessary in extremely bitter disputes, especially those in which the parties have been engaged for long periods and are locked into public postures that appear to make compromise impossible without seriously jeopardizing the domestic positions of their leaders. It is also appropriate where the parties have the most profound distrust of each other's intentions, where cultural differences present an additional barrier to communication (Cohen, 1997), and where at least one of the parties refuses to recognize the other.[1]

The presence of mediation in international conflicts, and also in civil wars, is extensive, though only occasionally does it attract great attention. A recent study cites research showing that 255 of 310 conflicts between 1945 and 1974 enjoyed some form of *official* mediation alone (Princen, p. 5). At the beginning of the twenty-first century it seems even more difficult to find conflicts in which intermediaries – unofficial as well as official – are not participating in one way or another. What does mediation involve? What motivates the mediator? What are the intermediary's ideal attributes? Should the start of a mediation effort wait until the time for a settlement is 'ripe'? And what are the drawbacks of involving third parties in disputes? These are the questions that this chapter will consider.

The nature of mediation

Mediation is a special kind of negotiation designed to promote the settlement of a conflict. In this negotiation a distinctive role is played by a third party, that is, one not directly involved in the dispute in question. The third party must have a special characteristic in addition to an inclination to behave in a special way. To be precise, it must be substantially *impartial* in the dispute, at least once the negotiation has started and on the issue actually on the agenda.[2] Certainly, the third party must want a settlement but *any* settlement with which the parties themselves will be happy. As to its role, in a mediation – which is not to be confused with being a 'facilitator' or providing 'good offices' (see Box 11.1) – the third party searches actively for a settlement. Typically this means drawing up an agenda, calling and chairing negotiating sessions, proposing solutions, and – where the third party is a powerful state – employing threats and promises towards the rivals. In short, mediation is the active search for a negotiated settlement to an international or intrastate conflict by an impartial third party.

Mediation may be distinct from the provision of good offices but it sometimes evolves from execution of this more limited role. Moreover, providing good offices, whether it succeeds in bringing the parties to a conflict into direct negotiations or, this proving impossible, progresses into mediation, is by no means just a question of providing the parties with a channel of communications and perhaps a secure and comfortable venue for their talks. Ideally, the third party will also assist with the

---

Box 11.1   Good offices

A third party acting as a 'facilitator' or providing 'good offices' has a more limited role than a mediator, usually involving no more than helping to bring the parties in conflict into direct negotiations. At this point it withdraws, though it will usually remain in the wings in case the talks threaten to founder and it is needed again. In short, its role is limited to the prenegotiations stage. Modern social-psychological versions of this traditional approach emphasize that an enduring settlement is one that the parties must arrive at themselves, and reflect basic attitude changes. Of course, it is quite common for a good offices mission to turn into a mediation but the activities remain distinct. Unfortunately, this does not prevent many mediations from being described as missions of 'good offices', and the separate chapters on 'Good Offices' and 'Mediation' have disappeared from the latest edition of *Satow's Guide to Diplomatic Practice*. Mediation should also be distinguished from *conciliation*. This is the attempt to resolve a dispute by having it examined in depth by an independent commission of inquiry or 'conciliation commission'. This then offers its recommendations for a settlement, which are non-binding. This had a short heyday in the interwar period. *Arbitration* is the same as conciliation except that the recommendation is binding. It is akin to but not the same as judicial settlement.

interpretation of messages and be able to show one or both parties how the style, as well as the content, of a message from one party can be made more palatable to the other. It should also provide reassurance to each party that the other means what it says and is sincere in seeking a negotiated settlement. This seems to have been at least one of the roles played by the government of General de Gaulle in the earliest stage of the Sino-American rapprochement in 1969. The French leader was a figure who still enjoyed enormous international respect and whose reassurances thus commanded attention (Nixon, pp. 370–4; Hersh, 1983, pp. 351–2).

Via the communications they have exchanged through the 'good offices' of the third party, the parties to a conflict may conclude that there is a basis for negotiation between them. In this eventuality, the third party may be required to facilitate this by arranging for a neutral venue for the talks.[3] This may be on its own territory, especially if it is a permanent neutral such as Austria, or it may be elsewhere. During the Angola/Namibia negotiations in 1988, which were mediated by the United States, meetings were held in London, Cape Verde, Brazzaville, Geneva, and Cairo, as well as in New York (Berridge, 1989). Talks mediated by the UN are commonly held in Geneva or New York but certainly not always.

Having brought the parties together, the subsequent role of the third party depends on a variety of factors. These include its own motives (see below), influence, diplomatic skill, and standing with the parties; and whether or not the latter have been brought to a stage where they can bear it to be known that they are talking face-to-face with their enemies. A third party may lack significant influence with the rivals and find that in any case they are by now prepared to talk directly. This was the case in the Sino-American rapprochement in the early 1970s in which Pakistan had emerged as the most important provider of good offices and now withdrew to the wings.[4] Conversely, the influence of the third party over the antagonists may be considerable, especially if it has the support of other important players (see below). Furthermore, the parties in dispute may not only find it impossible to meet without the face-saving presence of the third party but also require a constant stiffening of their resolve to continue talking. In such circumstances, third parties – now full-blown mediators – have the chief responsibility for driving the negotiations forward. To reassure the rivals that calamity will not follow non-compliance with any agreement reached, the mediator may also provide tangible guarantees, a vital feature of American mediation in the Arab–Israeli conflict in the 1970s (Touval, 1982, chs 9 and 10). And the mediator may make a final contribution to face-saving on the part of one or both of the antagonists by assisting in construction of an agreement the form of which suggests (however implausibly) that any concessions made have been granted to the mediator rather than to the opponent. In the Iran hostages negotiations, for example, the final agreement took the form of a 'Declaration of the Government of the Democratic and Popular Republic of Algeria' (Sick, p. 332; *International Legal Materials*, pp. 224ff).

Different mediators and different motives

In a much-quoted though not altogether original line,[5] Touval says that 'mediators, like brokers, are in it for profit' (Touval, 1982, p. 321). There is no doubting this. It has been true at least since resident ambassadors in early modern Europe were given handsome and valuable personal gifts by foreign monarchs grateful for their assistance in helping to bring peace to their conflicts.[6] Today the nature of the profit sought by mediators still depends on who they are and what kind of dispute they are trying to mediate but ambassadors seeking the role for personal gain are no longer prominent among them. First of all, then, who are today's mediators? It is now conventional to divide them into official and unofficial categories, or into 'track one' and 'track two'.[7]

Track one

The most important mediators in international relations are states, whether acting singly or collectively, or via the international organizations such as the United Nations that are largely their creatures. The major powers, which held a virtual monopoly over mediation until the twentieth century (Princen, p. 6), generally involve themselves in it in pursuit of three main policy goals.

First and generally foremost, they seek the mediator's mantle in order to defuse crises that threaten the global stability, including global economic stability, in which they have such an important stake. These were certainly major considerations prompting successive US administrations to make a settlement of the Arab–Israeli conflict a high priority after the Yom Kippur War in October 1973. For this not only strained US–Soviet détente but produced such a massive increase in the price of oil that the economies of the West were severely rocked.

Secondly, the major powers generally think it prudent to mediate in conflicts if these occur within alliances or looser associations of states in which they play leading roles. The motive here is even clearer: they are anxious to maintain internal solidarity and pre-empt offers of 'assistance' from outside. In some cases this inclination is reinforced by a lingering sense of imperial responsibility and 'ethnic' lobbying at home. These have been key factors leading the United States and Britain to interest themselves in the Cyprus dispute, which, of course, involves two of the most important members of NATO's southern flank – Turkey and Greece. Britain also has legal guarantor obligations towards the Republic of Cyprus, which itself contains important NATO military installations and is a member of the Commonwealth. Considerations of in-group solidarity and leadership have also no doubt been behind Britain's long-standing attempts to mediate in the dispute over Kashmir between prominent Commonwealth members, India and Pakistan.

Finally, it is clear that the major powers also see mediation in general as a means of extending their networks of dependent clients. In other words, they see it not only as a means of preserving existing influence but also of projecting it into areas where previously it had not been great, especially if this means displacing an important rival. This prompted Soviet mediation in the India–Pakistan conflict, at Tashkent in January 1966, at a time when both of these South Asian powers were disgruntled with the West, and, as Humphrey Trevelyan observes, 'must have made Lord Curzon turn in his grave' (Trevelyan, 1971, p. 200). It was also behind the American role in the Angola/Namibia negotiations that were finally brought to success at the end of 1988 (Berridge, 1989).

The major powers, however, are not the only kind of states that involve themselves in mediation efforts. Middle powers, or regional 'great powers', periodically play this role and for reasons similar to those that lead to its adoption by the major powers, not the least their interest in *regional* stability. Among the middle powers, however, Switzerland and Austria should be mentioned as special cases by virtue of their permanent neutrality, which provides them with an outstanding qualification to provide good offices or engage in international mediation. Both Vienna and Geneva have been the venues of much sensitive diplomacy, and Geneva hosts the European headquarters of the UN. In 1979 – at very considerable cost to the Austrian taxpayer – a new International Centre for the use of UN agencies was opened in Vienna (Stadler, p. 14). And both Switzerland and Austria are frequently employed by states in conflict as 'protecting powers'.[8] It is true that with a particularly purist conception of neutrality, and aware that genuine mediation involves the kind of active diplomacy that risks the charge of bias, Switzerland has tended to confine itself to the provision of good offices. By contrast, Austria has prided itself on its 'active neutrality', especially during the period when it was led by Dr Bruno Kreisky (see Box 11.2.)

Box 11.2 Dr Bruno Kreisky

Kreisky, a Jewish but anti-Zionist Socialist, was Austrian minister of foreign affairs from 1959 until 1966 and federal chancellor from 1970 until 1983. He took a strong interest in the Arab–Israeli conflict in the mid-1970s, and was the first Western statesman to recognize the PLO, allowing it to open an information office in Vienna. In 1977 he also hosted a famous encounter in the city between South African prime minister, John Vorster, and US vice-president, Walter Mondale, and later visited Tehran on behalf of the Socialist International in an unsuccessful attempt to break the impasse in the hostages crisis (Stadler, pp. 16–17). According to Henry Kissinger, Kreisky was 'shrewd and perceptive ... [and] ... had parlayed his country's formal neutrality into a position of influence beyond its strength, often by interpreting the motives of competing countries to each other' (Kissinger, 1979, p. 1204). However, with the election to the federal presidency in 1986 of Dr Kurt Waldheim, the former secretary-general of the UN whose war record had shortly before received much unfavourable press scrutiny, Austria's ability to act as a mediator was seriously impaired. Waldheim himself was barred from visiting the United States.

However, permanent neutrality provides Austria and Switzerland with a motive as well as an opportunity to provide good offices and play the role of mediator. This is the need to deflect the 'free-rider' criticism of their neutrality. By their unusual diplomatic exertions in the causes of peace, they are able to take the edge off the complaint that, like non-unionized workers who take the pay rises secured by trade unions without paying their dues, they enjoy the security provided by NATO without contributing to its military strength.

It is important to note that small states, too, sometimes mediate in international conflicts, including those involving far larger states than themselves. A case in point is the mediation of Algeria in the hostages crisis between the United States and Iran at the beginning of the 1980s. Clearly, Algeria was interested in both the huge prestige that successful mediation in this most serious crisis would bring in its train and the increased influence in Tehran and Washington that it would produce as well. Another interesting example under this head is the Holy See, for which mediation is a spiritual duty as well as a political requirement. It is worth noting in passing, however, that for much the greater part of the post-war period Communism and religious divisions together severely restricted the mediating capacity of the Vatican diplomatic service. Not in diplomatic relations with any Communist state (including Communist China) until the end of the 1980s, and refusing to recognize the State of Israel, the Holy See was as much in need of mediation itself as it was available as an appropriate intermediary. In practice, its activities under this heading were confined to the Catholic world, as, for example, in Pope John Paul II's mediation of the Beagle Channel dispute between Argentina and Chile, diplomacy which began in 1979 and culminated successfully six years later (Lindsley; Princen, ch. 8).

Finally, it is important to note that states also mediate in international and intrastate conflicts under the authority of the charter obligations of the international organizations that they have established. As well as the United Nations, these include regional bodies such as the Organization of American States (OAS) and the Organization of African Unity (OAU). With their councils dominated by their weightiest members, it is hardly surprising that the interests of the latter should be most influential in shaping the mediations in which these intergovernmental bodies are involved. Nevertheless, their secretariats are not entirely puppets. The secretary-general of the UN, for example, now has some limited capacity to engage in independent mediation. This derives not least from the tradition going back to the Middle East crisis of 1956 in which the Security Council gave the then secretary-general, Dag Hammarskjöld, the right to use his discretion in seeking fulfilment of the purposes and principles of the UN Charter and the Council's decisions (Bailey and Daws, pp. 119–20; De Soto, p. 350). Among other things, it is also reinforced by the express and implied provisions of the Charter, especially Article 99 (see Box 11.3). Successive secretaries-general have pointed out that they cannot form an opinion of the sort envisaged in this article without the ability to appoint staff, authorize research, make visits, and engage in diplomatic consultations (Bailey and Daws, pp. 111–13).

Track two

Mediation (as well as the provision of good offices) by private individuals and non-governmental organizations was known in the United States as 'citizen diplomacy' until it was christened 'track two' by the American diplomat, Joseph Montville, in 1981. It has increased exponentially over recent decades. Prominent among private individuals engaged in these activities are well-connected businessmen such as the legendary Armand Hammer (Box 11.4) and 'Tiny' Rowland, the former managing director of Lonrho (Hall, 1987, 1992; Hume). Such people are prompted by any mixture of corporate interests, political ambitions, and charitable instincts – and perhaps just by a simple desire to show off. As for NGOs, the current edition of the *Directory of Conflict Prevention Organizations* published by the European Centre for Conflict Prevention

---

Box 11.3 Mediation in the UN Charter

Article 33
1. The parties to any dispute, the continuance of which is likely to endanger the maintenance of international peace and security, shall, first of all, seek a solution by negotiation, enquiry, mediation, conciliation, arbitration, judicial settlement, resort to regional agencies or arrangements, or other peaceful means of their own choice.
2. The Security Council shall, when it deems necessary, call upon the parties to settle their disputes by such means. . . .

Article 36
1. The Security Council may, at any stage of a dispute of the nature referred to in Article 33 or of a situation of like nature, recommend appropriate procedures or methods of adjustment.

Article 37
1. Should the parties to a dispute of the nature referred to in Article 33 fail to settle it by the means indicated in that Article, they shall refer it to the Security Council.
2. If the Security Council deems that the continuance of the dispute is in fact likely to endanger the maintenance of international peace and security, it shall decide whether to take action under Article 36 or to recommend such terms of settlement as it may consider appropriate.

Article 38
Without prejudice to the provisions of Articles 33 to 37, the Security Council may, if all the parties to any dispute so request, make recommendations to the parties with a view to a pacific settlement of the dispute. . . .

Article 99
The Secretary-General may bring to the attention of the Security Council any matter which in his opinion may threaten the maintenance of international peace and security.

---

now lists 475 organizations active in this area.[9] Among these, religious bodies have long been important and new ones are still emerging. The Quakers, with their strong pacifist leaning, have been energetic in this work since the seventeenth century,[10] while the Rome-based religious order of Sant'Egidio came to prominence for its role in the ending of the civil war in Mozambique in the early 1990s (Hume; Carnegie Commission, ch. 5, p. 6). However, secular NGOs dedicated to conflict prevention and resolution, as it is known in trade jargon, are now also extremely numerous. Sometimes referred to as 'track two professionals', these include such bodies as the very effective Carter Center, formed by former US president Jimmy Carter.

Box 11.4 Armand Hammer

Hammer was an American tycoon whose Russian father had emigrated to the United States in the late nineteenth century. During the Cold War Hammer, who died in 1990, received much carefully engineered publicity for his attempts as a 'citizen-diplomat' to promote East–West détente, though – for good reasons – less so for his efforts on behalf of Soviet Jews at the instigation of Israel. Exploiting to the full his huge experience of the Soviet Union, his vast wealth, and his remorseless energy, Hammer seemed to open doors in Moscow that others found closed. He certainly had political achievements to his credit. However, there were many in the US State Department who did not trust him and some of his efforts on behalf of East–West détente were rendered superfluous by the fact that diplomatic relations between the superpowers were never actually broken off (Hammer; Weinberg; Blumay and Edwards).

Multiparty mediation

So far, and despite occasional hints to the contrary, it has been assumed that mediation is an activity carried out by a single party. However, the involvement of more than one mediator in the attempt to settle a conflict, including those in both track one and track two, is now so common as probably to be the norm. According to the editors of a recent major study, 'multiparty mediation' consists of 'attempts by many third parties to assist peace negotiations in any given conflict' (Crocker et al., p. 9). Is this a good definition? Are different forms of multiparty mediation observable?

In fact, multiparty mediation divides up into a variety of species. It may, to begin with, involve either simultaneous or sequential participation in a mediation by two or more parties. In the former case, it may further separate into uncoordinated or coordinated mediation. Where it is an uncoordinated, competitive mediation, the parties to the conflict simultaneously exploit rival brokers seeking the sole 'contract'. This happened in the early stages of the Sino-American rapprochement at the beginning of the 1970s, although in the event these turned out to be only competitive good offices. In the opposite situation, that is, when a simultaneous multiparty mediation is coordinated, it is sometimes described as 'collective mediation' and the coordinating body involved as a 'contact group'. Typically having four or five members, the most important example of a contact group in recent years is the Contact Group on Bosnia, which was created in April 1994 and was revived in an attempt to grapple with the Kosovo crisis in 1999. It consisted of Germany, France, Russia, Britain and the United States. When there are only two mediators, as for example in the original UN/EU mission to broker a settlement in Bosnia,[11] the designation 'joint mediation' is more common. In all such mediations, responsibility is formally shared between equals.[12]

As for 'sequential' multiparty mediation, this occurs when single mediators execute deliberate 'hand-offs' at watersheds in the 'life cycle' of a conflict (rising, followed by falling, levels of violence) when different kinds of mediator appear to be more appropriate (Crocker et al., p. 10). This sort of mediation was seen in Haiti in the early 1990s. Here, responsibility for the mediation started with the Organization of American States (OAS), was then passed to the UN, and finally – when the threat of real force seemed necessary – came to rest with the United States (McDougall). It is important to stress that not all successive single mediations are examples of this species of 'multiparty mediation', and certainly not if they are random, unconnected, and separated by years.

The ideal mediator

Obviously, the attributes of the ideal mediator will vary according to the nature of the conflict with which it is called upon or aspires to deal. For example, the Holy See is in principle well suited to the mediation of a conflict between two Catholic states, provided the exertion of material power over them is not required. Small states may be appropriate as mediators between major powers since the latter will not feel threatened by them. The UN often seems best for the mediation of conflicts that appear intractable but are of relatively marginal concern to the major powers. Track two NGOs may well have a role in the settlement of a conflict in which at least one of the parties believes that track one intervention would give too much legitimacy to its rival, or in which the major powers would dearly like to see progress but, for one reason or another, cannot risk direct involvement themselves. As for the major powers themselves, and at the risk of appearing tautological, they are usually the most suitable to the mediation of conflicts that are amenable only to power.

It also seems likely that the ideal mediator may vary with the stage of the 'conflict cycle', as remarked in the discussion of 'sequential' multiparty mediation above, or with the stage of the mediation. It is, for example, a commonplace of analysis of this subject that track two diplomacy may have a key role in preparing the ground for a mediation, that is to say, in the prenegotiation stage, but that it must stand down in favour of the more muscular track one once the mediation is properly launched. This is an oversimplification, as the Oslo channel which produced the historic agreement between Israel and the PLO in September 1993 and other mediations have demonstrated (Abbas; Corbin; Heikal). Be that as it may, whatever the nature of the conflict or the stage that it has reached, all mediators should have certain common characteristics in addition to routine diplomatic skills, which include the ability to generate 'creative formulas' (Crocker, 1999, p. 243).

In the first place, all mediators should be perceived as impartial on the specific issues dividing the parties to a conflict. In the second, they should have influence, if not more effective power, relative to them. In the third, they should possess the ability to devote sustained attention to their dispute. And in the fourth place, all mediators should have a strong incentive to achieve a durable settlement.

Mediation, by definition, requires a third party that is impartial on the issue of the moment even if the parties to the conflict are not in general held in equal affection. However, it is still necessary to explain the advantages of impartiality. The key point is that impartiality enables the third party to be trusted by both parties. This is important for many reasons. Among these, it is important if the parties are to believe that the mediator will convey messages between them without distortion, that its reassurances about their mutual sincerity are well-founded, and that their confidences will be kept. It is also important if they are to believe that any compromises it proposes are of equal benefit to both, and that it will implement any guarantees if this is required by any defaulting on the settlement achieved – irrespective of which party is guilty. Of course, a third party with close ties to only one of the parties to the conflict may be attractive as a mediator to the party without such ties as a means of drawing the third party away from its traditional relationship to its rival. This may also strengthen the hand of such a mediator, once the mediation has started, by enabling it to play on the fears of desertion of the one and the hopes of consolidating a new friendship of the other (Touval, 1982). The fact remains, however, that the party that has not hitherto enjoyed friendly relations with the third party is only likely to accept it as a mediator on two conditions. First, it must believe that it will be impartial on the issue actually on the table and secondly that it is able to 'deliver' its traditional friend. This is why the Egyptians accepted American mediation with the Israelis in the late 1970s. They knew that Washington was bound by close ties to the government in Jerusalem but they also knew that its attitude on the 'occupied territories' was even-handed. It was disposed to see their return to the Arabs but in a manner that did not compromise Israel's security. In the event, then, the mediator must be impartial once the mediation has started. The notion of a 'biased intermediary' is a contradiction in terms.

What next of the value to the mediator of influence or more effective power relative to the parties? This may not be of great importance if the 'mediation' is in the good offices stage – provided 'ripeness' does not need engineering. However, it is clearly vital to a genuine mediation, when the parties will probably need cajoling to a settlement; it is even more so if it is necessary to provide guarantees against the consequences of any subsequent non-compliance with its terms. Mediator influence has many sources (Rubin, 1992; Crocker, 1999, pp. 240–1). It may, for example, derive from a record of past success and the lack of alternative mediators acceptable to both parties at a critical point, which seems to have helped Algeria during the Iran hostages negotiations. It may even derive from spiritual authority, as in the case of the Holy See. It seems most effective of all, however, when it is based on the ability to manipulate tangible rewards and sanctions, including increased or reduced levels of economic and military aid. Thus Jimmy Carter said that he was wary of 'buying peace' in the Camp David negotiations between Egypt and Israel – but he did.[13]

Whatever the source of the mediator's influence relative to the parties, it will also be increased to the extent that it is allied to that of other states or track two bodies pushing in the same direction.[14] For example, America's influence in the Angola/Namibia negotiations in 1988 was clearly enhanced by the support of a considerable list of states, among them the Soviet Union, Britain, Portugal, and the African Front Line States, together with members of the UN and OAU secretariats (Crocker, 1999, pp. 229–39). If, as in this case, the external patrons of the parties to the conflict are all on the list, the game is usually up. If a settlement is achieved against this background, it also increases the cost of any subsequent default by multiplying the ranks of those who will be directly affronted by it. It is important to add that in principle the same effect – maximizing power relative to the parties – can be achieved by multi-party mediation in the form of a contact group. However, in practice the disadvantages of this form of mediation tend to weaken it, as we shall see later.

Next, it is important that the mediator should be able to give continuous attention to a conflict, possibly over many years. The conflicts that require mediation are the most intractable, and intractable conflicts are not settled overnight. Continuous involvement produces familiarity with the problem and key personalities, enables relationships of personal trust to develop that reinforce calculations of interest, and fosters a routine that reduces the likelihood of false expectations being generated. It also makes possible procedural breakthroughs and even breakthroughs of principle that in turn make seizing a propitious moment for settlement that much easier. This is where track two diplomats and the secretariats of international organizations, notably the UN, tend to have the edge over states, especially in the mediation of disputes where major power interest is at most moderate. This applies even to stable political regimes like that of the United States. Such states may have foreign ministries capable of pursuing consistent policies over long periods but electoral cycles as well as a constantly changing international context tend to condemn mediation to being an episodic rather than a continuous affair (Quandt, ch. 1). This has been a marked feature of American mediation in the Middle East. It is fair to note, however, that Chester Crocker, the US assistant secretary of state for African affairs who successfully negotiated the Angola/Namibia Accords of December 1988, was able to devote the full period of both Reagan administrations to the task. Not surprisingly, Crocker himself emphasizes the value of continuity in his memoir of this negotiation (Crocker, 1992, pp. 468–70).

Finally, it is clear that the ideal mediator should have a strong incentive to obtain a settlement. The different motives of different kinds of mediators have already been discussed and it is clear that often these are sufficient to sustain a mediator through what often turns out to be a lengthy, trying and costly negotiation. Nevertheless, a successful mediation also increases the reputation of the mediator for diplomatic skill and political weight ('prestige'), at home as well as abroad. It is for this reason that the ideal mediator, while being able to rely on the support of 'friends', is also usually not one who shares formal responsibility for the mediation with them. The clear allocation of responsibility to one party alone is uniquely energizing. This is because not only will it take all the blame for failure but also all the credit for success. By contrast, where responsibility is formally divided, as in a contact group, individual third parties can pass on the blame for failure and will have to share the credit for any success. Their incentive to make settlement of the conflict a high priority is thereby reduced.[15] It is thus perhaps no accident that the real breakthroughs tend to come when one of the members of a contact group seizes the reins of the mediation itself and puts its prestige directly on the line. This is well illustrated by the success of American mediation in south-western Africa in the late 1980s subsequent to Washington's withdrawal from the Western Contact Group on Namibia (Berridge, 1989). It is also demonstrated by its even more spectacular success at

Dayton, Ohio, in November 1995 following President Clinton's decision to take the lead in Bosnian diplomacy from the Bosnia Contact Group (Holbrooke).

It will thus be clear that the attributes of the ideal mediator are one thing; the attributes of the ideal mediation are another. Single mediation, albeit assisted by 'friends', is better than simultaneous multiparty mediation. In some conflicts, for example that in Haiti already mentioned, the most effective mediation may be one conducted by an orchestrated sequence of different, single mediators – sequential multiparty mediation.

The ripe moment and whether there is such a thing as a premature mediation

Provided there is to hand an ideal mediator appropriate to a particular dispute, mediation is most likely to succeed in the circumstance in which any negotiation is most likely to succeed. This is when the antagonists have both arrived at the conclusion that they will probably be better off with a settlement than without one, when, in other words, the situation is 'ripe' for a settlement (Haass, 1988).[16] But does this mean that no move to launch a negotiation should be contemplated before this point is reached?

There is a view that any attempt to launch a mediation before the time is 'ripe' will not only fail but make matters worse. Failure is one thing, and in such circumstances this is not difficult to comprehend. By definition, at least one of the parties to the conflict will believe that it can get what it wants by other means, such as force, or that the passage of time will deal it a better hand in resumed talks. By contrast, why a 'premature' attempt at mediation should also be counter-productive is not self-evident, and is positively disputed by many scholars (Rubin, 1991). In fact, 'premature' mediation need not always exacerbate a conflict; it depends on the form that it takes and the goals that those bent on this course set themselves. If the former is low-key (track two, for example) and the latter modest, there is no reason to suppose that the situation will deteriorate when the negotiations stall and certainly not that it will become impossible of resolution. On the contrary, useful advances on procedure, in the building of trust, and even on broad principle may be made which will make seizing the opportunity that much easier when the time really is ripe for substantive negotiations (Crocker, 1992, p. 471). Besides, diagnosing 'ripe moments' is not exactly a scientific exercise and it is not always possible to tell if these circumstances exist until they are put to the test, that is, by negotiation.[17] The very fact that such a move is made can itself also affect the degree of 'ripeness' for settlement.

It remains true, however, that if a mediation launched in unpropitious circumstances is ambitious and conducted with much fanfare, and if in consequence it fails, then it can indeed be counter-productive. There are at least three reasons for this. In the first place, the leaders and domestic groups on which political support for negotiations rests will be at least temporarily discredited.[18] In the second, pessimism about reaching an agreement will be deepened where optimism is so important if the risks of restarting negotiations are to be taken; these include exploitation by the other side and charges of weakness, or even treason, by radical elements at home. In other words, the view that the conflict is intractable will be strengthened.[19] And in the third place, one or both of the parties to the conflict may take provocative measures in reaction to the failure of the negotiations (Haass, 1990, p. 139).

In any event, having secured the agreement of the parties – however reluctantly – to collaborate with its efforts, the mediator also needs to judge whether it is best to seek a 'comprehensive' solution to the dispute, or approach it in a 'step-by-step' manner. Since conflicts would not require mediation if they were not very deep, it is often best to adopt the latter approach. This emphasizes the need to build both trust and momentum by confining the initial negotiations to subjects of only limited political implications, such as the disengagement of military forces (Golan; Zartman and Berman, pp. 33–4). Besides this, the mediator needs to employ a judicious combination of carrots and sticks, together with deadlines and press manipulation in order to sustain diplomatic momentum (see Chapter 4). A fair share of luck is also needed. This is because a local incident can sour the atmosphere at a critical juncture while the eruption of a major international crisis can at best distract attention from the dispute in question and at worst seriously alter the calculation of interests on which one or more of the parties – including the mediator – had previously agreed to proceed. Recent successes in some of the most intractable conflicts – notably the Israel–PLO agreement in 1993 and the Bosnian peace settlement at Dayton, Ohio, two years later – show that mediation can produce handsome dividends.

The drawbacks of mediation and the lure of direct talks

The willingness to accept mediation is sometimes prompted by the need to secure guarantees of any settlement from the mediator, as has generally been the case in the Arab–Israeli conflict. In this event, the parties to a dispute will seek it even if in different circumstances they would have been prepared to negotiate without an intermediary. However, when the antagonists are major powers and when, as a result, it is extremely unlikely that any external guarantee of a settlement between them will be available, they have an incentive to dispense with the mediator or mediators as soon as possible. This is because, to return to the major theme of Touval's work, 'mediators, like brokers, are in it for profit', and some of this may be anticipated in the form of direct payment from the antagonists themselves, albeit generally in kind rather than in cash. It is well known, for example, that the American 'tilt' to Pakistan in its conflict with India in the early 1970s was in part precipitated by Nixon's indebtedness to Yahya Khan for acting as intermediary in the early approaches to Peking. Rewarding intermediaries in this manner, or simply enabling them to increase their prestige by acting in this role, may also be distasteful for another reason. Since the intermediary also has to have good contacts with one's enemy, dislike for the former may be only marginally less evident than hostility to the latter. This sort of consideration encouraged US Secretary of State John Foster Dulles to keep at arm's length the repeated offers to mediate between the United States and Communist China that were made by neutralist India in the mid-1950s.

But minimizing the rewards of intermediaries is not, of course, the only reason for dispensing with their services at the earliest moment decently possible. Using mediators inevitably causes delays, increases the number of foreigners who share one's secrets, and carries the risk that messages may be garbled in transmission. Furthermore, it usually brings into the negotiations an additional source of complaint about one's own 'reasonable' demands as well as a source of support in the diplomatic campaign against the wholly 'unreasonable' position of one's enemy, and how this will all work out is rarely predictable. Not surprisingly, Hersh records, apropos the budding Sino-American rapprochement, that as early as mid-1970 both Nixon and Kissinger were anxious 'to get rid of all the middlemen' (Hersh, 1983, p. 364; and Kissinger, 1979, pp. 722–3).

Summary

Mediation is the active search for a negotiated settlement to an international or intrastate conflict by an impartial third party. Mediators come in all shapes and sizes, as well as singly and in groups. The attributes of the ideal mediator vary with the nature of the conflict in question and sometimes with the stage reached by the conflict or the mediation itself. However, all mediators should be perceived as impartial once the mediation is in progress. They should also have influence if not more effective power relative to the parties, the ability to devote sustained attention to the dispute in question, and a strong incentive to achieve a durable settlement. This incentive will usually be the greater if one third party alone has sole responsibility for the mediation because this means that its prestige, as well as the more specific policy goals in which it is interested, will be at stake. Mediation is often needed and often accepted; but it is often refused as well, and, if accepted, sometimes discarded. The lure of direct talks, even at a high political price, is usually strong.

Notes

1 It is important to note, though, that non-recognition does not necessarily make mediation essential to communication between the parties concerned, as illustrated by the direct Sino-American contacts in the 1950s and 1960s (Berridge 1994, ch. 5).

2 It is sometimes said that the most successful 'mediations' are those in which the 'mediators' are partial to one side rather than impartial between them. I believe that this is a category error. Negotiations involving biased third parties certainly exist and are sometimes successful; they are just not mediations. This point is discussed further below.

3 This is by no means essential. In the final Iran hostages negotiation, the Americans shuttled between Washington and Algiers, the Algerians shuttled between Algiers, Tehran and Washington, and the Iranians stayed at home.

4 After Kissinger's secret visit to Peking in July 1971 Chou En-lai suggested to him that they should continue to use the Pakistani channel occasionally since there was a saying in China that 'one shouldn't break the bridge after crossing it' (Kissinger 1979, p. 745).

5 For example, in a memorandum of 29 April 1955, Robert Murphy, US deputy under-secretary of state, having noted that 'volunteer intermediaries [between the US and China] are not wanting', added that 'this might be profitable brokerage for them ... ' (*Foreign Relations of the United States*, p. 532).

6 This was especially good business for ambassadors in Istanbul, in the constant cycle of war and peacemaking between Sultan and Tsar and Sultan and Emperor.

7 However, it should be noted that supporters of the term 'multitrack diplomacy', popularized by Louise Diamond, now restrict the term 'track two' to NGOs dedicated to conflict prevention and resolution. Classes of organization for which this activity is just one aspect of their work, for example religious bodies and organs of the mass media, are thus described as 'track three', 'track four', and so on (states remain 'track one'). This trivializes the profound distinction between states and the rest and is a case of advocacy confusing understanding.

8 Strictly speaking – but only strictly speaking – this is not a mediating role since a protecting power acts for one party only. See Chapter 8.

9 This extremely useful directory is available free online at http://www. oneworld.org/euconflict/publicat/directin.htm

10 The late Sydney Bailey, author of the classic text on *The Procedure of the UN Security Council* (see 'References'), was a Quaker who was very active in this work (*The Times*, 11 January 1991).

11 This example is typical of current joint mediations: a joint effort between the UN and the regional organization with the closest interest in the dispute concerned. It was the model proposed by the UN Secretary-General in *An Agenda for Peace*, where he used the phrase 'complementary effort' to describe it (Boutros-Ghali, ch. vii). However, it is also not unusual still to find two major powers playing this role, for example the USA and the USSR at the conferences on the Arab–Israeli conflict at Geneva in December1973 and Madrid in November 1991.

12 It is a moot point as to whether a mediation formally charged to a single party but which is assisted by a group of 'friends' – 'herded', like cats, with difficulty – should also be described as an example of 'multiparty' mediation, as has been claimed (Crocker et al., pp. 9–10). Where the third party with the 'lead' in the negotiations is a small, track two body and one of the 'friends' is a major power, the label would seem appropriate. In the opposite situation it would not. In between, there are bound to be borderline cases. Resisting the excessively broad definition of multiparty mediation in *Herding Cats* is the excellent chapter on El Salvador by Alvaro de Soto.

13 With $3 billions in concessional loans in order to enable the Israelis to build new airfields in the Negev to compensate for the ones they would have to surrender in Sinai (Quandt, p. 241). As for Egypt, by 1980–81 (the year following signature of the Egypt–Israel Peace Treaty) Egypt was the top recipient of US official development assistance (Berridge, 1997, Table 7.2).

14 Track two diplomats now routinely acknowledge that their own efforts are most effective when coordinated with those of track one.

15 Contact groups can also invite 'forum shopping' by the parties to the conflict (Crocker et al., pp. 674–5).

16 Of course, ripeness itself can be engineered by a prospective mediator, especially if it is a major power and a party to the dispute is one of its clients or at least a state over which it has significant influence. This was part of Kissinger's approach to the Arab–Israeli conflict after the Yom Kippur War (Touval, 1982, pp. 228–38) and equally part of Crocker's strategy in south-western Africa (Berridge, 1989; Crocker, 1992, pp. 469–72; Crocker, 1999, pp. 213, 217).

17 This argument is not, as sometimes suggested, tautological, since ripe moments can be botched as well as missed altogether.

18 In Pruitt's language (though unfortunately he does not consider the question of premature negotiation), these would be 'perceived valid spokesmen' and the ' "bridge" people on both sides who have sufficient contact with and understanding of each other to spring into action when a period of motivational ripeness arrives' (Pruitt, 1997). See also the Introduction by Kriesberg (Kriesberg and Thorson, eds, 1991, p. 19).

19 The importance of optimism as a component of ripeness (or 'readiness') is persuasively emphasized by Pruitt (Pruitt, 1997) and Kriesberg (Kriesberg and Thorson, eds, 1991, p. 20).

Further reading

Abbas, Mahmoud ['Abu Mazen'], *Through Secret Channels – The Road to Oslo* (Garnet: Reading, 1995), esp. chs 6–8.

Bailey, Sydney D. and Sam Daws, *The Procedure of the UN Security Council*, 3rd edn (Clarendon Press: Oxford, 1998), ch. 3(1), 'Secretary-General'.

Bercovitch, J. (ed.), *Resolving International Conflicts: The Theory and Practice of Mediation* (Lynne Rienner: Boulder, Colorado, and London, 1996).

Bercovitch, Jacob and J. Z. Rubin (eds), *Mediation in International Relations* (Macmillan – now Palgrave: Basingstoke, 1992), ch. by Kelman [on track two].

Berman, Maureen R. and Joseph E. Johnson (eds), *Unofficial Diplomats* (Columbia University Press: New York, 1977).

Berridge, G. R., *Return to the UN: UN Diplomacy in Regional Conflicts* (Macmillan – now Palgrave: Basingstoke, 1991).

Berridge, G. R., *Talking to the Enemy: How States without 'Diplomatic Relations' Communicate* (Macmillan – now Palgrave: Basingstoke, 1994).

Bourantonis, D. and M. Evriviades (eds), *A United Nations for the Twenty-First Century* (Kluwer Law International: The Hague, London and Boston, 1996), esp. Part II.

Boutros-Ghali, B., *An Agenda for Peace: Preventive Diplomacy, Peacemaking and Peace-keeping* (United Nations: New York, 1992).

Brinkley, D., 'Jimmy Carter's modest quest for global peace', *Foreign Affairs*, Nov/ Dec. 1995, pp. 90–100.

Carnegie Commission on Preventing Deadly Conflict, *Preventing Deadly Conflict: Final Report* (1997), www.ccpdc.org/pubs/rept97/toc.html

Christopher, W. and others (1985), *American Hostages in Iran: The Conduct of a Crisis* (Yale University Press: New Haven and London).

Cohen, Herman J., *Intervening in Africa: Superpower Peacemaking in a Troubled Continent* (Macmillan – now Palgrave: Basingstoke, 2000).

Corbin, Jane, *Gaza First: The Secret Norway Channel to Peace Between Israel and the PLO* (Bloomsbury: London, 1994).

Crocker, C. A., *High Noon in Southern Africa: Making Peace in a Rough Neighbourhood* (Norton: New York and London, 1992).

Crocker, C. A., Fen Osler Hampson, and Pamela Aall (eds), *Herding Cats: Multiparty Mediation in a Complex World* (US Institute of Peace Press: Washington, DC, 1999).

Diamond, Louise and John McDonald, *Multi-Track Diplomacy: A Systems Approach to Peace* (Kumarian Press: West, Hartford, Connecticut, 1996).

European Centre for Conflict Prevention, *Directory of Conflict Prevention Organisations*, http://www.oneworld.org/euconflict/publicat/directin.htm

European Centre for Conflict Prevention, *People Building Peace*, http://www.oneworld.org/euconflict/pbp/

Druckman, D. and C. Mitchell (eds), *Flexibility in International Negotiation and Mediation* (Sage: London, 1995), chs by Botes and Mitchell, and Touval.

Fisher, R. J., 'The third party consultant', *Journal of Conflict Resolution*, 16(1), 1972, pp. 67–94.

Gore-Booth, Lord (ed.), *Satow's Guide to Diplomatic Practice*, 5th edn (Longman: London, 1979), pp. 351ff.

Heikal, Mohamed, *Secret Channels* (HarperCollins: London, 1996), esp. chs 11–15.

Holbrooke, Richard, *To End a War* (Random House: New York, 1998).

Hume, Cameron, *Ending Mozambique's War: The Role of Mediation and Good Offices* (US Institute of Peace Press: Washington, DC, 1994).

Jones, Deiniol L., *Cosmopolitan Mediation? Conflict Resolution and the Oslo Accords* (Manchester University Press: Manchester, 1999).

Kriesberg, L. and S. T. Thorson (eds), *Timing the De-Escalation of International Conflicts* (Syracuse University Press: Syracuse, New York, 1991).

Lindsley, L., 'The Beagle Channel settlement: Vatican mediation resolves a century-old dispute', *Journal of Church and State*, vol. 29, no. 3, 1987.

Luard, Evan, *The United Nations: How it works and what it does*, rev. by Derek Heater (Macmillan – now Palgrave: Basingstoke, 1994).

Owen, David, *Balkan Odyssey* (Indigo: London, 1996).

Princen, T., *Intermediaries in International Conflict* (Princeton University Press: Princeton, New Jersey, 1992).

Pruitt, D. (1997), 'Ripeness theory and the Oslo talks', *International Negotiation*, vol. 2, no. 2.

Quandt, W. B., *Camp David: Peacemaking and Politics* (Brookings Institution: Washington DC, 1986).

Roberts, Adam and B. Kingsbury (eds), *United Nations, Divided World*, 2nd edn (Clarendon Press: Oxford, 1993), chs 5 and 6.

Rouhana, N. and H. C. Kelman, 'Promoting joint thinking in international conflicts', *Journal of Social Issues*, 50(1), 1994, pp. 157–78.

Rubin, Barry, et al (eds), *From War to Peace: Arab–Israeli relations, 1973–1993* (Sussex Academic Press: Brighton, 1994), esp. Parts I and III.

Stedman, Stephen J., *Peacemaking in Civil War: International Mediation in Zimbabwe, 1974–80* (Lynne Rienner: Boulder, Colorado, and London, 1990).

Touval, S., *The Peace Brokers: Mediators in the Arab–Israeli Conflict, 1948–1979* (Princeton University Press: Princeton, New Jersey, 1982).

Touval, Saadia and I. William Zartman (eds), *International Mediation in Theory and Practice* (Westview: Boulder, Colorado, and London, 1985), esp. chs by Sick and Thornton.

Watkins, Michael and K. Lundberg, 'Getting to the table in Oslo: driving forces and channel factors', *Negotiation Journal*, vol. 14, no. 2, 1998, pp. 1156–136.

Zartman, I. W. and S. Touval (1985), 'International mediation: conflict resolution and power politics', *Journal of Social Issues*, vol. 41, no. 2, pp. 27–45.

Track Two on the Web

This is a subject on which there is a wealth of information and ideas on the world wide web. Key 'track two diplomacy' into www.google.com, for example, and you will find over thirty thousand sites. These are mainly concerned with examples of track two diplomacy or institutes engaged in it, like the Carter Center in Georgia (www.cartercenter.org/)

Conclusion

Negotiation is the most important function of diplomacy because, as stressed in the Introduction to Part I, the world diplomatic system now encompasses considerably more than the work of resident missions. And negotiation becomes more and more the operational focus of diplomacy as we move into the realms of multilateral diplomacy, summitry, and, above all, into that other growth sector of the world diplomatic system – mediation. Furthermore, it is the process of negotiation that grapples directly with the most threatening problems, whether they are economic dislocation, environmental catastrophe, sporadic ethnic violence, or outright war. It is because negotiation is the most important function of diplomacy broadly conceived that the first part of this book was dedicated to it.

Most negotiations proceed through three stages: prenegotiations, the formula stage, and the details stage. In prenegotiations it is necessary to agree on the need to negotiate, the agenda, and procedural questions such as the venue of the talks. In prenegotiations between recently or still warring parties these matters are often so difficult to conclude that it is testimony not only to the pressure generated by a 'hurting stalemate' but also to the sheer professionalism of modern diplomacy that the substantive stages of negotiations are ever reached at all. In the formula stage the broad principles of a settlement are agreed and in the details stage these are fleshed out. The first and last stages are generally the most difficult, though it would seem (this is an area in which more research needs to be done) that this varies significantly with the kind of negotiation and the kind of parties involved. If the momentum of a negotiation falters, even though the parties remain keen to press on, deadlines and other techniques (also generally ignored by modern research) may be employed with some reasonable hope of reviving it. If the momentum is maintained, or – if lost – regained, and if agreement is finally reached, it still needs to be 'packaged'. Saving face is often an important consideration here and how this should be achieved is not always straightforward. As a result, the presentation of any agreement itself provides considerable scope for negotiation.

While negotiation is the most important function of diplomacy, it is not of course the only one. As a result, Part II of this book expanded its focus to embrace its other activities, while employing as its organizing principle the *different channels* through which all of the functions of diplomacy are pursued.

Direct telecommunication between governments is now a very important channel for the conduct of diplomacy, both in crises and in more normal times. Nevertheless, even some of its most enthusiastic supporters acknowledge that its limitations remain considerable, especially in negotiations between hostile states. As for bilateral diplomacy via the resident mission, this has survived the communications revolution chiefly because it remains an excellent means by which to support if not lead in the execution of key diplomatic functions. These include lobbying, commercial work, and consular activities, as well as negotiation. Furthermore, the communications revolution has made the resident mission both more responsive and more able to make inputs into policy-making at home. Bilateral diplomacy has also proved inventive in its unconventional dimension, which in itself is powerful evidence of its indispensability.

What of multilateral diplomacy? This blossomed in the twentieth century under the press of events, the steady increase in the number of states and, among other things, the growing popularity of the liberal-democratic notion that power should rest on consent. The inter-war League of Nations and the post-war United Nations are the most eloquent testimonies to the twentieth century faith in this mode of diplomacy. Over recent decades, however, this faith has been severely tested and there has been evidence of a crisis of multilateralism. Third world states have expressed disillusionment with its results, especially in the economic sphere; the United States, finally reacting savagely to years of having to finance programmes to which it was opposed, began to withhold funds from the UN system; and the number of intergovernmental organizations began to drop. Nevertheless, there remains little doubt that multilateral diplomacy, which is so valuable when urgent attention has to be given by many parties to a particular question, and when it is important to advertise the fact that this is being done, is here to stay. What has helped to guarantee this is the now widespread acceptance that important decisions must be based on consensus.

Unlike the position in respect to multilateral diplomacy, there seems to be no prospect of the enthusiasm for summitry being deflated, despite its well-known drawbacks. The involvement of political leaders in diplomacy tends too often to inject sloppiness where there should be precision, publicity where there should be confidentiality, ignorance where there should be intimate acquaintance with detail, and personal considerations where there should only be objective consideration of the requirements of the national interest. Nevertheless, summits – especially serial summits – can make a broad contribution to diplomacy as well, not least because of their ability to revive the momentum of a flagging negotiation.

Mediation is as popular as summitry, no doubt because it is often one and the same thing. Whether conducted at or below the summit, it is a distinctive form of multilateral diplomacy, involving the active attempt of an impartial third party to cajole rivals to a settlement of their differences. Events in Africa, the Middle East, the Balkans, and elsewhere, demonstrate that it is a vital feature of the world diplomatic system.

There is room for optimism about the future of diplomacy. What are the reasons for making this statement? For one thing, 'open diplomacy', always a contradiction in terms, is a dead slogan. For another, there is at last broad understanding that majority voting in multilateral meetings is incompatible with a radically unequal distribution of power. There is also now a more accurate appreciation of the enduring value of resident missions for those states that can afford them, and the legal regime under which these missions function has, under the Vienna Convention on Diplomatic Relations, been firmly secured since 1961. Finally, the revolution in telecommunications is making diplomacy a vastly more flexible instrument. It is at least in part against this background that the new states that have emerged from the former Soviet Union have lost no time in creating their own diplomatic services, and that severing diplomatic relations is no longer the crisis reflex that it was in the 1960s and 1970s.

It is as well that there are grounds for optimism about the future of diplomacy because while power remains dispersed between states – while there remains, in other words, a states-system – international diplomacy, bilateral or multilateral, direct or indirect, at the summit or below, remains essential. Only this activity can produce the enormous advantages obtainable from the cooperative pursuit of common interests and prevent violence from being employed to settle remaining arguments over conflicting ones. When violence breaks out nevertheless, diplomacy remains essential if the worst excesses are to be limited and if, in addition, the ground is to be prepared against the inevitable day of exhaustion and revised ambition.

References

Abbas, Mahmoud ['Abu Mazen'] (1995), *Through Secret Channels – The Road to Oslo* (Garnet: Reading)

Acheson, D. (1969), *Present at the Creation: My Years in the State Department* (Norton: New York)

Adair, E. R. (1929), *The Exterritoriality of Ambassadors in the Sixteenth and Seventeenth Centuries* (Longman: London)

Adcock, Sir F. and D. J. Mosley (1975), *Diplomacy in Ancient Greece* (Thames & Hudson: London)

Adelman, K. L. (1989), *The Great Universal Embrace: Arms Summitry – A Skeptic's View* (Simon & Schuster: New York)

Ahmad, Z. H. (1999), 'Malaysia', in B. Hocking (ed.), *Foreign Ministries: Change and Adaptation* (Macmillan – now Palgrave: Basingstoke)

Akokpari, J. (1998), 'Globalization, the emerging market economy and the Ghanain Foreign Ministry', *International Insights*, vol. 14, Special Issue 1998, pp. 87–98

Algosaibi, G. A. (1999), *Yes, (Saudi) Minister! A Life in Administration* (London Centre of Arab Studies)

Ambrose, S. (1989), *Nixon, Volume Two: The Triumph of a Politician, 1962–1972* (Simon & Schuster: London and New York)

Anderson, M. S. (1993), *The Rise of Modern Diplomacy* (Longman: London and New York)

Armstrong, D. (1982), *The Rise of the International Organization: A Short History* (Macmillan – now Palgrave: Basingstoke)

Augusta Chronicle Online (1999), 'Cold War-era hot line still in place', 26 July

Aurisch, K. L. (1989), 'The art of preparing a multilateral conference', *Negotiation Journal*, vol. 5, no. 3

Bailey, S. D. and S. Daws (1998), *The Procedure of the UN Security Council*, 3rd edn (Clarendon Press: Oxford)

Baldi, S. (2000), 'The internet for international political and social protest: the case of Seattle', *Research paper no. 3*, April (Ministero degli Affari Esteri, Unita' di Analisie Programmazione: Roma)

Ball, G. (1976), *Diplomacy for a Crowded World* (Bodley Head: London)

Ball, G. (1982), *The Past has another Pattern* (Norton: New York)

Barber, J. and J. Barratt (1990), *South Africa's Foreign Policy: The Search for Status and Security, 1945–1988* (Cambridge University Press: Cambridge)

Bergin, P. E. (1999), 'Bureau of the month: Diplomatic Security Service', *State Magazine*, November

Bergus, D. C. (1990), 'U.S. diplomacy under the flag of Spain, Cairo, 1967–74', in D. D. Newsom (ed.), *Diplomacy Under a Foreign Flag* (Hurst: London; St. Martin's Press – now Palgrave: New York)

Berridge, G. R. (1987), *The Politics of the South Africa Run: European Shipping and Pretoria* (Clarendon Press: Oxford)

Berridge, G. R. (1989), 'Diplomacy and the Angola/Namibia Accords', *International Affairs*, vol. 65, no. 3

Berridge, G. R. (1991), *Return to the UN: UN Diplomacy in Regional Conflicts* (Macmillan – now Palgrave: Basingstoke)

Berridge, G. R. (1992a), *South Africa, the Colonial Powers and 'African Defence': The Rise and Fall of the White Entente, 1948–60* (Macmillan – now Palgrave: Basingstoke)

Berridge, G. R. (1992b), 'The Cyprus negotiations: divided responsibilty and other problems', *Leicester Discussion Papers in Politics*, no. P92/7

Berridge, G. R. (1994), *Talking to the Enemy: How States without 'Diplomatic Relations' Communicate* (Macmillan – now Palgrave: Basingstoke)

Berridge, G. R. (1996), 'Funeral summits', in David H. Dunn (ed.), *Diplomacy at the Highest Level: The Evolution of International Summitry* (Macmillan – now Palgrave: Basingstoke)

Berridge, G. R. (1997), *International Politics: States, Power and Conflict since 1945*, 3rd edn (Prentice Hall/Harvester Wheatsheaf: Hemel Hempstead)

Berridge, G. R. and N. Gallo (1999), 'The role of the diplomatic corps: the US–North Korea talks in Beijing, 1988–94', in J. Melissen (ed.), *Innovation in Diplomatic Practice* (Macmillan – now Palgrave: Basingstoke)

Berridge, G. R. and A. James (2001), *A Dictionary of Diplomacy* (Palgrave: Basingstoke)

Berridge, G. R. and A. Jennings (eds) (1985), *Diplomacy at the UN* (Macmillan – now Palgrave: London)

Berridge, G. R., Maurice Keens-Soper, and T. G. Otte (2001), *Diplomatic Theory from Machiavelli to Kissinger* (Palgrave: Basingstoke)

Binnendijk, H. (ed.) (1987), *National Negotiating Styles* (Center for the Study of Foreign Affairs, Foreign Service Institute, US Department of State: Washington, DC)

Blake, J. J. (1990), 'Pragmatic diplomacy: the origins and use of the protecting power', in D. D. Newsom (ed.), *Diplomacy Under a Foreign Flag* (Hurst: London; St. Martin's Press – now Palgrave: New York)

Blancké, W. W. (1969), *The Foreign Service of the United States* (Praeger: New York)

Blumay, C. and H. Edwards (1992), *The Dark Side of Power* (Simon & Schuster: New York)

Boutros-Ghali, B. (1992), *An Agenda for Peace: Preventive Diplomacy, Peacemaking and Peacekeeping* (United Nations: New York)

Bower, D. (1994), 'Summit and symbol: Franco-German relations and diplomacy at the top', unpubl. dissertation (University of Leicester)

Bozeman, A. D. (1994), *Politics and Culture in International History: From the Ancient Near East to the Opening of the Modern Age*, 2nd edn (Transaction: New Brunswick and London)

Bradshaw, K. and D. Pring (1973), *Parliament and Congress* (Quartet: London)

Brown, J. (1988), 'Diplomatic immunity – state practice under the Vienna Convention', *International and Comparative Law Quarterly*, vol. 37

Brzezinski, Z. (1983), *Power and Principle: Memoirs of the National Security Adviser 1977–1981* (Farrar, Straus, Giroux: New York)

Bull, H. (1977), *The Anarchical Society: A Study of Order in World Politics* (Macmillan – now Palgrave: Basingstoke)

Bulmer, S. and W. Wessels (1987), *The European Council: Decision-making in European Politics* (Macmillan – now Palgrave: Basingstoke)

Buzan, B. (1981), 'Negotiating by consensus: developments in technique at the United Nations Conference on the Law of the Sea', *American Journal of International Law*, vol. 72, no. 2

Cahier, P. (1969), 'Vienna Convention on Diplomatic Relations', *International Conciliation*. no. 571

Callaghan, J. (1987), *Time and Chance* (Collins: London)

Callières, F. de (1994), *The Art of Diplomacy*, ed. by H. M. A. Keens-Soper and K. Schweizer (University Press of America: Lanham, New York and London)

Carnegie Commission on Preventing Deadly Conflict, *Preventing Deadly Conflict: Final Report* (1997), www.ccpdc.org/pubs/rept97/toc.html

Carter, J. (1982), *Keeping Faith: Memoirs of a President* (Bantam: New York)

Cecil, A. (1923), 'The Foreign Office', in Sir A. W. Ward and G. P. Gooch (eds), *The Cambridge History of British Foreign Policy, 1783–1919, vol. 3, 1866–1919* (Cambridge University Press: Cambridge)

Central Policy Review Staff (1977), *Review of Overseas Representation* ['The Berrill Report'] (HMSO: London)

Clapham, C. (ed.) (1978), *Foreign Policy Making in Developing States: A comparative approach* (Saxon House: Farnborough)

Cohen, R. (1987), *Theatre of Power: The Art of Diplomatic Signalling* (Longman: London and New York)

Cohen, R. (1997), *Negotiating across Cultures: International Communication in an Interdependent World*, rev. edn (US Institute of Peace Press: Washington, DC)

Cohen, R. and R. Westbrook (eds), *Amarna Diplomacy: The Beginnings of International Relations* (Johns Hopkins University Press: Baltimore)

Coles, J. (2000), *Making Foreign Policy: A Certain Idea of Britain* (Murray: London)

Corbin, Jane (1994), *Gaza First: The Secret Norway Channel to Peace between Israel and the PLO* (Bloomsbury Publ.: London)

Cradock, P. (1994), *Experiences of China* (Murray: London)

Crocker, C. A. (1992), *High Noon in Southern Africa: Making Peace in a Rough Neighbourhood* (Norton: New York and London)

Crocker, C. A. (1999), 'Peacemaking in Southern Africa: The Namibia–Angola settlement of 1988', in Crocker et al., *Herding Cats: Multiparty Mediation in a Complex World* (United States Institute of Peace Press: Washington, DC)

Crocker, C. A. et al. (eds) (1999), *Herding Cats: Multiparty Mediation in a Complex World* (United States Institute of Peace Press: Washington, DC)

Cross, C. T. (1999), *Born a Foreigner: A Memoir of the American Presence in Asia* (Rowman & Littlefield: Lanham, Maryland)

De Magalhães, J. C. (1988), trsl. by B. F. Pereira, *The Pure Concept of Diplomacy* (Greenwood: New York)

Denza, E. (1976), *Diplomatic Law: Commentary on the Vienna Convention on Diplomatic Relations* (Oceana: Dobbs Ferry, New York. British Institute of International and Comparative Law: London)

Denza, E. (1998), *Diplomatic Law: A Commentary on the Vienna Convention on Diplomatic Relations*, 2nd edn (Clarendon Press: Oxford)

De Soto, A. (1999), 'Ending violent conflict in El Salvador', in Crocker, C. A., et al. (eds), *Herding Cats: Multiparty Mediation in a Complex World* (United States Institute of Peace Press: Washington, DC)

Detmold, C. E., trsl. and ed. (1882), *The Historical, Political, and Diplomatic Writings of Niccolo Machiavelli*, vols. 3 and 4 (Osgood: Boston)

Dickie, J. (1992), *Inside the Foreign Office* (Chapman & Hall: London)

Dimbleby, D. and D. Reynolds (1988), *An Ocean Apart: The Relationship between Britain and America in the Twentieth Century* (Hodder & Stoughton: London)

Donelan, M. (1969), 'The trade of diplomacy', *International Affairs*, vol. 45, no. 4

Ducci, R. (1980), 'Bidding a Fond Farewell to The Career', *The Times*, 14 January

Dunn, D. H. (ed.) (1996), *Diplomacy at the Highest Level: The Evolution of International Summitry* (Macmillan – now Palgrave: Basingstoke)

Eagleton, W. L., Jr. (1990), 'Evolution of the U.S. Interests Sections in Algiers and Baghdad', in D. D. Newsom (ed.), *Diplomacy Under a Foreign Flag* (Hurst: London; St. Martin's Press – now Palgrave: New York)

Eban, A. (1977), *Abba Eban: An Autobiography* (Random House: New York)

Eban, A. (1983), *The New Diplomacy: International Affairs in the Modern Age* (Weidenfeld & Nicolson: London)

Edwards, R. D. (1994), *True Brits: Inside the Foreign Office* (BBC Books: London)

Eubank, K. (1966), *The Summit Conferences, 1919–1960* (University of Oklahoma Press: Norman, Oklahoma)

Faber, R. (2000), *A Chain of Cities: Diplomacy at the End of Empire* (Radcliffe Press: London and New York)

Far Eastern Economic Review (1989), 12 January

Fennessy, J. G. (1976), 'The 1975 Convention on the Representation of States in their Relations with International Organizations of a Universal Character', *American Journal of International Law*, vol. 70, no. 1

Fleming, P. (1959), *The Siege at Peking* (Hart-Davis: London).

Foreign Relations of the United States, 1955–1957, Vol. II, China (1986), (US Government Printing Office: Washington DC)

Franck, T. M. and E. Weisband (1979), *Foreign Policy by Congress* (Oxford University Press: New York and Oxford)

Franklin, W. M. (1947), *Protection of Foreign Interests: a study in diplomatic and consular practice* (US Government Printing Office: Washington DC)

Geldenhuys, D. (1984), *The Diplomacy of Isolation: South African Foreign Policy Making* (Macmillan: Johannesburg)

Gilbert, F. (1953), 'Two British Ambassadors: Perth and Henderson', in G. A. Craig and F. Gilbert (eds), *The Diplomats, 1919–1939* (Princeton University Press: Princeton, New Jersey)

Glennon, M. J. (1983), 'The Senate role in treaty ratification', *American Journal of International Law*, vol. 77

Global Policy Forum (2001), *Security Council Reform: Crucial Documents*, http://www.globalpolicy.org/security/reform/

Golan, M. (1976), *The Secret Conversations of Henry Kissinger: Step-by-Step Diplomacy in the Middle East* (Bantam: New York)

Goldstein, E. (1996), 'The origins of summit diplomacy', in D. H. Dunn (ed.), *Diplomacy at the Highest Level: The Evolution of International Summitry* (Macmillan – now Palgrave: Basingstoke)

Gore-Booth, P. (1974), *With Great Truth and Respect* (Constable: London)

Gore-Booth, Lord (ed.) (1979), *Satow's Guide to Diplomatic Practice*, 5th edn (Longman: London and New York)

Gotlieb, A. (1991), *I'll be with you in a minute, Mr. Ambassador: The education of a Canadian diplomat in Washington* (University of Toronto Press: Toronto)

Grenville, J. A. S. and B. Wasserstein (1987), *The Major International Treaties since 1945: A history and guide with texts* (Methuen: London and New York)

Haass, R. N. (1988), 'Ripeness and the settlement of international disputes', *Survival*, May/June

Haass, R. N. (1990), *Conflicts Unending: The United States and regional disputes* (New Haven, Connecticut: Yale University Press.

Hale, J. B. (1957), 'International relations in the West: diplomacy and war', in Potter, G. R. (ed.), *The New Cambridge Modern History*, I (Cambridge University Press: Cambridge)

Hall, R. (1987), *My Life with Tiny: A Biography of Tiny Rowland* (Faber: London)

Hall, R. (1992), 'Private diplomats: Tiny in Africa', *The Economist*, 26 September

Hamilton, K. and R. Langhorne (1995), *The Practice of Diplomacy: Its evolution, theory and administration* (Routledge: London and New York)

Hammer, A. with N. Lyndon (1987), *Hammer: Witness to History* (Simon & Schuster: London)

Hankey, Lord (1946), *Diplomacy by Conference: Studies in Public Affairs, 1920–1946* (Benn: London)

Harahan, J. P. (1993), *On-Site Inspections Under the INF Treaty, A History of the On-Site Inspection Agency and Treaty Implementation, 1988–1991* (Government Printing Office: Washington DC), repr. at
http://www.fas.org/nuke/control/inf/infbook/ch3b.html

Hardy, M. (1968), *Modern Diplomatic Law* (Manchester University Press: Manchester. Oceana, Dobbs Ferry, New York)

Harris, S. (1999), 'Australia', in B. Hocking (ed.), *Foreign Ministries: Change and adaptation* (Macmillan – now Palgrave: Basingstoke)

Harrison, S. (1988), 'Inside the Afghan talks', *Foreign Policy*, Fall

Hayter, Sir W. (1960), *The Diplomacy of the Great Powers* (Hamilton: London)

Heikal, M. (1996), *Secret Channels* (HarperCollins: London)

Henderson, N. (1984), *The Private Office* (Weidenfeld & Nicolson: London)

Henderson, N. (1994), *Mandarin: The Diaries of an Ambassador, 1969–1982* (Weidenfeld & Nicolson: London)

Henkin, L. (1979), *How Nations Behave: Law and Foreign Policy*, 2nd edn (Columbia University Press: New York)

Herman, M. (1996), *Intelligence Power in Peace and War* (Cambridge University Press: Cambridge)

Herman, M. (1998), 'Diplomacy and intelligence', *Diplomacy & Statecraft*, vol. 9, no. 2, July

Hersh, S. M. (1983), *Kissinger: The Price of Power* (Faber: London)

Hersh, S. M. (1991), *The Samson Option: Israel, America and the Bomb* (Faber: London and Boston)

Herz, F. M. (ed.) (1983), *The Consular Dimension of Diplomacy* (Institute for the Study of Diplomacy: Washington DC)

Hocking, B. (1999), 'Introduction. Foreign ministries: redefining the gatekeeper role', in B. Hocking (ed.), *Foreign Ministries: Change and adaptation* (Macmillan – now Palgrave: Basingstoke)

Hoffmann, S. (1978), *Primacy or World Order: American Foreign Policy since the Cold War* (McGraw-Hill: New York)

Holbrooke, R. (1998), *To End a War* (Random House: New York)

Horn, D. B. (1961), *The British Diplomatic Service 1689–1789* (Clarendon Press: Oxford)

Hume, Cameron (1994), *Ending Mozambique's War: The Role of Mediation and Good Offices* (United States Institute of Peace Press: Washington, DC)

Hunter, J. (1987), *Israeli Foreign Policy: South Africa and Central America* (Spokesman: Nottingham)

Hurd, D. (1997), *The Search for Peace* (Warner Books: London).

The implications of establishing reciprocal interests sections with Vietnam (1989). Hearing before the Subcommittee on Asian and Pacific Affairs of the Committee on Foreign Affairs, House of Representatives, 28 July 1988 (US Government Printing Office: Washington DC)

International Legal Materials (1981), vol. 20, pp. 224ff

Jackson, G. (1981), *Concorde Diplomacy: The Ambassador's Role in the World Today* (Hamilton: London)

James, A. M. (1980), 'Diplomacy and international society', *International Relations*, vol. 6, no. 6

James, A. M. (1992), 'Diplomatic relations and contacts', *The British Yearbook of International Law 1991* (Clarendon Press: Oxford), pp. 347–87

Jenkins, R. (1989), *European Diary, 1977–1981* (Collins: London)

Jenks, C. W. (1965), 'Unanimity, the veto, weighted voting, special and simple majorities and consensus as modes of decision in international organisations', *Cambridge Essays in International Law: Essays in honour of Lord McNair* (Stevens: London; Oceana: Dobbs Ferry, New York)

Johnson, L. K. (1984), *The Making of International Agreements: Congress confronts the Executive* (New York University Press: New York and London)

Kaiser, P. M. (1992), *Journeying Far and Wide: A Political and Diplomatic Memoir* (Scribner's: New York)

Kampfner, J. (1999), *Robin Cook* (Phoenix: London)

Kear, S. (1999), 'The British Consulate-General in Hanoi, 1954–73', *Diplomacy and Statecraft*, vol. 10(1), March, pp. 215–39

Keeley, R. V. (1995), 'Crisis avoidance: shutting down Embassy Kampala, 1973', in J. G. Sullivan (ed.), *Embassies Under Siege* (Brassey's for the Institute for the Study of Diplomacy: Washington DC)

Keeley, R. V. (ed.) (2000), *First Line of Defense: Ambassadors, Embassies and American Interests Abroad* (American Academy of Diplomacy: Washington, DC)

Keens-Soper, M. (1985), 'The General Assembly re-considered', in Berridge, G. R. and A. Jennings (eds), *Diplomacy at the UN* (Macmillan – now Palgrave: Basingstoke)

Kennan, G. F. (1967), *Memoirs, 1925–1950* (Hutchinson: London)

Kerley, E. L. (1962), 'Some aspects of the Vienna Conference on Diplomatic Intercourse and Immunities', *American Journal of International Law*, vol. 56

Kirton, J. J. (1989), 'The significance of the Seven Power Summit', in Hajnal, P. I. (ed.), *The Seven Power Summit: Documents from the Summits of the Industrialized Countries 1975–1989* (Kraus: Millwood, New York)

Kirton, J. J. (1991), 'The significance of the Houston Summit', in Hajnal, P. I. (ed.), *The Seven Power Summit: Documents from the Summits of the Industrialized Countries. Supplement: Documents from the 1990 Summit* (Kraus: Millwood, New York)

Kissinger, H. A. (1979), *The White House Years* (Weidenfeld & Nicolson and Michael Joseph: London)

Kissinger, H. A. (1982), *Years of Upheaval* (Weidenfeld & Nicolson and Michael Joseph: London)

The Kissinger Transcripts: Notes and Excerpts (1999), http://www.gwu.edu/nsarchiv/nsa/publications/DOC-readers/kissinger/notes.htm

Klieman, A. (1988), *Statecraft in the Dark: Israel's Practice of Quiet Diplomacy* (Jaffee Center for International Studies: Tel Aviv)

Kornienko, G. M. (1994), *The Cold War: Testimony of a Participant* (International Relations: Moscow), translated extract: 'A "Missed Opportunity" ... with introduction by Mark Garrison (Cold War International History Project: Woodrow Wilson International Center for Scholars), http://cwihp.si.edu/cwihplib.ns

Kriesberg, L. and S. T. Thorson (eds) (1991), *Timing the De-escalation of International Conflicts* (Syracuse University Press: Syracuse, New York)

Lakoff, G. and M. Johnson (1980), *Metaphors We Live By* (University of Chicago Press: Chicago and London)

Langhorne, R. (1981), 'The development of international conferences, 1648–1830', in *Studies in History and Politics*, vol. 11, part 2

Langhorne, R. (1992), 'The regulation of diplomatic practice: the beginnings to the Vienna Convention on Diplomatic Relations, 1961', *Review of International Studies* vol. 18, no. 1

Langhorne, R. and W. Wallace (1999), 'Diplomacy towards the 21st century', in B. Hocking (ed.), *Foreign Ministries: Change and adaptation* (Macmillan – now Palgrave: Basingstoke)

Lawford, V. (1963), *Bound for Diplomacy* (Murray: London)

Lindsley, L. (1987), 'The Beagle Channel settlement: Vatican mediation resolves a century-old dispute', *Journal of Church and State*, vol. 29, no. 3

Liverani, M. (2001), *International Relations in the Ancient Near East, 1600–1100 BC* (Palgrave: Basingstoke)

Loeffler, J. C. (1998), *The Architecture of Diplomacy: Building America's Embassies* (Princeton Architectural Press: New York)

Lowe, V. (1990), 'Diplomatic law: protecting powers', *International and Comparative Law Quarterly*, 39(2), April

Luard, E. (1994), *The United Nations: How It Works and What It Does*, 2nd edn rev. by D. Heater (Macmillan – now Palgrave: Basingstoke)

Lukacs, Y. (ed.) (1992), *The Israeli–Palestinian Conflict: A Documentary Record* (Cambridge University Press: Cambridge)

McDougall, B. (1999), 'Haiti: Canada's role in the OAS', in Crocker et al., *Herding Cats: Multiparty Mediation in a Complex World* (United States Institute of Peace Press: Washington DC)

Mattingly, G. (1965), *Renaissance Diplomacy* (Penguin: Harmondsworth)

May, E. R. (1994), 'The news media and diplomacy', in G. A. Craig and F. L. Loewenheim (eds), *The Diplomats 1939–1979* (Princeton University Press: Princeton, New Jersey)

Meerts, P. (1999), 'The changing nature of diplomatic negotiation', in J. Melissen (ed.), *Innovation in Diplomatic Practice* (Macmillan – now Palgrave: Basingstoke)

Meier, S. A. (1988), *The Messenger in the Ancient Semitic World* (Scholars Press: Atlanta)

Merillat, H. C. L. (ed.) (1964), *Legal Advisers and Foreign Affairs* (Oceana: Dobbs Ferry, New York)

Miles, D. (2000), 'Diplomatic couriers: on the road, from Rangoon to Russia and back!' *State Magazine*, February-March, http://www.state.gov/www/publications/statemag/statemag-feb2000/feature1.html

Monroe, E. (1963), *Britain's Moment in the Middle East, 1914–1956* (Methuen: London)

Montgomery, K. (2000), 'The Office of Casualty Assistance: a recommendation becomes a reality', *State Magazine*, September, http://www.state.gov/www/publications/statemag/statemag-sept2000/bom.html

Morgenthau, H. J. (1978), *Politics Among Nations: The Struggle for Power and Peace*, 5th edn (Knopf: New York)

Moser, M. J. and Y. W. -C. Moser (1993), *Foreigners within the Gates: The Legations at Peking* (Oxford University Press: Hong Kong, Oxford and New York)

Naff, Thomas (1963), 'Reform and the conduct of Ottoman diplomacy in the reign of Selim III, 1789–1807', *Journal of the American Oriental Society*, vol. 83, pp. 295–315

Nicol, D. (1982), *The United Nations Security Council: Towards Greater Effectiveness* (UNITAR: New York)

Nicholas, H. G. (1975), *The United Nations as a Political Institution*, 2nd edn (Oxford University Press: London and New York)

Nicolson, H. (1937), *Peacemaking 1919* (Constable: London)

Nicolson, H. (1954), *The Evolution of Diplomatic Method* (Constable: London)

Nicolson, H. (1963), *Diplomacy*, 3rd edn (Oxford University Press: London)

Nixon, R. M. (1979), *The Memoirs of Richard Nixon* (Arrow: London)

Oakeshott, M. (1962), *Rationalism in Politics and Other Essays* (Methuen : London)

Parsons, A. (1984), *The Pride and the Fall: Iran 1974–1979* (Cape: London)

Peters, J. (1994), *Building Bridges: The Arab–Israeli Multilateral Talks* (RIIA: London)

Peterson, M. J. (1986), *The General Assembly in World Politics* (Allen & Unwin: Boston)

Peterson, M. J. (1997), *Recognition of Governments: Legal Doctrine and State Practice, 1815–1995* (Macmillan – now Palgrave: Basingstoke)

Peyrefitte, A. (1993), trsl. by J. Rothschild, *The Collision of Two Civilizations: The British Expedition to China in 1792–4* (Harvill: London)

Platt, D. C. M. (1968), *Finance, Trade and Politics in British Foreign Policy, 1815–1914* (Clarendon Press: Oxford)

Platt, D. C. M. (1971), *The Cinderella Service: British Consuls since 1825* (Longman: London)

Plischke, E. (1974), *Summit Diplomacy: Personal Diplomacy of the United States' Presidents* (Greenwood Press: New York)

Princen, T. (1992), *Intermediaries in International Conflict* (Princeton University Press: Princeton, New Jersey)

Pruitt, D. (1997), 'Ripeness theory and the Oslo talks', *International Negotiation*, vol. 2, no. 2

Putnam, R. (1984), 'The Western Economic Summits: a political interpretation', in Merlini, C. (ed.), *Economic Summits and Western Decision-making* (Croom Helm: London. St. Martin's Press – now Palgrave: New York)

Quandt, W. B. (1986), *Camp David: Peacemaking and Politics* (Brookings Institution: Washington)

Queller, D. E. (1967), *The Office of Ambassador in the Middle Ages* (Princeton University Press: Princeton, New Jersey)

Raghavan, C. (2001), 'WTO sets Doha as venue, but stumbles on dates ... ', *Third World Network*, 30 January, http://www.twnside.org.sg/title/doha.htm

Ragsdale, L. (1993), *Presidential Politics* (Houghton Mifflin: Boston)

Rana, K. S. (2000), *Inside Diplomacy* (Manas: New Delhi)

Randle, R. F. (1969), *Geneva 1954: The Settlement of the Indochinese War* (Princeton University Press: Princeton, New Jersey)

Rawnsley, G. D. (1999), 'Monitored broadcasts and diplomacy', in J. Melissen (ed.), *Innovation in Diplomatic Practice* (Macmillan – now Palgrave: Basingstoke)

Reagan, R. (1990), *An American Life* (Hutchinson: London)

Review Committee on Overseas Representation (1969), *Report of the Review Commitee on Overseas Representation 1968–1969* ['The Duncan Report'] (HMSO: London)

Richelieu, Cardinal (1965; first published 1688), *The Political Testament of Cardinal Richelieu: the significant chapters and supporting selections*, trsl. H. B. Hill (University of Wisconsin Press: Madison)

Robertson, J. (1998), 'Introduction: Contemporary Developing Country Foreign Ministries', *International Insights*, vol. 14, summer, special issue on 'The Foreign Ministry in Developing Countries and Emerging Market Economies'

Rothstein, R. L. (1972), *Planning, Prediction, and Policymaking in Foreign Affairs: Theory and Practice* (Little, Brown: Boston)

Rozental, A. (1999), 'Mexico', in B. Hocking (ed.), *Foreign Ministries: Change and adaptation* (Macmillan – now Palgrave: Basingstoke)

Rubin, J. Z. (1991), 'The timing of ripeness and the ripeness of timing', in L. Kriesberg and S. J. Thorson (eds), *Timing the De-escalation of International Conflicts* (Syracuse University Press: Syracuse, New York)

Rubin, J. Z. (1992), 'International mediation in context', in J. Bercovitch and J. Z. Rubin (eds), *Mediation in International Relations* (St. Martin's Press – now Palgrave: New York)

Safire, W. (1975), *Before the Fall: An Inside View of the Pre-Watergate White House* (Doubleday: New York)

Satow, Sir E. (1922), *A Guide to Diplomatic Practice*, 2nd edn (Longman: London)

Saunders, H. (1985), 'We need a larger theory of negotiation: the importance of pre-negotiating phases', *Negotiation Journal*, vol. 1

Schlesinger, A. M. Jr. (1965), *A Thousand Days: John F. Kennedy in the White House* (Deutsch: London)

Seale, P. and M. McConville (1978), *Philby: The Long Road to Moscow*, rev. edn (Penguin: Harmondsworth)

Seitz, R. (1998), *Over Here* (Weidenfeld & Nicolson: London)

Shaw, M. N. (1991), *International Law*, 3rd edn (Grotius: Cambridge)

Shultz, G. P. (1993), *Turmoil and Triumph: My Years as Secretary of State* (Scribner's: New York)

Shultz, G. P. (1997), 'Diplomacy in the Information Age', Keynote Address at the Virtual Diplomacy Conference, April 1997,
http://www.usip.org/pubs/pworks/virtual18/dipinfoage_18.html

Sick, G. (1985), *All Fall Down: America's Fateful Encounter with Iran* (Random House: New York)

Simpson, S. (1967), *Anatomy of the State Department* (Houghton Mifflin: Boston)

Simpson, S. (1980), *The Crisis in American Diplomacy: Shots Across the Bow of the State Department* (Christopher: North Quincy, Massachusetts)

Smith, G. (1980), *Doubletalk: The Story of the First Strategic Arms Limitation Talks* (Doubleday: New York)

Smith, G. S. (1999), *Reinventing Diplomacy: A Virtual Necessity* (http://www.usip.org/oc/vd/vdr/gsmithISA99.html

Solomon, R. H. (1997), 'The Information Revolution and International Conflict Management', Keynote Address at the Virtual Diplomacy Conference, April 1997, http://www.usip.org/pubs/pworks/virtual18/inforev_18.html

Stadler, K. R. (1981), 'The Kreisky phenomenon', *West European Politics*, vol. 4, no. 1

Stearns, M. (1996), *Talking to Strangers: Improving American Diplomacy at Home and Abroad* (Princeton University Press: Princeton, New Jersey)

Stein, J. G. (1989), 'Getting to the table: the triggers, stages, functions, and consequences of pre-negotiations', *International Journal*, vol. 44, no. 2

Steiner, Z. (ed.) (1982), *The Times Survey of Foreign Ministries of the World* (Times Books: London)

Stimson Center Project on the Advocacy of U.S. Interests Abroad (1998), *Equipped for the Future: Managing U.S. Foreign Affairs in the 21st Century*, October (Stimson Center) http://www.stimson.org/pubs/ausia/ausr1.pdf

Sullivan, W. H. (1981), *Mission to Iran* (Norton: New York)

Taylor, P. M. (1992), *War and the Media: Propaganda and Persuasion in the Gulf War* (Manchester University Press: Manchester and New York)

Thant, U (1977), *View from the UN* (David & Charles: London)

Thatcher, M. (1993), 'The Downing Street Years', *Booknotes Transcript* (Booknotes on C-Span, http://www.booknotes. org/transcripts/10117.htm)

Thatcher, M. (1995), *The Downing Street Years* (HarperCollins: London)

Thompson, K. W. (1965), 'The new diplomacy and the quest for peace', *International Organization*, vol. 19

Touval, S. (1982), *The Peace Brokers: Mediators in the Arab–Israeli Conflict, 1948–1979* (Princeton University Press: Princeton, New Jersey)

Touval, S. (1989), 'Multilateral negotiation: an analytic approach', *Negotiation Journal*, vol. 5, no. 2

Trask, D. T. (1981), 'A short history of the U.S. Department of State, 1781–1981', *Department of State Bulletin*, vol. 81, no. 2046

Trevelyan, H. (1971), *Living with the Communists* (Gambit: Boston)

Trevelyan, H. (1973), *Diplomatic Channels* (Macmillan – now Palgrave: London)

Urban, Mark (1996), *UK Eyes Alpha: The Inside Story of British Intelligence* (Faber and Faber: London and Boston)

US Department of State Dispatch (1991), 13 May

Vance, C. (1983), *Hard Choices: Critical Years in America's Foreign Policy* (Simon & Schuster: New York)

Vattel, Emmerich de (1964), *Le Droit des Gens*, first published 1758 (Oceana: New York), vol. 3

Ware, R. (1990), 'Treaties and the House of Commons', *Factsheet*, FS.57 (Public Information Office, House of Commons: London)

Watson, A. (1982), *Diplomacy: The Dialogue between States* (Eyre Methuen: London)

Watt, D. (1981), 'Do summits only lead to trouble at the top?' *Financial Times*, 3 July

Webster, Sir C. (1961), *The Art and Practice of Diplomacy* (Chatto & Windus: London)

Weihmiller, G. R. and D. Doder (1986), *US–Soviet Summits* (University Press of America: Lanham, Maryland, and London)

Weinberg, S. (1989), *Armand Hammer: The Untold Story* (Little, Brown: Boston)

Weizman, E. (1981), *The Battle for Peace* (Bantam: Toronto, New York and London)

Werts, J. (1992), *The European Council* (North-Holland: Amsterdam)

Whelan, J. G. (1990), *The Moscow Summit 1988* (Westview Press: Boulder, Colorado)

Wilenski, P. (1993), 'The structure of the UN in the post-Cold War period', in Roberts A. and B. Kingsbury (eds), *United Nations, Divided World*, 2nd edn (Clarendon Press: Oxford)

Wilson, H. (1974), *The Labour Government, 1964–70: A Personal Record* (Penguin: Harmondsworth)

Wood, J. R. and J. Serres (1970), *Diplomatic Ceremonial and Protocol: Principles, Procedures and Practices* (Macmillan – now Palgrave: London)

Wriston, W. B. (1997), 'Bits, Bytes, and Diplomacy'. Keynote Address at the Virtual Diplomacy Conference, April 1997, http://www.usip.org/pubs/pworks/virtual18/bitbytdip_18.html

Yearbook of the International Law Commission, 1956, vol. II; 1957, vols I and II; 1958, vols I and II; 1960, vol. II.

Yearbook of International Organizations (1999), *Edition 36, 1999/2000*, vol. 1B (K. G. Saur: Munich)

Young, E. (1966), 'The development of the law of diplomatic relations', *British Yearbook of International Law 1964*, vol. 40 (Oxford University Press: London and New York), pp. 141–82

Young, J. W. (1986), 'Churchill, the Russians and the Western Alliance: the three-power conference at Bermuda, December 1953', *English Historical Review*

Zamora, S. (1980), 'Voting in international economic organizations', *American Journal of International Law*, vol. 74

Zartman, I. W. and Berman, M. (1982), *The Practical Negotiator* (Yale University Press: New Haven and London)

Index

see also Reykjavik summit (1986)
recognition   132, 155, 187
regional organizations   204 n. 11
   see also under individual organizations
    and summits
representation   107, 112–13, 117–18
representative offices   140–1, 142
resident embassy
  and access   110, 118–19, 120
  alleged redundancy of   103 n. 12,
    116–17
  and clarification of intentions   121
  and commerce   124–5
  consular sections of   123
  in diplomatic law   112–17
  and foreign aid administration   127
  freedom of movement of staff
    of   114
  and friendly relations   113, 118
  functions of generally   15, 113
  information gathering by   16, 106,
    114, 116, 122–3
  inspections of   10–11
  interests sections in   133–8, 139,
    140
  and intervention in domestic
    affairs   115, 121, 127
  inviolability of premises of   113–14,
    115, 134
  lobbying by   120–1
  and localitis   109–10
  and negotiations   41, 106, 113
  origins of   2, 106
  and policy advice   123
  public diplomacy by   125–6
  and rotation of staff   110
  and summitry   169–73
  see also aristocracy and the foreign
    service; consuls; diplomatic
    corps; diplomatic relations;
    proxenos; representation;
    Richelieu
Reykjavik summit (1986)   39, 41, 185
  n. 13
Rhodesia   67, 68
Richelieu, Cardinal   1, 5, 106
Rio Branco Institute   20 n. 9
ripeness   200–1
  see also stalemate

Rogers Act (1924)   8
Romania   11
Russia   9, 17, 156–7
  see also Soviet Union

SAARC Summit   175, 177
Sadat, Anwar   62, 67–8, 82, 84, 122
  see also Camp David talks (1978)
salami tactics   54 n. 5
SALT I   47, 50, 179
SALT II   76
Sant' Egidio, order of   194
Satow, Sir Ernest and telephones   99
Saudi Arabia   62
  diplomatic quarter of   22 n. 26
secrecy   107
secret intelligence   12, 115, 122
Senegal   9, 12, 19, 103 n. 12
separation of powers   184 n. 7
service attachés   115, 125, 136
Shanghai Communiqué   47, 185 n. 14
sherpas   178, 182
Shultz, George   94, 97
side letters   81–2
Simonstown Agreements (1955)   78
Simpson, Smith   14
Slovenia   19
Smith, Gordon S.   101
Smuts, General Jan C.   172–3
South Africa   30
  and agendas   34, 35
  and Britain   41, 78
  Department of External Affairs
    of   14
  and international
    organizations   158
  and Kreisky   192
  and Soviet Union   135–6
  and UN   160
  unconventional diplomacy of   141,
    144 ns. 11, 14
  see also Angola/Namibia talks;
    Britain; Smuts
Southern Department of FO   20 n. 1
South Korea, *see* Korea, Republic of
Soviet Union
  and China, People's Republic
    of   183
  Cold War embassies of   127